The Road to Colossus

THE ROAD TO
COLOSSUS

A Celebration of
American Ingenuity

Thomas Kiernan

WILLIAM MORROW AND COMPANY, INC.
New York

Library of Congress Cataloging in Publication Data

Kiernan, Thomas.
    The road to colossus.

    Bibliography: p.
    Includes index.
    1. United States—Social conditions.   2. United States
—Economic conditions.   3. Technology—Social aspects—
United States.   I. Title.
HN57.K525   1985   306'.0973   84-10861
ISBN: 0-688-00456-3

Printed in the United States of America

First Edition

1 2 3 4 5 6 7 8 9 10

BOOK DESIGN BY ELLEN LO GIUDICE

For Sam . . . Who Asked the Question

CONTENTS

INTRODUCTION

Imagine that you're living in the United States of two hundred years ago. It is the mid-1780s, and by virtue of the 1783 Treaty of Paris, formally ending the Revolutionary War, the country has just achieved its independence. You reside, necessarily, somewhere within the eastern sliver of the continent, the region of the original colonies-turned-states. You might live in a principal city such as Boston, New York or Philadelphia, then still little more than extended villages. If not, you likely inhabit a smaller community—a Pittsfield or Springfield, Massachusetts, for example, or a Williamsburg or Richmond, Virginia. If not that, then your abode is in a rural hamlet or on a small subsistence farmstead not far away.

Wherever you place yourself, try to envision what your life is like. Unless you are among the elite, wealthy few, no matter where you live your quarters are small, crude and cramped. If you are the typical man and do not earn your livelihood from the land or the sea, you operate a small business in one of a limited number of crafts or trades, or you work for someone who does. If you are a woman, you probably manage a crowded household and, between periodic birthings, tend to your numerous children and to the endless chores necessary to help support your family. For half the year—more if you live in the North—much of your daily existence is devoted to the never-ending task of keeping warm.

This rotelike aspect of life extends to just about everything else you do. As a workingman—whether farmer, forester or fisherman, mechanic or craftsman, merchant, laborer or clerk—your hours are long and exhausting, spanning twelve to sixteen hours a day, six and often seven days a week. As a woman, your time is consumed by the perpetual toil of home and hearth. You see few people outside your family or workplace. Travel is unheard of except among those who pull up roots to settle elsewhere, and then it is arduous and fraught with hardship and peril. Once you are settled, your longest trek is usually to Sunday church or to a market town to hawk your wares. You either walk or, if you are fortunate enough to own one, go by horse or horse-drawn carriage.

Aside from churches and a scattering of men-only taverns, there are few if any diversions in your life. There is, naturally, no television, no radio, no cinema, no theater, no circuses, no amusement parks—nothing in the way of spectator entertainment. Those of you who are sufficiently literate might get to see a newspaper once a week, a single smudged, dog-eared sheet reporting events in your general region that are weeks if not months old. There are no organized sports or sporting events at which to while away an afternoon or evening. There is no electricity, of course, and except for candles, most of you do not possess illumination of any kind in your homes; when darkness comes your day is effectively ended. Aside from the family Bible, books are few and far between.

A typical day in your life goes something like this: First you rise, almost always at dawn if not before. You spend the next hour, if you are a man, reviving the wood fire for warmth and hot water. If you are a woman you busy yourself at the fireplace, preparing breakfast for your family out of sacks of flour and grain, and tending to those among your children who are ill. (Sickness is a common component of your life and you are likely to lose almost half your children to disease before they reach their teens.) Thereafter, man or woman, you embark on your respective day's physical work, which will keep you occupied until dusk. Then, most of your energy spent, you go through the tedious preparation of your evening meal, generally cooking the same dull food every night. Thereafter you eat and clean up. Finally you bank the fire and, between eight and nine o'clock, retire to your hard, mattressless bed until the next day's dawning.

And so your life goes, as it did for the great majority of Americans who lived in the United States of the 1780s. Hard to imagine? Perhaps not in the abstract. But imagining yourself an inhabitant of the infant nation suggests an existence that is doubtless exceedingly difficult to comprehend in real terms when compared to what you are accustomed to today. A world with no television or radio? No automatic central heating or air conditioning? No cars or paved roads? No packaged foods or supermarkets? No refrigerators or toilets or hot and cold running water? No telephones or movies? No golf courses or racetracks or stadiums or tennis courts? No trains or airplanes, few newspapers, hardly any books? No doctors or dentists to speak of, no corner drugstores or fast-food shops? The list is virtually endless.

When the United States took root as an independent nation two hundred years ago, its social and political infrastructure was as fragile as a leaf in April. Its economic underpinning had only the barest substance—there was no such thing as a Gross National Product. Raw and unsettled in its traditions and institutions, the country's commercial foundation consisted largely of a disorganized aggregate of tiny farms, one-man maritime pursuits and cottage industry. It is unlikely that a single citizen, even among the visionary Founding Fathers, was capable of imagining that the primitive nation of just over 2 million souls would become what it is today.

Today, it goes without saying, the United States—economically, socially, industrially and technologically—is the richest and most variegated country in the history of the world. No other nation, no other society, has approached America in the tremendous diversity of material comforts, conveniences, advantages, opportunities, experiences and diversions it affords its populace. Even the most sophisticated foreigners are awed by the immensity of choice the average American has at hand to ease and enrich his or her personal existence.

We Americans, however, marvel little if at all at our astonishing abundance. As individuals we reflect little if at all on our status as the chief beneficiaries of the country's seemingly depthless well of material and economic largesse. And, conditioned by the very pragmatic traditions that have generated our material plenitude to take that plenitude for granted, we possess little in the way of a vivid, unified, concrete idea of how it all came about. In a mere two hundred years the United States has transformed itself from a weak, loosely—almost accidentally—organized society of subsistence farmers, fishermen, merchants and cottage craftsmen into the richest, most powerful colossus of industrial and technological prowess and variety the world has ever known. Two hundred years is akin to a split second in the history of man's recorded time on earth. How has America managed to pack so much achievement and progress into such a seeming instant of time?

The primary vehicle of the country's historic—some would say miraculous—transformation has been its evolving social, scientific, technological and industrial machine. How and why the United States became the material Goliath it did, providing not only its own people but much of the rest of the modern world with a standard of living and quality of life unimagined just a few generations ago, is the principal subject of this book. It is in this still-wondrous history, I believe, that the key to a comprehensive understanding and appreciation of the America of today lies.

But today many expert observers claim that the American colossus, having grown so huge and muscle-bound, has become immobilized by its bulk, has started to wallow helplessly in its elderly complacency, and is well on the road to both apathy and atrophy, if not decay and death.

It is a durable fact of history that sooner or later every mighty nation or society declines and dies. Equally durable is the axiom that the seeds of every society's death lie in its own imperfections. Is America dying? A modest attempt to answer that question is the subsidiary purpose of this book.

CHAPTER 1

THE HERITAGE

Rub your hands together briskly for a few seconds. Do you feel the heat the friction creates in your palms?

That simple exercise, carried out by Francis Bacon in early seventeenth-century England, inspired the beginning of the scientific, technological and industrial transformation of the world. Because the transformation reached its zenith three centuries later in the United States, Bacon can fairly be called the "grandfather" of our country. Without the conceptual contributions he made to science and the principles of mechanics, it is likely the United States would not have evolved as it did. In fact there probably would have been no America, at least as we know it today.

Until Bacon's time, scientific and technological development and its application to the improvement of the human condition had progressed at a snail's pace. Indeed, there had been hardly any connection made between scientific inquiry and the material enhancement of earthly life. Such inquiry was concerned mainly with understanding the cosmic and the abstract, with explaining in rational terms phenomena no longer satisfactorily explained by religious dogma and mysticism. Copernicus, then Kepler and Galileo—astronomers all—were the leading scientific names of the period. Others in Europe, metaphysicians and mathematicians, grappled with phenomenological questions through different methods but with similar rational goals in mind.

It remained for Francis Bacon to direct science and technology onto a more practical track. It was a track that diverted scientifically minded men from the realm of abstract speculation into one of pragmatic application. Bacon, in short, was the spiritual founder of organized human invention and industry.

13

What motivated Bacon was not only his own scientific outlook but the fact that he was a politician, statesman and humanist. He lived at a time when the notion of the machine as a replacement for human labor was in its ascendancy, a notion that had been shaped by the Renaissance and refined by the Reformation. It was a time when the seeds of capitalism were being sown throughout northwestern Europe and the monarchies of the region were vying for economic and territorial dominance. In his time, too, England was on the verge of exhausting its forests as the primary source of its heating fuel and building material.

England was in the process of developing the recently discovered resource known as coal as its principal medium of heating. In addition it was turning to cast iron for construction. The smelting of iron required heat, of course, which also meant coal. The problem was getting the coal out of the ground in quantity and at a cost that would make the new fuel practicable. The solution was machinery.

Ideas about mechanical power had developed as early as the ancient Greek, Egyptian and Chinese eras, and were based on observations of nature. Later, primitive methods of harnessing the power of wind and water were perfected—the windmill, the waterwheel—and even a man-made power source was discovered in the weight and spring, a compound device created to drive clocks and other small, lightweight mechanisms. But a source of power to turn self-contained heavy machinery was still in the sphere of dreams during Francis Bacon's time.

The dream's possibilities were growing conceptually clearer, however, and it was Bacon who first articulated them. While writing his scientific masterwork, *Novum Organum*, late in the second decade of the seventeenth century, he rubbed his hands together vigorously—as I asked you to do at the start of this chapter. On the basis of the sensation he received, he made the observation that motion plus friction equals heat. He already knew, of course, that fire equaled heat and that heat equaled energy. He knew, too, that energy was translatable into motive power, and that the energy from heat, when concentrated, could move things with a particularly distinct power. (For example, toss a feather atop a chimney flue below which a fire is burning and observe how the hot draft propels the feather into the sky.)

But how to reconcile all these qualities into a workable formula of mechanical power eluded Bacon. So he put out the call to his scientific contemporaries to pursue such a formula, in the process providing them with key hints. The hints were water and air. Bacon contended that water and air (the wind) were proven energy sources. He reasoned from there that a way must exist to apply fire, the third known energy producer, to water and air in order to synthesize a kind of superenergy source. If such a synthesis were to be achieved, an entirely new and more versatile and efficient class of heavy machinery would be possible—the kind of machinery needed for the mining and transport of coal, and for the manufacture of heavy iron.

Bacon was less a pure scientist than a gifted scientific thinker and conceptualizer. Published in 1620, the year of the first Pilgrim settlement in Massachusetts, his *Novum Organum* had a riveting effect on England's tight circle of pure scientists, particularly because of the revolutionary "scientific method" it advanced. It had a similar impact on the country's wider community of merchants, craftsmen and tradesmen, who were by then beginning to cultivate the garden of capitalism. For underlying Bacon's detailed outline of his scientific method was his declaration "that the true and lawful end of the sciences is that human life be enriched by new discoveries and powers." A few years later, moreover, he told his biographer:

> Now, among all the benefits that could be conferred on mankind, I found none so great as the discovery of new arts, endowments and commodities for the bettering of man's life. For I saw that among the rude people in the primitive times, authors of inventions and discoveries were consecrated and numbered among the gods. And it was plain that the good effects wrought by the founders of cities, law-givers, fathers of the people, extirpers of tyrants, and heroes of that class, extend but over narrow surfaces and last but for short times; whereas the work of the inventor, though a thing of less pomp and show, is felt everywhere and lasts forever.

Bacon was saying, in other words, that the time had come for abstract science and human industry to join forces. Which is exactly what they began to do after his death. Inspired by Bacon's ideas, a group of English capitalists and scientists banded together under a 1662 charter from King Charles II to form the Royal Society of London. The Royal Society's mission, as first articulated, was specifically to finance concerted practical scientific studies devoted to solving the immediate problems of industry and navigation. In a more general sense its goal was:

> To improve the knowledge of natural things, and all useful Arts, Manufactures, Mechanick practices, Engynes and Inventions by Experiment—(not meddling with Divinity, Metaphysics, Morals, Politics, Grammar, Rhetorick or Logicks).

But how could science do its job and not "meddle" in matters relating to divinity and morals? Because of these strictures, the Royal Society was able to achieve little at first in the way of practical solutions to the problems that continued to restrain the development of British industry and trade. Its founding and early years did have a monumental significance for the future, however.

The significance was threefold. First, the Royal Society imbued experimental scientific study for the first time with an organized social character, bringing it out of the university and making it a part of everyday life, especially commercial life. Second, it attracted such gifted abstract scientists as Robert Boyle and Robert Hooke, both of whom, in their pioneering studies in chemistry, mechanics, physics and biology—hindered only by their shortcomings in mathematics—anticipated and made possible the much greater practical scientific discoveries soon to come.

The third and most vital impact of the Royal Society derived from the combination of the first two. Until the late seventeenth century, experimental science in England had been almost exclusively the province of Oxford University—both Boyle and Hooke were Oxford mainstays.* Isaac Newton, a contemporary, had been educated at England's other principal university, Cambridge. Also a scientist, he chose to remain there rather than join the Royal Society-sponsored circle at Oxford, primarily because he could not accept the religious restraints implicit in the society's charter. As a consequence, a rivalry grew between the gifted

---

*Robert Hooke was England's first major scientist-inventor. Among the many useful devices he created, the most noteworthy was the universal joint.

Newton at Cambridge and his counterparts at Oxford. It was a rivalry that would culminate in the single most important scientific breakthrough in history up to that time and would launch the beginning of the Industrial Revolution.

In 1684, under the auspices of the Royal Society, Robert Hooke and his young protégé Edmund Halley (after whom Halley's Comet is named) were working at Oxford on a definitive scientific explanation of the principles and mechanics of gravity, based on the speculations of Kepler and Descartes, the French mathematician. Obstructing their path was their inability to produce a precise mathematical formulation by which to express their findings in terms of hard-and-fast law. Nor had they been able to solve vital questions relating to the elliptical orbits of the planets and the modes of interaction between large attractive bodies.

By 1684, the forty-two-year-old Isaac Newton had become well known in the scientific community for his work at Cambridge in optics and mathematics. Newton was struggling to create a "new" mathematics that, in the spirit of Bacon's scientific method, would establish a definitive methodology by which all scientific experimentation could be quantified and verified. Robert Hooke wrote to Newton for advice on the problems he and Halley were having with their investigations, revealing in the process their mathematical deficiencies. Newton declined to respond. Thereupon Halley, the scion of a wealthy family, offered a prize to anyone who could solve his and Hooke's difficulties. Thus sufficiently motivated, Newton decided to look into the matter.

The result, three years later, was Newton's *Principia Mathematica*. The publication of this seminal treatise, which Halley generously financed after reading it, far exceeded in import the mere solution of the Hooke-Halley dilemma. It rattled late-seventeenth-century science to its very foundations, not just in England but, as it rapidly became known, throughout Europe. One of the reasons it did so was because Newton had finally succeeded in perfecting his new mathematics, "the infinitesimal calculus." The system was to function as an unerring method by which to render the mysteries of the various sciences intelligible, to prove or disprove what theretofore had been only speculative and vaguely certain.

The second reason the *Principia* had the effect it did was because it established once and for all, through its precise calculus, the laws of motion and gravitation. Newton had devised a revolutionary new method, absolute in its certainty, toward the understanding of variables and motion. The method would enable scientists in a variety of different fields of research to progress much more rapidly. In addition, he created the groundwork for the immediate solution of many of the mechanical and hydraulic problems that plagued England's industrial development, and he advanced a conceptual template for the mastery of technical engineering in all its contemporary forms.

Newton transformed not only abstract science, then, but mechanical technology and late seventeenth-century man's outlook on life as well. His discoveries almost single-handedly launched England's Industrial Revolution early in the eighteenth century. That revolution would untether completely the impulses of capitalism, individualism and free enterprise that had been generated by social and economic philosophers during the century before. And it would trigger a simultaneous revolution in human affairs called the Enlightenment, or the Age of Reason. These two developments would lead in turn to the more vigorous colonization of North America, to the eventual establishment of an independent United States, and ultimately to the America we know today.*

Of course at the time of Newton's death in 1727, America as it then existed—a primitive amalgam of colonies and territories controlled variously by England, Holland, France and Spain—had no inkling of what it was to become. In England, meanwhile, the Industrial Revolution was fast gathering force.

During the sixty-seven-year span between Francis Bacon's *Novum Organum* and Isaac Newton's *Principia Mathematica*, Robert Boyle had emerged as England's most fecund scientist. His empirical, Bacon-inspired experiments in chemistry and physics, particularly in the properties of the vacuum and air pressure, had led in 1662 to the formulation of Boyle's Law, which held that the pressure of a given amount of a gas, multiplied by its volume, is constant at constant temperature.† Boyle's Law, coming just be-

---

*So celebrated did Newton become that the English poet Alexander Pope memorialized him upon his death with the following verse:

> Nature, and Nature's laws lay hid in night.
> God said, *Let Newton be!* and all was light.

†It was Boyle's enunciation of this law that led directly to the formation of the Royal Society in the same year; it was widely recognized that his finding had important practical implications for British industry and commerce.

fore the rise to eminence of Newton, unlocked the door to the possibilities of steam as the manifestation of Francis Bacon's superenergy force. It remained for Newton to open the door with his infinitesimal calculus and laws of motion, which shed authoritative light on the theretofore barely understood principles of thermal mechanics, hydrodynamics and atmospheric pressure.

During the early 1700s, while England was tightening its proprietary grip on much of colonial America, several British experimenters, impelled by their understanding of Boyle's Law and Newtonian physics, developed primitive piston-operated steam engines for use in coal mining. But these devices operated only under extremely high temperatures and pressures; they were at once unreliable and unsafe, due to the metallurgical fragility of the iron used in their fabrication. Nevertheless, a practical trend, based on abstract scientific investigation, had begun.

In 1712 Thomas Newcomen, an ironmonger with no formal scientific training, improved on these early devices by developing an engine that did not require such high pressures. Its use was also limited, however, because its mechanical action was too irregular for anything but pumping water out of coal mines and blowing air into iron-smelting furnaces. Yet it remained the sole practical steam engine for the next half century—that is, until 1765, when a Scottish instrument maker, James Watt, invented the separate steam condenser.

The separate condenser, which made the steam engine immensely more efficient, was only the first of Watt's improvements. Thereafter, by introducing the combination of flywheel, throttle and centrifugal governor, Watt made an engine capable of driving machinery at steady speed against changing loads.*

Watt's innovations occurred at a time when English industry was in the process of changing from scattered, small-scale, local cottage manufacture to centralized factory production. This initial phase of the Industrial Revolution had been triggered largely by the invention of the manually operated loom and by the discovery and increasing availability of cotton in the American colonies. Cotton and the loom, first a manually operated machine and then one powered by water, together with the intensifying capitalist spirit in England, had gradually created a mechanical textile in-

*It was James Watt who first coined the term *horsepower*.

dustry in that country. In its northern regions, where the sources
of waterpower were most abundant and the labor cheapest, large
complexes of textile factories had been established, while teeming
industrial towns began to sprawl around them.

The first steam engines had been useful only for pumping and
blowing. The engine devised and improved by James Watt, representing the first major advance in self-contained mechanical
power, climaxed the opening stage of the Industrial Revolution. It
in fact rerevolutionized the revolution. Thereafter Watt's engine—
improvements on it, miniaturizations of it—was applied to a
widening spectrum of English industrial endeavor. As a result, at
about the time of the American Revolution, the Industrial Revolution in England was shifting into high gear. With man-made machines driving other man-made machines, and with the fuel that
powered the former produced by still other man-made machines,
the Age of the Machine had truly arrived, at least in England and
northwestern continental Europe.

We now cross the Atlantic to the America of that period—to an
America soon to transform itself from a loose agglomeration of
British colonies into an infant independent nation.

The outline of the country's political, social and economic history up to that time is well known. To summarize, in the early
1600s the English and, to a lesser extent, the Dutch began to colonize what is today the Eastern Seaboard of North America. Soon
the Dutch foothold was eroded by England's rising power in the
world. The Eastern Seaboard came under the principal control of
England, while the French and Spanish empires laid claim to
other portions of the continent. Eventually, what had been scattered primitive maritime settlements—Plymouth, Massachusetts
Bay, Rhode Island, New Amsterdam (New York), Philadelphia,
Baltimore, Jamestown, Charleston—were expanded by continuing immigration, mostly from the British Isles, and by English law and custom, into a string of separate British-governed
colonies.

Many of those first involved in the establishment and expansion of the American colonies had journeyed to the New World to
escape religious persecution and social disenfranchisement. But by
the early 1700s the colonies had fallen firmly under England's dominion. Moreover, because of their natural and agricultural re-

sources, they had become collectively the British Empire's most valuable foreign asset. They continued to grow in importance as a source of timber, cotton, tobacco and other raw-material and commercial imports throughout the mid-1700s, those imports figuring vitally in England's ongoing industrial transformation. As a consequence, the character of the continuing immigration from England to the colonies changed, becoming motivated less by religious emancipation and more by economic opportunism as England's need for colonial labor increased. With the increase, immigration from other parts of the British Isles accelerated as well, particularly from Scotland and Ireland. And as machine industrialism spread from England into continental Europe, Germans and Scandinavians began to make their way across the Atlantic.

But with the increased migratory tide came new social, economic and political impulses launched by the Enlightenment, itself a reaction to the changes capitalism and industrialism had wrought on traditional notions of monarchy and the divine right of kings. The Enlightenment was the philosophical equivalent of the Industrial Revolution. Where industrialism and capitalism were in the process of releasing the common man from the enslaving yoke of physical feudalism (while creating for him other problems), the Enlightenment was beginning to free him, at least partially, from the restraints of spiritual serfdom. That every man had a natural right to life, liberty and property, so long as he exercised that right legally and in the context of a higher common good, was the principal conclusion of the philosophical architects of the Enlightenment. It was a conclusion that, as it caught hold in the mid-1700s, would lead first to the American and then to the French Revolution—political and economic events destined in their own way to transform the Western world.

The America of the mid-1700s, then, was a mixing bowl of old traditions and new ideas, some of them as raw and untested as its colonial frontiers. Physically the colonies were still largely maritime and agricultural in nature, the original seaside settlements having evolved into socially and religiously structured villages, and then into larger commercial towns based on the earlier English industrial-crafts model. There was no town that could yet be called properly a city, at least not in the context of the English or European concept of *city*, not even Boston, Philadelphia or New York. These communities were minuscule as compared to

London, Paris or, say, Frankfurt, and their amenities, architecture and physical infrastructures, such as they existed, were not even remotely comparable. Beyond the maritime towns, settlement had stretched into the colonies' principal inland river valleys. Few but the most daring or desperate, however, had ventured farther westward into the frontier wilderness that lay past the Appalachian mountain chain.

It was the French and Indian Wars of the early 1760s that opened up the colonials' interest in the wilderness. Mainly further installments in the longstanding imperial combat between England and France during the seventeenth and eighteenth centuries, the French and Indian Wars unleashed the specific string of events that climaxed in the American Revolution. The colonies, having feared the native Indians since the time of the first settlements, had assisted the English only reluctantly in Britain's territorial struggle against the French and their Indian mercenaries in North America, and sporadically at that. Once the wars were concluded in 1763, the British government in London decided to subsidize the colonies no longer but to force them to pay their own way. That decision produced the succession of increasingly repressive tariff and taxation acts which, within the colonies, fomented the debate over the concept of "taxation without representation." And the debate, sharpening and widening in intensity as the British imposed each new economic sanction, stirred the colonists to rebellion in 1776.

By the time of the American Revolution, the Industrial Revolution in England was about to reach full flower. The British invention of the spinning jenny in 1764 and the water frame in 1769 had stepped up the manufacture of cotton textiles enormously.* The only problem was that the mills in which these machines were installed were still being powered by water from the relatively small, sluggish rivers next to which they had been built. The streams, with their modest currents and limited volume, did not have the capacity or consistency to drive the complex new machinery so as to exploit its full potential. It was not until 1785, two years after the formal end of the American Revolution, that

*The jenny, a machine for spinning several threads at once, was the idea of James Hargreaves of Blackburn, England. As news of the invention spread, it caused a public uproar of the kind occasioned today by most new machines that promise to put people out of work.

James Watt's steam engine was finally adapted to power England's textile industry. Once that happened, steam power quickly spread to all other forms of light and heavy industry in England and the countries of northwest Europe.

Most inhabitants of the colonies were only vaguely aware of the remarkable industrial changes that were occurring across the Atlantic in the years leading up to and during the War of Independence. Piety, liberty and self-sufficiency were the cultural concepts that dominated American colonial life. Subsistence labor and individual industry, the practical correlatives of self-sufficiency, were held in high esteem, but it was the labor of the craftsman—the cottage fabricator and small-shop manufacturer—that was exalted, not that of the machine. Tools were necessary to many kinds of work, of course: small hand tools that themselves were handcrafted. So toolmaking was as important an industry as any other manufacturing enterprise in the colonies. But the idea of large machines, powered by external sources and stamping out products in a kind of primitive mass production, was not only foreign to the sensibilities of most colonists, it would have been alien.

Much of the colonists' ignorance of the industrial developments abroad was the result of their own inherent, religiously inspired lack of interest in the machine as a substitute for honest and productive human labor. Much of it, too, derived from the prohibitions the English put on the export of contemporary industrial ideas and techniques. The mother country was happy to send the products of its increasingly mechanized industry to the colonies to be sold there—another way of holding them in thrall. But England was fully committed to keeping the secrets of its new inventions and manufacturing techniques at home in order to bar competition with its industry. Not until the colonies were two or three years into their rebellion did they begin to grow aware of the need for better and more expeditious manufacturing facilities to assist in the war effort.

A similar situation existed with regard to the colonists' attitudes toward the scientific underpinnings of industrial progress. To many, formal scientific study—even curiosity—was contrary to the precepts of religion. Science was still viewed as little more than a component of philosophy, and a minor one at that. The colonists, for all their progressive ideas about liberty, individualism and democracy, remained largely rooted in the Middle Ages when it came to contemplating science. Here, too, the English abetted the colonists' ignorance. The colonial population was made up almost exclusively of people with limited education or of descendants of people with limited education. Most of the significant English scientific works of the period—Newton's *Principia*, for one—were written in Latin. Few colonists could read Latin. And when the works were translated into English and the translations published, England severely limited their export to the New World. Had it not been for a few curious Americans in the period between 1725 and 1775, the colonies would have had no scientific sensibility at all.

Foremost among those Americans was Benjamin Franklin. Often pictured in our popular histories as an avuncular, homely eccentric, Franklin was actually an ideal Baconian blend of the practical and the abstract, and as such was truly *the* Founding Father of the nation. Born in Boston in 1706 of a poor English-immigrant father, he was thrust into child labor as a printer's apprentice at the age of twelve and ran away five years later to Philadelphia to establish his own printing business. Shortly thereafter he sailed to England, where he became exposed to the intensive post-Newtonian application of science to industry and discovered his own aptitude for scientific experimentation. When he returned to Philadelphia three years later at the age of twenty, Franklin was imbued both with the new practical scientific spirit and with the advanced capitalist ethic of England.

Franklin channeled these twin drives into the accomplishment of many things during the next forty years, not the least of which were discoveries in electricity that established the definitive foundation of electrical theory, until then a barely understood branch of abstract science even in England and Europe. Not only that, but early on he managed to apply his scientific talents to the betterment of everyday life with his discovery of the principle of the lightning rod, a device that was quickly hailed throughout the industrial world for its simple ingenuity and its function as a protector of life and property.

Franklin might have gone on to become a scientific pioneer of the first rank had he had the necessary equipment and laboratory facilities. But there was little in the way of such necessaries in colonial America, which was why he concentrated on electricity. Franklin was basically, and by necessity, what we would call today a "backyard scientist." What with its kites and iron poles, Franklin's brand of experimentation and observation lent itself perfectly to a backyard environment. Although he was interested in many other sciences, living in colonial Pennsylvania, with its severely limited laboratory resources, effectively barred his pursuit of those interests. And his attempts to acquire scientific equipment and literature from England were frequently discouraged, usually by nothing more than the colonial religious prejudices against science. Certain religionists even blamed Franklin and his lightning rod for a severe earthquake that occurred in Boston in 1755, on the theory that the iron rods, having been erected in great numbers on Boston rooftops, had drawn huge amounts of electricity from the sky into the earth, thus causing the earth to rumble with God's wrathful vengeance.

Another distraction to Franklin was the increasing tension between England and the colonies as a result of the French and Indian Wars, which turned his attention to trying to forge a new political arrangement between the two. During his earlier stay in England, Franklin had taught himself Latin in order to be able to read the scientific treatises of Bacon, Newton and others. After returning to the colonies, and while pursuing his electrical experiments, he became exposed as well to the writings of the early Enlightenment philosophers, the first to raise substantive questions about the nature and validity of the absolute authority exercised by Europe's imperial monarchies.

In 1754, Franklin played a key role at the Albany Congress, a gathering of representatives from several of the colonies convened originally to try to dissuade the Indians from joining the French in their colonial war against Britain. Although the congress failed in its principal purpose, out of it grew the first hard notions of a union of the colonies. The notion was implanted almost single-handedly by Franklin, who went so far as to propose a "plan of union" and then persuaded the congress to vote favorably on it. The plan was later rejected both by the colonies themselves and by England, for different reasons. But by virtue of Franklin's politicking at Albany, the practical seeds of union, and of independence, were for the first time firmly planted.

Once he was centrally involved in the politics of the colonies,

Franklin proceeded to devote most of his energies to the subject. He spent much of his time between 1757 and 1775 in London as an agent-lobbyist for Pennsylvania and several other colonies. There, while further cultivating his scientific interests and learning more at first hand about the life-enhancing symbiosis between science and capitalism, he became increasingly immersed in the rising political agitation between England and its American dominion. He also became acquainted, among others, with the British philosopher David Hume, whose essays on authority and liberty were contributing mightily, along with those of Voltaire in France, to the establishment of Enlightenment thought; with Adam Smith, whose pioneering work in economics, embodied later in his *Wealth of Nations*, published in 1776, would form the blueprint of modern capitalism; with Joseph Black, who was in the forefront of British science at the time and in the process of revolutionizing the science of chemistry; with William Small, the tutor of a younger American contemporary of Franklin who would become in many ways Franklin's spiritual heir—Thomas Jefferson; and with Joseph Priestley, the discoverer of oxygen, who would later migrate to the newborn United States and carry on Franklin's scientific and technological interests.

Franklin also witnessed the beginning stages of the application of James Watt's steam engine to British industry. Although Friedrich Engels has been credited with having first coined the phrase *Industrial Revolution* in 1848 to characterize what occurred in England in the 1700s, Benjamin Franklin, in a letter from London to a friend in Philadelphia in 1768, wrote, "There can be no doubt that what we see in these parts is a revolution of industries in all its forms."

It was politics, though—its theory and practice as between England and the colonies—that most consumed Franklin's energies during the years he was in England following the conclusion of the French and Indian Wars. As England began to impose its stiffening fiscal sanctions against the colonies in the mid-1760s, Franklin became less an agent and more a political lobbyist for the colonies. He was even instrumental in persuading Parliament to repeal the 1765 Stamp Act, the first in a series of onerous tax burdens heaped upon the colonies.

But it was too late. The Stamp Act had transformed the 1750s' mood of loose, semi-autonomous colonial union under English dominion, as reflected in the Albany Congress, into a spirit of permanent separation from England. Although the Stamp Act was repealed a year after its enactment, on the same day of its repeal, in 1766, Parliament issued its Declaratory Act, asserting Britain's full authority over the colonies and its right to impose whatever binding laws it wished. That, coupled with the series of subsequent, increasingly punitive tax and tariff acts that issued from London, once again transformed the mood in the colonies, this time from one of negotiated separation to outright armed rebellion.

Throughout this time Franklin in England, as well as several leading political and philosophical thinkers in the colonies, began to see that the political and humanistic ideas of the Enlightenment philosophers extended only so far as to promote what came to be called "enlightened despotism." Suddenly the theories of the Enlightenment lost some of their appeal, both among American "Patriots" and among activists in France who were pursuing a realignment of the repressive monarchial system there. Proceeding from the concept of enlightened despotism, however, these thinkers began to formulate even newer and more radical ideas—in a nutshell, a society without monarchy; a society with representative self-government that answered to no higher authority, as the English Parliament did to the king; a society of the "common man."

So began the American "age of reason." At its forefront in the late 1760s and early 1770s was Benjamin Franklin, still in England. Franklin was among the first of the colonists during the period to recognize that some radical change in the relationship between America and England was inevitable, undoubtedly because he was so close to the seat of British thinking and power. He began to send dispatches and essays back to America which contained carefully thought-out ideas for separation and independence. Inspired in part by Franklin's long missives and in part by the growing public debate in America itself, other colonists also started to contemplate concrete blueprints for independence.

But then events began to overtake thought. The Quartering Act and Townshend Acts triggered a string of minor citizen rebellions throughout the northern colonies, particularly in the maritime cities, which led to the Boston Massacre in 1770 when British troops sought to restore order. The enmity between the colonies and the mother country spread like flame in a hay barn, as did the sense of spiritual unity among the colonies. The freedom the early settlers had achieved had clearly been eroded by England's increasingly oppressive, militaristic determination to maintain its economic and political domination. Within the colonies, patriot groups such as the Sons of Liberty were formed— quasi-guerrillas devoted to retrieving the early colonists' ideas of individual freedom and self-determination, by then more political and economic than religious in character. Then came the Boston Tea Party, followed by England's attempts to censure and discredit Benjamin Franklin, its coercive Boston Port Bill, its dismantling of the colonial government of Massachusetts, and its harsh military occupation of various "rebellious" cities.

These and other restrictive measures finally produced the convening of the first Continental Congress in Philadelphia in September of 1774, a mix of radical and conservative delegates from twelve of the thirteen colonies who agreed among other things to mount an organized economic resistance against England and to form a unified association of colonies to be controlled by the Congress. Thus was born the actual revolution, although by no means were the colonists, or the colonies, genuinely united.

After the war commenced in earnest in 1775, first with the improvised militia battles at Lexington and Concord in April, then with the second Continental Congress's June commission to George Washington to form an integrated and cohesive colonial army, the leaders and representatives of the twelve colonies (the thirteenth, Georgia, had still not joined the shaky union) got down to the task of hammering out a political agenda for the future. By that time Benjamin Franklin was recently returned from London. Considered by many rebellious colonists to be the elder statesman of the separation movement, his advice was eagerly sought out. Fully committed to separation and independence, he had plenty of advice to give. Yet because he was almost seventy years old, and probably because he had spent so many of his latter years in close proximity to the English institutions—king and Parliament—against which the colonists had risen up, he temporized and counseled caution in the face of the clamor of the more radical and impatient backers of full-scale revolt.

But then came the publication of Thomas Paine's pamphlet *Common Sense*, a strident call to action that converted even the most timid fence-straddlers to the cause of revolution. So it was, then, that the Declaration of Independence was overwhelmingly ratified by the second Continental Congress on July 4, 1776. Prominent among its authors, besides Thomas Jefferson of Virginia and John Adams of Massachusetts, was Benjamin Franklin.

The only substantive matter that remained to be resolved was that pertaining to the future structure of the thirteen colonies. The Declaration described the "united" colonies as "free and independent states." In the parlance of eighteenth-century political thought, a state was essentially an independent and sovereign nation. Did the Declaration's wording mean that the colonies were thereafter to function as thirteen separate nations, each free and independent of the other? Or did the "united" qualification suggest that they were to be linked into a component whole?

The question remained debated but unresolved for well over a year as the Revolution spread and intensified in the face of Britain's resolve to crush it. Then, impelled largely by such "aristocrats" of Virginia as Thomas Jefferson, James Madison and Richard Henry Lee, the Congress reconvened late in 1777 to consider the merger of the thirteen states into a unified confederation under the control of a central "federal" representative government.

That this plan emanated for the most part from Virginia might have seemed ironic: The Virginians, of all the colonists, had remained the most "Anglified" throughout the colonial period. Yet it was not so ironic, for Virginia as a whole, through its House of Burgesses-style of internal colonial government, had become politically the most sophisticated of the colonies. Virginians had experienced the least tradition of religious restraint of any of the colonies during the previous century and a half. Concepts of free speech, assembly, equality and representative government were well advanced there—albeit only within its white population, most of which was wealthy, well-educated and "democratically aristocratic" in its aspirations. Indeed, it can be said that the constitutional form of federal government eventually adopted by the states was almost totally a Virginia invention, and that in inspiring that form, the Virginians had nothing more in mind than to make the United States an extension of Virginia.

The Articles of Confederation were debated and then agreed upon in mid-November 1777, but they were not formally and completely ratified until more than three years later. In the meantime the war raged on, often badly for the American cause. Then the embattled new nation, increasingly outarmed and outfinanced by the British, entered into an alliance with France. Gradually, reinforced by French money, arms and, eventually, troops, Washington's army began to turn the tide. In March 1781, when it appeared that Washington would succeed against the British after all and that the war would produce a viable sovereign independent nation, the thirteen states formally ratified the Articles of Confederation. One final effort by the British forces failed. In October 1781, aided by the French, Washington's army defeated British General Cornwallis's troops at the Battle of Yorktown in Virginia. Cornwallis was forced to surrender his army of almost eight thousand men.

The Cornwallis defeat sucked the wind out of the sails of Britain's resolve, and early in 1782 Parliament voted to seek peace with the new United States. While Washington engaged in a few minor clean-up skirmishes in the American South, preliminary peace talks began in Paris between Benjamin Franklin, representing the United States, and Richard Oswald on behalf of England. Formal negotiations continued in June with Franklin leading an American delegation augmented by John Jay and John Adams. In November the British signed the Preliminary Articles of Peace, the terms of which, extremely favorable to the United States, had been wrought largely by the then seventy-six-year-old Franklin.

Franklin had gone from youthful scientist and inventor to elder statesman and diplomat of the first rank. Nevertheless he was not yet finished with science. It is symbolically fitting that early America's premier scientist and inventor should have been the man to gain the things he did for the new nation in the political and diplomatic realms. These included the alliance with France and the peace terms with England that firmly established the infant United States as a new star in the international firmament. They included, too, a unique and progressive new form of governance, the invention of which Franklin had a strong hand in. This invention vividly symbolized the inherent ingenuity of the new America.

Yet for all the uniqueness represented by the United States in social and political terms in 1782, it was woefully behind the times scientifically and technologically. True, there were scientists in colonial America besides Franklin, but few were more than ill-educated interpreters and teachers, men restrained in their investigative aspirations by the scientific conservatism of their religions and cowed by the monumental discoveries of Newton, awareness of which had finally begun to spread through the colonies during the early 1770s. There were inventors and mechanical devisers as well, but again few who were more than amateur home tinkerers and repairmen.

The Treaty of Paris, formally ending the Revolutionary War and granting recognition to the United States as an independent nation, was signed in September 1783—exactly two hundred years ago as these words are written. As generations are measured today, that was about seven generations ago. To measure it in another fashion, if the average modern-day lifetime spans seventy-five years, it was considerably less than three lifetimes ago.

No matter how it's measured, the transformation of the United States from a scientifically, technologically and materially barren backwater into the land of its current state of material and creature-comfort variety and sophistication, over the course of a few successive lifetimes and in the context of everything that came so gradually before, borders on the miraculous. There were, then, really two American revolutions. The first was political and cultural. The second—the country's stunning scientific, technological, economic and material revolution—was no less important and in many ways has had significantly more personal impact on each of us living today.

In the pages ahead, we will learn something about how the second revolution happened, and about what it suggests for America's future.

CHAPTER 2

AN UNCERTAIN BEGINNING

At the time Benjamin Franklin was negotiating in Paris with the British to win a formal peace, he was increasingly plagued by eyesight problems. In common with many people of advancing age, then as today, he suffered from a combination of farsightedness and nearsightedness. Spectacles had long been in existence; one of the most valuable early practical inventions of mankind, they were first developed in the Western world in Italy about 1350 from earlier Oriental influences. By Franklin's time, the ability to correct faulty vision through carefully ground glass lenses—what we now call prescription lenses—was one of the world's more advanced technologies. But the craft of the lens grinder, a skilled, highly exclusive cottage industry, remained mostly in Europe. American colonists who required and could afford to purchase eyeglasses got them from England and Holland for little in the way of an eyeglass technology as such existed in pre-Revolutionary America. Nor had optical science yet arrived at an understanding of the causes of the various forms of faulty eyesight.

Franklin had been distracted by poor eyesight for most of his life. When he first went to England in 1723, in addition to acquiring his first set of spectacles, he read Isaac Newton's *Opticks*, the celebrated scientist's last important work. Published in 1704, *Opticks* had opened up a whole new field of discovery to astronomers and set down much of the vital theory that produced later advances in microscopy, the study of microorganisms, and European medical research. The young Franklin, upon reading Newton's work, became keenly interested in the subject. Back in the colonies thirty years later, as his eyesight problems were compounded by blurred vision both near and far, he took to carrying several pairs of spectacles, alternating them as required, and—most frustrating—frequently losing or misplacing one or the other.

There is no documentation for this, but one can easily imagine Benjamin Franklin saying to a fellow colonist at some point in his exasperation: "Why doesn't someone invent a lens that corrects nearsightedness and farsightedness at the same time so that I don't have to carry all of these confounded different spectacles around with me?" And his fellow colonist saying, "Why don't *you* invent such a lens?"

With the help of several Parisian lens grinders, Franklin finally did just that—creating the bifocal lens. When he brought his unique double-focus glasses back to the newly sovereign United States, they were instantly in demand. After the lightning rod, then, Franklin's invention of bifocal eyeglasses was the first significant practical device to be produced by the infant republic. It was a device that in more refined form is used to beneficial effect by millions throughout the world today, and it makes an apt symbol of the ingenuity that would in so short a time transform the United States. As was typical of most of Franklin's inventions and discoveries, this one was inspired by a pressing personal need.

The same spirit of need became the engine that eventually propelled the United States in its rise to the pantheon of industrial and technological achievement, and shaped its role as principal provider of the world's material progress, convenience and life enhancement. Yet Franklin's 1783 invention was a reverse symbol, too. It was a lonely beacon in a part of the world that had made hardly any material or technological progress on its own during the almost two hundred years since its first settlement.

For most people in the United States of 1784, life was not that markedly different from what it had been for their forebears in Virginia and Massachusetts a century earlier. To be sure, for some, housing conditions were slightly less crude, less cramped. And towns and villages had streets instead of footpaths. But people still lived much as they had a century earlier, drawing their water from streams and wells, obtaining their warmth from wood-burning fireplaces (Franklin's iron stove, though he had devised it in 1740, was not yet in widespread use), traveling by horse and ox, and so on. The same was basically true in Europe. The difference was that in Europe such modes of living were considerably more refined and organized. Working conditions were similar. Indeed the early United States, with its handcrafts and tiny shop industries, was a good hundred years behind England and northern Europe industrially and technologically.

This was not entirely the fault of the early Americans, since they were a broad ocean away from the source of the Industrial Revolution and had been deliberately saddled by their parent nation with a kind of perpetual industrial and scientific immaturity. (One can legitimately wonder whether, if he had not spent so much time in England, Franklin would have achieved what he so singularly did in the colonies.) Not only did the British discourage the transport of their own scientific ideas and discoveries, they also imposed repeated embargoes on the transfer of industrial know-how to the colonies. A parliamentary act of 1750, for instance, had decreed: "No mill or other engine for slitting or rolling of iron, or any furnace for making steel shall be erected . . . in His Majesty's Colonies of America." The penalty for infringement was a powerful deterrent: £200, more than an able-bodied American could save in a lifetime.

Although England was forced to give up its "Colonies of America," it did not quite so readily relinquish its habit of denying the secrets of its industrial technology to the United States. Soon after the war, Parliament amended the 1750 Act to read: ". . . no export of tool, engine or *persons* connected with the iron industry . . ." (Emphasis added.) This was understandable, perhaps, since England feared the infringement of its own highly lucrative and monopolistic industrial-products markets by the new republic. It made good business sense, but it was also vindictive and, in the end, shortsighted. It was not so much the export of tools and engines the English needed to worry about, but "persons connected with the iron industry." And persons connected with the variety of other progressively mechanized industries then proliferating in Britain as well.

The shortsightedness was to prove itself later, though. The seven years of war between America and England had cut off the steady migrant stream of skilled workers from Britain, further drying up sources of mechanical knowledge and innovation in

America. What little industrial progress had occurred in the colonies during the pre-Revolutionary period derived mostly from the word-of-mouth of English industrial workers who had crossed to the New World in search of a better life. Aside from their skills in individual handcrafts, however, they had had little to offer in the way of contributions to technological progress. They were prideful artisans who had been made redundant by the rapid mechanization of industry in Britian. Although most were filled with tales of the new machines, and some could even roughly diagram the machines' designs and engineering, their prevailing attitude toward them was one of skepticism and denigration. It was precisely the newfangled machines, after all, that had put them out of work and driven them to America in the first place.

Attitudes were not much different after the Revolution. As immigration from England resumed in 1883, mostly among those seeking better economic opportunity, it was skilled handcraftsmen who, next to farmers, dominated their numbers. Native American small industrialists were eager to hire craftsmen who arrived with advanced and sophisticated tools. But it would be several years—a decade, even—before the immigrant traffic from England and the rest of northern Europe began to bring with it an appreciation for the remarkable industrial happenings abroad. It came primarily through the iron industry—that industry whose techniques, both before and after the Revolution, England had so assiduously tried to keep from America.

The reasons for the British prohibition of the export of iron technology to the colonies before the Revolution were not only to preserve their own widespread markets for iron products, but also to deprive America of the means of making cannon and other armaments for waging war. The Revolutionary War demanded a vast increase in the manufacture of arms and munitions within the rebellious colonies. Prior to the French and Indian Wars, the only significant types of arms that had been made in America were muskets and rifles—these hand-fabricated by colonial gunsmiths primarily for use by hunters. In the mid-1750s, the French and Indian Wars had brought an influx of guns and cannons into America from Britain and France, and local gunsmiths were able to copy European improvements. Twenty years later, as the Revolution gathered momentum and an integrated colonial army was formed, native arms-making became an urgent enterprise. This required a sharp increase in the output of iron. Both industries were still rooted in the manual-labor past, and every step in the process—from the mining of ore to the casting of gun barrels and cannonballs—was accomplished exclusively by hand and body toil. The iron and arms industries gave plenty of people work into the early 1780s. But it was the kind of slow, tedious and exhausting work that the English, and other northern European people after them, had started to replace fifty years before.

In terms of output, then, the iron industry was the first to make significant advances in the young republic. After the war, however, with the withdrawal of French financing and the continuation of the English embargo on iron-finishing technology, the industry was forced to settle back into the manufacture of the crude products of the past.

"Iron-finishing" meant this: The iron industry in early America had originally been developed to provide crude iron, in the form of bars of "pig," for the mills and forges of the English Midlands, which would then turn the colonial iron into specific "finished" iron products. That had been another reason for the Iron Acts the English had levied against the colonies in 1750: to prevent the colonists from being able to make their own finished products, and thus to create an exclusive market in America for the products of their own manufacturers. Crude iron was shipped from the colonies to the Midlands, then returned in the form of finished products for sale to the colonists at steep prices. The English manufacturers paid little for American pig iron at its source and were exempted from having to pay a duty on it when it arrived in England. When it returned to the colonies in specific product form, the products not only cost a great deal to purchase but were additionally freighted with large import tariffs. This was just one of the many ways in which England had increasingly exploited the colonies in the years leading up to the War of Independence.

So, although the capacity to forge crude iron increased considerably in the United States as a result of the Revolution, the technical ability to fabricate finished iron products remained seriously retarded. American iron making was caught in a vicious circle. In order to create a more complex and lucrative industry in finished iron, machinery—itself made of finished iron—was required. But without the means to produce finished iron, such machinery could not be made. The problem was compounded by the fact that the post-Revolution immigrants from England who were familiar with the more advanced methods of iron fabrication were at first either still disdainful of machinery or not gifted enough to reproduce the secrets of England's finished-iron technology. The true beginnings in the United States of heavy industry as we know it today were still almost fifty years away.

The same could be said, more or less, of every other industry, major and minor, that later contributed to America's emergence as the world's preeminent industrial power. In contrast to the relatively brief time it took for the country to transform itself into an industrial and technological colossus, it took a remarkably long time to get started.

There were many reasons for this, some of them already alluded to. In addition to the general lack of colonial interest in the basic sciences, and to England's stifling of native American initiative in the industrial and technological realms, the newly emancipated United States simply lacked the capitalistic sophistication and financial wherewithal to carve out a workable industrial base immediately after the Revolution. The only true large native industries up to the time of independence had been fishing and whaling. I say "true" because this was the only industry most of the fruits of which went in trade not to England but to the colonies. Lumbering and iron making, the other American "heavy" industries, were conducted primarily for the benefit of England.

The British Isles were forest-depleted. Timber was harvested in its greatest quantities in the colonies for the building of British ships, and by-products such as tar, pitch and turpentine were extracted for the benefit of British naval stores. As we have seen, crude iron was made primarily for shipment to England's Midlands. But fishing was a genuine native commercial enterprise, used to feed the coastal regions of America where the largest concentrations of population were, and to trade inland for such agricultural staples as flour and tobacco. Whaling flourished to supply the demand for spermaceti, the basic raw material of the candlemaking industry, which was concentrated in colonial Rhode Island, and for sperm oil and whalebone.

Fishing and lumbering, then, and to a lesser extent crude iron and food agriculture, were the major raw-material industries of the colonies up to the time of the Revolution. With the exception of the fishing industry, all were financed to a great extent by British investment, as were such subsidiary industries as shipbuilding, flour milling, and tobacco and cotton culture. Most of that financial support collapsed during the Revolution, and it was a decade and more after the war before enough native American capital, along with foreign trade credits, could be accumulated to restore the basic raw-material underpinnings of the new nation. Those relatively few Americans who had large sums of liquid capital at hand preferred to invest it in land and land speculation rather than in industry. And even among them, many fell into financial ruin because of their inexperience in capitalistic enterprise, their greed, and the fragile foundations of the early American economy.

Let it never be said that the United States started as some glorious adventure in idealistic altruism, with all of its roughly 2.5 million citizens pulling together in common cause to establish the first truly democratic utopia on earth. The facts were quite different. The Revolutionary War had been fought to regain the liberties the colonies had lost under England's expanding political dominion, and also to wrest a larger slice of the world economic pie away from the English. It is true enough that once the Revolution was launched there emerged sensible and learned men who, exposed to the rise in Enlightenment thought, saw an opportunity to create a new, cooperative and representative form of political government and social order, and that to a certain extent they succeeded. But the Revolution was essentially an economic one. It was engineered mostly by men who were thoroughly English in their instincts and outlook, and who sought to transfer whole the British economic system and way of life to America, *sans* monarchy. It was only the ferocity of Britain's resistance during the Revolution, and its unforgiving intransigence in the years immediately after, that compelled the Founding Fathers to formulate a more radically (for the times) republican and constitutional style of government. This was reflected vividly by the long stretch of time it took the separate states, after the Revolution, to arrive at a settled blueprint for the future federal government—six years. It was not until 1788, when a federal Constitution was adopted in the face of much opposition, some of it violent, that the final framework of the American "experiment" was erected and a national government was able to proceed.

In the meantime, between 1782 and 1788, economic depression set in. Among those with capital as well as those without, it was every man for himself. Notwithstanding their lofty political aspirations for the country, the early American monied groups had not yet learned that the monarchical capitalism of England, which still clung to the feudal past by concentrating wealth among a relatively small class and then regulating and restricting enterprise so as to preserve that concentration, was not what the progressive economic and political theories of the Enlightenment were about. A healthy, productive economy was certainly the prerequisite of success of any political system, no matter how new, no matter how revolutionary. But to apply the economic principles and practices of industrial monarchy to the nonindustrial nonmonarchy that revolutionary America represented would be folly. A revolution not only in the political nature of the United States but in the nature of its English-derived capitalism was necessary. Without a democratization of the economic system, the proposed democratic political system was sure to fail.

Fail it almost did in the first decade of its existence. The near failure was due partly to England's potent retaliatory measures against the young republic. The scorned parent not only slowed the transfer of industrial know-how and capital investment to its offspring, but it also closed off lucrative export markets for those goods America *was* capable of producing, particularly in nearby Canada and the West Indies.

But the difficulties could also be attributed in large part to the attempts of early America's wealthy class to carry on economically as if there had been no revolution. The new nation's wealth was concentrated in that small portion of the colonial population, mostly English by tradition and genetic heritage, that had orchestrated the War of Independence: the Cavaliers of Virginia, the Brahmins of Massachusetts, the Barons of Pennsylvania. (Although the majority of the population of Pennsylvania at the time of the Revolution was divided between English and German, the English "Barons," one of whose leading lights was Benjamin Franklin, were those who most avidly supported independence.) It was also the most highly educated class. Authors of the Declaration of Independence in 1776, strategists of the Articles of Confederation in 1778, and framers of the national Constitution in 1788, its members were well read in the political theories of the leading Enlightenment philosophers of England and Europe.

They were, however, considerably less well informed about the ideas of the Enlightenment's principal economic theorist, Adam Smith.

In his *Wealth of Nations*, Adam Smith, the Scottish intellectual, had laid the groundwork for the transformation of Britain's monarchical and feudalistic economic system into a modern capitalism that was congruent with, and even refined, the Enlightenment's ideas of political and social democracy. Ironically, *Wealth of Nations* was not published until 1776. Thus its theories on the division of labor, mercantilism and monopoly, the economic nature of man, value and exchanges, and *laissez-faire* free enterprise did not have a chance to penetrate American sensibilities until well after the political revolution had been won.

Typical of the immediate post-Revolution neo-British capitalist approach, and of its contrariness to the democratic political and social structure being shaped in the mid-1780s, was the story of Robert Morris. Morris, English-born in 1734, had immigrated to Philadelphia. In 1754 he began to accumulate a considerable private fortune as a partner in one of that city's largest shipping and mercantile houses (precursors of today's merchant and investment banks). Although at first he resisted the drive for separation, he was finally coaxed into signing the Declaration of Independence a few weeks after its adoption in 1776. Thereafter he became probably the most important financial cog in the Revolutionary War, raising money (including his own) domestically and obtaining loans from France to supply Washington's troops with arms and munitions. Morris's financial legerdermain contributed directly to Washington's war-ending defeat of the British at Yorktown and he was hailed as one of the heroes of the Revolution. He capped off his Founding Father career by becoming a delegate to the Constitutional Convention in 1787 and by serving as the first United States senator from Pennsylvania.

In contrast to many Patriots of the immediate post-Revolution years, Morris firmly believed in a strong, centralized federal system of governance and championed the novel—even radical—political principles that shaped the character of early American government. As noted, during the six years between Independence and the Constitution in the 1780s, debate raged over the proper form the government should take—indeed, over the proper form the entire society should take. One major faction, led by

Thomas Jefferson, advocated a government that would favor a democratic agrarian order, a broad diffusion of wealth, and relative freedom from industrialism, urbanism and organized finance typified by Britain. Jefferson's philosophy derived from his oft-stated belief in the perfectibility of man and his certainty that people, acting through simply structured representative systems, could be left to govern themselves.

The chief spokesman for the other major faction was Alexander Hamilton, who promoted the concepts of a representative but complex central government under strong executive leadership (the presidency), a balanced and diversified economic order based as much on industrial pursuits as on agriculture, and active governmental involvement in finance, industry and commerce.

Although some of Jefferson's ideas were incorporated in the subsequent constitutional blueprint, Hamilton and his Federalist supporters prevailed for the most part. Robert Morris, who like Hamilton retained a residual belief in the monarchical theory that ordinary men did not have the capacity to govern themselves and that the best government was one composed of a society's elite, thoroughly supported the Hamiltonian approach. For his support, Morris was given the honor of nominating George Washington to be the nation's first President.

After declining Washington's invitation to become Secretary of the Treasury in 1789 (Hamilton took the job and thus became the prime architect of the early American economy), Morris went into the Senate. Encouraged by Hamilton's elitism, or perhaps feeling vindicated by it, Morris in the meantime had set out to expand his personal fortune by land speculation. One of his first acquisitions was a large portion of what is today Washington, D.C., then a swampy Potomac River backwater that was ten years away from becoming the nation's capital. Morris's aggressive and haughty English style of land acquisition proved the contradiction between the old economic order and the new, however, even though the new economic order had yet to be codified. When Morris's lands were appropriated by congressional fiat for the nation's capital in 1790, he was suddenly and unexpectedly thrust to the brink of financial ruin. Fighting desperately to salvage his reduced real-estate empire by means of private loans, he failed. In 1798 he was sent to debtor's prison, where he remained for three years. Five years later he died, a disgraced and humiliated public ward.

Robert Morris's financial downfall was just one of many that occurred during the first troubled decade of the republic. In the meantime, beginning to recognize the need for a new economic approach to deal with the actualities of political democracy, Alexander Hamilton and his Federalist compatriots had begun to debate the most appropriate course for the nation's economy. The message of Adam Smith's capitalist economics had yet to penetrate deeply into the sensibilities of the Federalists. After the nation paused in 1790 to mourn the death of its gray eminence, Benjamin Franklin, Hamilton, as the first Secretary of the Treasury, devised a fiscal program based on the heavy taxation of business and industrial enterprises. As part of that program he proposed a national bank to control the flow of capital investment.

Both of these measures met with strong and vocal opposition from Hamilton's by-then traditional adversaries, the Jeffersonians. Out of their differences arose the new nation's first constitutional crisis. Jefferson and his supporters argued that Hamilton's plans were unconstitutional, particularly in view of the fact that the Constitution had not specifically provided for the incorporation of a national bank or for "selective" taxation. It was against this very sort of British-derived, underhanded economic methodology that the colonies had rebelled. For their part, the Hamiltonians insisted that the Constitution contained "implied" powers that granted the executive branch and Congress the right—nay, the duty—to finance the government.*

The Jeffersonian posture gave birth to the "strict constructionist" view of constitutional government, whereas the Hamiltonians begat the "loose constructionist" approach. This in turn produced the beginnings of the two-party mode of politics in America, with the Jeffersonians (minimal government) sowing the seeds of the modern-day Republican party and the Hamiltonians (maximal government) engendering today's Democratic party. (Of course, the political differences and similarities between and among the two have melded over the past two hundred years; both parties today give lip service to Jefferson's philosophy while arguing over the extent to which modern "hands-on" government is excessive and economically debilitating.) The split also produced an increasingly activist role for the Supreme Court in American life.

*The Hamilton faction won this initial debate when, in 1791, the federal Bank of the United States was established.

While the conflict between Hamilton and Jefferson raged on (Jefferson was Secretary of State in George Washington's first administration), Hamilton released a "Report on Manufactures" at the end of 1791. The report, in addition to proposing bounties to encourage agriculture, recommended a program of federal financial sponsorship of domestic manufacturing industries. The report passed from the scene without any significant notice. The nation was still caught up in constitutional politics and the ideological feud between Hamilton and Jefferson. Industrial production and cohesion, the lifeblood of any modern nation of the time, remained of secondary concern. As did scientific endeavor.

CHAPTER **3**

SYNTHESIS

It was not until 1793, when Jefferson resigned from the Washington administration in protest of Hamilton's increasing authority in the government, that Hamilton gained enough influence to commit the country to a future to be based heavily on industry. Hamilton, still often accused of being excessively pro-English in his sensibility, envisioned his plan as a catching-up process. He recognized that the fledgling United States was well behind England and northern Europe in industrial expertise and technique. He knew that the country was committed to expanding westward—it had already acquired most of the territory as far as the Mississippi River as a result of the treaty that ended the Revolution—and that the West promised to be rich in natural raw-material resources.

Future economic prosperity lay in the exploitation of those resources, Hamilton insisted in his "Report on Manufactures." But such exploitation meant their conversion into goods and products. If the matter was left to the Jeffersonian faction of the nation, which advocated leisurely development, the country might wither and die from economic starvation before its natural wealth could be tapped. Although increasingly embroiled in European war in reaction to the Napoleonic revolution in France, the British still had designs on restoring dominion over their former colonies and other territories in North America. If the United States failed to become economically independent in quick fashion, it could fall prey once again to English rule. Hamilton, then, once rid of the political restraints imposed by the Jeffersonians, persuaded the Washington administration to support a rapid buildup of industry, to be shaped and controlled by the federal government.

In the 1790s, the "state of the art" in American industry was well behind that of England, and so was agriculture. Great strides in agricultural production had been made in Britain and northern Europe in the previous century, strides almost as revolutionary as those in manufacturing. The rotation of crops had been the standard European practice for several centuries prior to the American Revolution. In America, crop rotation would not become the rule until well into the 1800s. Although the plow was commonly in use in the United States, it remained made of wood and was much inferior to the more advanced and varied iron versions of England and Holland. And the discovery of the fertilization of soil in Europe had yet to make an impact on American agriculture.

Advances in agriculture in England and northern Europe had transformed farming there from a subsistence to a commercial enterprise in the early 1700s. In the process, much of the labor previously required for farming was released to the burgeoning manufacturing industries of mid-century. In the America of the late 1700s, on the other hand, farming was still largely a subsistence occupation. Tobacco, rice and indigo had been produced in quantity in the southern colonies for export, but that was about the extent of America's cash-crop base. Cotton cultivation had recently been introduced (and would soon become the major agricultural export), but commercial farming—especially of foods and foodstuffs—was scarcely done.

The great majority of the country's 4 million population in the 1790s was engaged to a greater or lesser degree in farming, both within the states and in the territories beyond the Appalachian Mountains that were being opened up by post-Revolution expansion and by the Washington administration's open-door immigration policy. But most farming was designed to feed only family and neighbors. Those few who were fortunate enough to possess enough land and labor to produce surpluses might trade them to other farmers or to local grinding mills for produce in kind, but that "commercial" aspect of early American agriculture was nothing like the large-scale commercialization of agriculture that had occurred across the Atlantic.

The nation's industrial base was similarly backward. While large factories, their new metal machinery increasingly powered by steam, had sprung up throughout England and northern Europe, American manufacture was still rooted in the cottage, in the village workshop and, on a widely scattered basis, in the small, creek-powered mill. In the mills the crude machinery was still made of bulky wood and stone. Driven by water wheels through mechanically ingenious but easily breakable gearing systems, the mills were at the mercy of seasonal floods and droughts. The most productive of the small industries were concentrated in workshops, which specialized in custom handcrafts such as hat making, cabinetmaking, shoemaking, clock making, silversmithing, candle making, and the like. The organized manufacture of clothing was conducted mostly through the "putting-out" system; that is, fabrics were woven in private homes (homespuns) on a piecework basis and then purchased by central tailoring workshops before being shaped and hand-sewn into finished garments.

It was in the spinning and weaving of fabrics that American industry took its first tentative steps toward modern methods, replacing tedious human handwork with the much faster pace of powered machinery. In the years just before and during the American Revolution, inventors in Britain had devised a series of huge spinning machines that so vastly increased textile output that England was suddenly hard put to keep up with its factories' demand for raw materials. By 1785 the last step in the transformation of the English textile industry was completed when Watt's steam engine was adapted to drive the new machinery.

Steam power was still but an abstract concept in America at the time of George Washington's first inauguration, although in England and Europe it was being perfected for a variety of uses, including railroad and marine transport. The renewal of English immigration to America after the Revolution, while it brought mostly skilled but embittered handcraftsmen disenfranchised by Britain's industrial transformation, also introduced a few men who possessed inside knowledge of the new industrial processes and did not nurse hostility toward the idea of mechanization. One of those immigrants was Samuel Slater, who had journeyed to America from Derbyshire, in England's industrial Midlands, in 1789.

As a fifteen-year-old in Derbyshire, Slater had been apprenticed in 1783 to the firm of Richard Arkwright, the Englishman who had invented or improved upon much of that nation's cotton textile machinery. Britain's ban on the export of mechanical and technical know-how to the United States was still being strictly enforced six years later, when Slater decided to emigrate. Before departing, he memorized the details of the machinery made by Arkwright and others, and when he arrived in Rhode Island he had a firm blueprint of a modern mechanized English textile mill in his head.

In 1790, a year after his arrival in Providence, the twenty-one-year-old Slater met financier Moses Brown. With Brown's financial backing, Slater managed to reproduce the English machinery. Within three years the two built a cotton spinning mill at Pawtucket, Rhode Island, that became the prototype for the revolution in textile manufacture in America and later served as the crude model for the development of the factory system in other American industrial enterprises. Thereafter, benefiting from the vast increase in domestic cotton growing made possible first by the territorial expansion of the American South and then by Eli Whitney's invention of the cotton gin, and applying the new capitalist theories of Adam Smith, Brown and Slater plowed much of their profits into building a succession of further textile plants in New England. They were the first to prove that the theories of "enlightened" capitalism, as espoused by Adam Smith, could work in the United States.

This combination of industrial espionage and improvisational capitalism, coupled with the invention of the cotton gin, produced the first major manufacturing entity in America and made its founders rich. Such was not the case with Eli Whitney, whose invention contributed so much to the fortunes of Brown and Slater. Indeed, although Whitney's cotton gin was a much more original piece of work, he quickly ran afoul of the new capitalism and came away practically penniless. Not that Slater and Brown were in any way responsible for Whitney's failure to realize the full potential of his device. Whitney had only himself to blame. Like Ben Franklin as a young man, he was initially more interested in the solutions of practical problems than in their financial rewards.

Tobacco and rice farming in the American South had plunged into a deep depression after the outbreak of the Revolution severed their primary markets in England and the West Indies. These enterprises, long the main commercial staples of southern colonial agriculture, had made a number of white planters, farmers and brokers wealthy, but they had thrived on the backs of slave labor. Although slave owning was a common practice at the time throughout the colonies, even among many of the celebrated architects of the nation, slavery was already being acknowledged by others as antithetical to the social principles upon which the nation had been established. As a result, antislavery sentiment gradually gathered force, particularly in the northern states. Nevertheless, Northerners did not protest too loudly against slavery after independence was won. They believed that the collapse of the once-lucrative tobacco and rice agriculture of the southern states would bring a natural end to it. They were unable, however, to foresee the revolution in cotton growing that was about to occur.

Cotton had been grown in the southern colonies as early as the mid-seventeenth century, when cotton textiles were still being hand-manufactured in England. But cotton agriculture throughout the colonial period had proved largely unprofitable because of the extensive time and labor involved in separating the seeds from the fibers of the only variety of cotton plant that flourished in the South: the "upland" plant.

The War of Independence not only brought the main southern agricultural enterprises to the verge of collapse, it also opened up the frontiers beyond the southern Appalachians—the valleys and plateaus that swept westward from the mountains into what is today Tennessee, Alabama and Mississippi. Many white farmers fled from the agricultural depression of the coastal South to stake out new farms and plantations for themselves in the western uplands. With them they brought their gangs of slaves. When it came time to begin planting, in the expectation that the ongoing conflict with England would soon generate a domestic market for it strong enough to overcome its previous unprofitability, they tried cotton. They were right—the cutoff of finished cotton goods from England did produce a marginally profitable domestic demand for raw cotton. And the establishment of the Slater-Brown mechanized cotton-spinning mills in New England a decade later was about to create a further demand, which the southern cotton growers would find it difficult to keep up with because of the slow hand process of separating seed from fiber. It took one slave an entire day, removing seeds, to produce a single pound of clean raw cotton. All these factors brought about not the hoped-for diminution of black slavery, but an intensification of it.

Enter, then, Eli Whitney. Whitney, an admirer of Benjamin Franklin, had been born on a farm in Massachusetts in 1765 and had tinkered extensively in his father's barn-side tool shop as a boy. Inspired by Franklin's writings on science, invention and philosophy, he entered Yale University in 1789 to acquire an education. Upon leaving in 1792, he was offered a summer tutoring job at a cotton plantation in Georgia. While there, he became exposed to the increasingly common complaint of plantation owners throughout the region: how the tedious hand method of separating seed from fiber was robbing cotton growing of its true profit potential.

With his tinkerer's outlook, the twenty-six-year-old Whitney spent several days watching slaves handpick green seeds from clumps of cotton fiber. It reminded him, he told his host, of the days on his father's farm when he was assigned the task of plucking the Sunday-dinner chicken; he had often thought about trying to devise a machine to do the job and had even written a letter to Benjamin Franklin in Philadelphia posing the problem. (The letter had gone unanswered.)

On the plantation, Whitney found what was known as a roller gin (short for *engine*), a hand-operated device with two opposed cylinders, much like the manual clothes wringer of later times, through which cotton was pressed forcing the seeds to pop out. The roller gin was useful for thin black-seed cotton but had little effect on the denser green-seed staple, the only variety that could be grown in the inland regions of the South. Nevertheless, his observation of the operation of the roller gin, and the recollection of his idle childhood discussions with his father about a mechanical chicken-plucking device, triggered an idea in Whitney's mind. Using scraps of metal he found on the plantation, he devised a hand tool, similar to a large hair comb, made of slim, wirelike tines extending from a metal grip. When he "combed" the tines through a thick clump of seed-filled green cotton, he observed the effect he had anticipated: The tines worked their way through the fiber and, because the seeds were too large to pass through the slits between the tines, they were swept out of the fiber by the comb.

Soon Whitney found a way to secure the tines perpendicularly around the circumference of a rotating wheel so that, as the wheel spun above a hopper filled with seeded cotton, the tines clawed the fiber away from the seeds. Then he devised a second opposed wheel by which wire brushes, secured to it, removed the seedless cotton fibers from the tines of the first wheel. Within the year Whitney put together a prototype water-driven machine, tested it on the plantation and demonstrated that it could process fifty times as much raw cotton each day as a single slave could.

Word of Whitney's invention—although it was more an innovation of an existing device, the roller gin, than a pure invention—spread quickly through the plantation region. Although Whitney applied for a patent in 1794, by the time he did so, copies of his mechanism, some of them improvements, were being sold throughout the South by others. He thus lost the chance to monopolize its manufacture and sale. He sued many of the imitators but did not receive a favorable verdict until 1807, by which time most of the money awarded to him was eaten up by legal debts.

Whitney managed to recover from his initial setback, however. In its earliest stages his machine had engaged the interest of Virginia plantation squire Thomas Jefferson, a slave owner despite his high-minded pronouncements about liberty and equality. Jefferson, at the time still Secretary of State in the Washington administration, was an inventor of sorts himself, and he was among those who had urged Whitney to secure a patent before making the existence of his new device known.

In 1798 the United States found itself on the verge of war with its former ally, France, over a variety of issues. As a result, the federal government put out a call for the quick manufacture of ten thousand muskets. Whitney by then had returned north and settled in New Haven, where he was pressing his claims against the exploiters of his cotton gin. However, he had maintained his contacts with Jefferson, who, after quitting the Washington administration in 1793, had returned to government as Vice-President in the administration of John Adams, Washington's successor. Jefferson suggested that Whitney, who had established a small gunmaking shop in New Haven, bid for the musket commission. Whitney did so, and with Jefferson's help he obtained the contract.

In the late 1780s Jefferson had been in France as successor to Benjamin Franklin in the post of American minister to that country. He had observed the beginnings of machine industry there and had brought back a number of firm ideas on how to improve the basic shop-manufacturing process. Between 1793 and 1796 he had shared his ideas with, among others, Whitney. Whitney had established his gun-making business largely to experiment with Jefferson's theories, the substance of which was the principle of using interchangeable parts. His acquisition of the government musket contract was to be the first practical test of the principle. If Whitney could manufacture a series of component parts for the ten thousand muskets, each part in each series identical to the other, all that would remain would be the task of assembling them into finished weapons.

To put the idea to the test, though, required the handcrafting of special precision tools and dies to mass-produce each musket part, since such equipment was unknown in the United States. Using the advance money from his government contract, Whitney painstakingly designed a collection of such machine tools. It took him two years to turn out the necessary drill presses, jigs and templates to begin making his precision musket parts, but when he was finished he had originated a new tool-and-die industry, the backbone of all subsequent mass-production manufacture.

As a commercial manufacturer, Whitney proved much less able than as a designer and inventor. He encountered a variety of technical problems trying to produce the ten thousand muskets, and it took him more than ten years to make delivery. Fortunately for him, Jefferson was President for much of that time and refused to foreclose on the contract, which had mandated delivery within two years. As a result, once Whitney had perfected his methods, he was able to supply the American Army with enough weaponry to repel the British in the War of 1812 and to make the fortune that had been denied him from his cotton gin.

Within the period of a decade, not just for the United States but for the entire world, Whitney had launched a revolution in agriculture, through cotton, and a second one in mass manufacturing, through gun making. Nor was it just the actual machines and tools he invented that generated the twin revolutions; it was the further possibilities they unleashed. Until 1793 agriculture in all its forms had been almost exclusively and intensively a human-labor enterprise. In the wake of the cotton gin came a flurry of ideas about applying machinery to other areas of agriculture in order to increase productivity and reduce costs. And following Whitney's invention of the precision tool, and his eventually successful testing of Jefferson's interchangeable-parts principle, there erupted in America a volcano of new notions about the traditional manufacture of "fine" goods and products. Previously, product manufacture had been conducted by skilled, deliberate, individual craftsmen, using hand tools in small workshops to painstakingly construct and shape their finished products. Whitney's system opened up the possibility of manufacturing a diverse variety of products with precision parts turned out by relatively inexperienced and unskilled workmen engaged in simple, compartmentalized machine-tool operations. The skill and craft would be reserved to those who conceived and designed the precision tools. Although it would be several more decades before the fruits of Whitney's work would be fully realized, it set the stage for a mass industrial revolution in America that would not only catch up with Europe's but eventually surpass it.

Benjamin Franklin had been basically—if a pun will be excused—a "static" inventor. Which is to say that his inventions were of devices that did not move and involved no mechanical parts: the lightning rod, the iron stove, bifocal spectacles. And although all proved to have valuable practical application, Franklin's discoveries were primarily conceptual in nature, owing no doubt to his long self-training in the abstract sciences.

Whitney, on the other hand, was America's first "dynamic" inventor. His devices moved and articulated, requiring increasingly complex and precise machinery to manufacture effectively. Too, they were concrete in nature, the inspiration less of an abstract mind than of a pragmatic one.

Two traditions thus finally began to merge in the United States of the early 1800s, auguring the next major domestic development in the combined realms of science and technology. That development was the first practical introduction to America of steam power and the steam engine.

Sketchy information about the evolution of steam technology in England had trickled to the colonies in the decade prior to the Revolution, but little in the way of hard knowledge had made the journey. It was not until the early 1780s, as the Revolution was drawing to a close, that a few American scientists began to investigate steam on their own. During the time the first useful and efficient industrial steam engines were being put into service in

England, early American experiments by scientists such as John Stevens and Oliver Evans only proved how far behind the United States was. But for the intervention of a young man who was less a scientist than an aspiring artist and entrepreneur, the gap might have lasted much longer than it did. The young man's name was Robert Fulton.

Born near Lancaster, Pennsylvania, in 1756, Fulton grew up wanting to sketch and paint. In his late teens he studied in Philadelphia; then, in 1786, at the age of twenty-one, he traveled to England in the hope of making his mark as an artist there. His initial years in London were a struggle, however, and he was forced to take a job as a mechanical draftsman. This awakened an interest in invention and engineering, and Fulton soon turned his hand to designing mechanical devices of his own.

Just before leaving Philadelphia for London, Fulton had witnessed efforts by local inventor John Fitch to build a steam-powered boat for carrying cargoes along the Delaware River. Much of the interior commerce of late eighteenth-century England was conducted over a system of rivers and interconnecting canals. During his first year in London, Fulton made several treks into southern England's canal country to paint landscapes. Recalling John Fitch's steamboat experiments on the Delaware, he was surprised that steam power had not already been applied to the boats that plied England's inland waterways. Thus, when Fulton wedded his artistic talents to engineering, his ambition focused on adapting steam to England's river and canal traffic.

Fulton educated himself in the principles of James Watt's steam engine, which had recently been further refined and was being deployed on a widening scale throughout industrial Britain. As he did so, he learned that several other English inventors were already hard at work on a steam-driven canal boat, so he concentrated on other aspects of the application of steam power to the canals. In the early 1790s he devised an apparatus for raising and lowering canal boats, then a power shovel for digging canal channels. These inventions earned enough money to enable Fulton to resume painting. Thinking that his chances for artistic success might be better in France, then in the midst of its own political revolution, he moved to Paris in 1797. Aside from a panoramic painting of the French capital, however, his art work went unacclaimed and he once again took up his engineering pursuits.

Fulton remained abroad and had a modest measure of success designing technologically advanced aqueducts and bridges. In 1806, though, after the French and then the British government refused to show interest in his experiments with a steam-powered submarine boat, he returned to the United States. When Fulton had demonstrated his submarine in 1803, he had done so in partnership with Robert Livingston, the wealthy American minister to Paris. Upon returning to America, Fulton learned that John Fitch's Delaware steamboat, though launched nineteen years earlier, had proved unfeasible, as had later versions by other builders. The basic problem was in the crude, dangerously high-pressured engines their inventors had fabricated.

In addition, the engines required huge amounts of fuel—so much that there was little room for cargo.

With his intimate knowledge of Watt's low-pressure steam engine—which had become standardized in England and was being manufactured in quantity—Fulton saw a new opportunity for himself. Settling in New York, he obtained financing from Robert Livingston and built a large, bargelike riverboat with two side-fixed wooden paddle wheels and an auxiliary sail. Then, in the spring of 1807, again with Livingston's help, he was able to acquire a standard Watt engine directly from the Boulton and Watt works in England and spent the next few months installing it in his boat.

He completed the job early in August of 1807. On August 16, with the grimy Fulton in the engine room, the vessel's boiler was fired. The next morning Fulton, freshly bathed, stood at the open helm. With steam and black, wood-scented smoke pouring copiously from its tall funnel, the boat eased away from the New Jersey wharf, opposite lower Manhattan, to which it had been tied. The wharf-side crowd gaped in a combination of wonder and skepticism. Once out in the North River's powerful seaward tidal flow, Fulton signaled his engine-room assistants to engage the piston connected to the driving gear that would transfer power to the twin paddle wheels.*

At first nothing happened. As the long, narrow craft was

---

*For the uninitiated, where the Hudson River flows seaward past New York City, it was, and is, known as the North River. Fulton named his boat "The North River Steamboat." Rebuilt and lengthened the following year, it soon came to be known as "The Clermont," after the upriver estate of Fulton's benefactor Livingston.

caught by the river's tidal current and began to drift aft toward New York Bay, the spectators on both the Manhattan and New Jersey shores guffawed and winked knowingly at one another. But then they saw the vessel's midships paddle wheels begin to rotate—at first with agonizing slowness, then with growing speed and force. The *Clermont*'s aftward drift slowed. Soon she was as though dead in the water, only her paddles in motion. Finally she began to inch forward against the current, her funnel belching with dark fury.

Making greater and greater headway, the *Clermont* labored northward, passing the upper tip of Manhattan Island a little over two hours later. Two mornings hence she had steamed 150 miles up the Hudson and had Albany in view.

Thanks to Robert Fulton, and no less to Robert Livingston, the age of steam had arrived in America. Important enough in itself, the feat heralded for the United States two even more significant events: the permanent wedding of science and mechanics, and that of technology and capitalism. Thomas Jefferson was President of the country at the time of Fulton's first river voyage. His vision of America as a simple, equality-based agrarian society went up in the smoke and cinders that spewed from the *Clermont*'s funnel.

CHAPTER **4**

THE PIVOTAL DECADE

In 1807 the quality of life in America essentially was no different from what it had been thirty years earlier, during the Revolution. Indeed, by most standards it was little different from what it had been a hundred years before. The addition of several states beyond the original states' borders, the acquisition of the huge midsection of the continent through the 1803 Louisiana Purchase, and a doubling of the population gave the country a distinctly changed physical character, however. The change was most apparent to the inhabitants of the major cities, which had begun to expand and grow more crowded at an unprecedented pace. New York, at the time of the Revolution a community of no more than 25,000 people packed into the tightly circumscribed lower reaches of Manhattan Island, had tripled its population and was spilling northward. Philadelphia, considerably larger than New York in population during the Revolutionary years, was on the verge of losing its preeminence to New York. Boston and Baltimore, too, had undergone population explosions, as to a lesser degree had virtually all the smaller cities and towns of the Eastern Seaboard.

Nevertheless life remained more or less as it had been for generations. There were few newspapers, and those that published regularly were for the most part limited in circulation and far outdated in their reporting of anything but local events. News of the English and French wars in Europe took months to reach the eyes of American newspaper readers, and even then the reports were laden with uncertainty and error. Information about signal events at the seat of power in Washington took weeks to reach Bostonians and Charlestonians via newspapers. Often the federal mail service, originated half a century earlier as a private colonial enterprise by Benjamin Franklin and others, was quicker in disseminating regional news. But that, too, carried with it a built-in unreliability, the accuracy of the reports dependent on the interpretive biases of those who wrote letters, and then of those who received them and shared their contents with others.*

Transportation was similarly slow and limited. The system of intercolonial dirt highways that had evolved prior to the Revolution, little improved thirty years later except for the addition of occasional stopping places (inns and taverns), remained the principal routes of land travel. Those who could afford it journeyed by the old familiar horse-drawn stage; those many more who couldn't used their own crude wagons or went on horseback, or walked. As time went on, many of the main arteries became toll roads and a few were even planked to combat mud and dust. But those developments improved neither the speed of land travel nor its general comfort.

Maritime transport was the only other form of long-distance movement. A traveler going from Boston to, say, Baltimore might opt to sail rather than make the overland trek. That meant the wind-powered packet boat, many of which plied the coast from Maine to Georgia, making countless stops along the way. Again, if one could afford decent accommodations, the journey, though slow, could be reasonably comfortable. Those who could not afford first-class accommodations usually found themselves sharing their space on board with livestock and lumber being shipped from one region to another. Fulton's steamboat and its successors would soon improve the comfort and speed of water transport, but only marginally as compared to the differences between modern train and jet airplane travel over long distances. The more far-reaching practical benefit of the steamboat was its introduction of the potentialities of steam power across a much broader spectrum of American enterprise. Possibly even more beneficial in the long term was its implantation in the American mind of the concepts of

---

*It does not seem farfetched to suggest that the modern American love of printed gossip, so profitably exploited by today's tabloid and magazine industry, is a matter of cultural inheritance stemming from the time when gossip and speculative reporting were the primary means of spreading news.

personal mobility and leisure, concepts that contributed as powerfully as any other to the shaping of the American colossus.

Territorial and population expansion were the principal features of change during the first thirty years of the United States'
existence. For many that meant nothing more than a revival of the
hardships experienced by the colonies' first generations of settlers.
As the descendants of those pioneering generations, driven by
post-Revolution hard times, pushed westward toward the Great
Lakes region and the Mississippi Valley to carve out new home-
steads, farms and villages, life for many early nineteenth-century
Americans took on the grim and difficult tenor of that of their
seventeenth-century forebears. The same held true for many of
the newer foreign immigrants who, finding little economic opportunity in the established seaboard cities, joined the westward trek.

Nor had there been any significant progress on a more personal level. Compared to today, daily life was an infinitely more
tedious and frequently tragic arrangement with nature.* This was
especially so with respect to health and health care. The average
life-span in 1810 was thirty-nine years; those who lived beyond
that age might have considered themselves the blessed winners of
a divine lottery. Communicable diseases were rampant: Typhus,
smallpox, yellow fever, scarlet fever and tuberculosis were only a
few of the mass killers. Bacterial infections and childbirth were
also great hazards, and unrelievable pain was often a daily component of many people's lives. Although a primitive medical profession had been established, and with it a few rudimentary medical
schools, the nation's physicians were helpless to cure illness; all
they could do was attempt to manage it, and then hope for the
best. For their patients, the best frequently was a final merciful
release from agonizing pain and wastage through death.

The reality of widespread disease and premature death was
not unique to early America; it existed throughout the world.
And, as elsewhere, it had created a powerful stoicism in the populace with regard to the fragility of human life. That stoicism was
reinforced by the country's deep religious strain. Thus, although
life was never considered cheap, most Americans accepted death,

---

*Of course, people living in the America of the early 1800s had no way of comparing
their situation with that of today, or of any time beyond their own. Like us, they could
make comparisons only to the past. Because there was little in the way of difference between their present and past, such comparisons were seldom made. Those that were generally bemoaned the deterioration of piety and religiosity in daily life.

even their own, with considerably less trepidation and resistance than they do today.

The stoicism of the period led also to a paradox. As the United States in the second decade of the 1800s began to perceive the potential of homegrown science, invention and technology to improve the conditions of temporal life, its vision remained limited to the more material aspects of life—to ideas and systems designed to enhance mechanization, productivity, commerce and the like. Little thought was given to applying science to the prevention or alleviation of disease, or to the prolongation of life. This, too, was due to the still-potent religious orientation of American society. To direct science toward the improvement of work and the proliferation of goods was a socially acceptable concept, since work and its fruits were at the heart of religion's earthly rationale. But to attempt to use science to interfere with the operation of the Divine Will, which is how most religious Americans rationalized the frequency of disease and death, was by silent consensus unacceptable.

Thus, although the nation's creative energy turned increasingly toward scientific and technological exploration around the time of the War of 1812, very little of that energy was devoted to the medical realm. As early as almost a hundred years before, the notorious colonial scientific theorist and religious evangelist Cotton Mather (notorious because of the contradictoriness of his professions) had promoted the idea of smallpox inoculations as a way of preventing that dread disease. Time had proved his theory sound. But so suspicious did early nineteenth-century society remain of mixing science and religion that few doctors dared to recommend such inoculation and fewer citizens were willing to risk it. It would not be until the middle of the century that science in America would begin to address itself seriously to the treatment of disease and the postponement of death. In the meantime, bloodletting and occasional desperate surgical procedures, without the benefit of anesthetics (which had yet to be discovered), were the only forms of "aggressive" medical treatment. More often than not, these techniques only complicated patients' problems through infection, thereby hastening death.

A similar if less life-threatening situation prevailed in what we know today as dentistry. To put it plainly, there was no such thing as dentistry in early nineteenth-century America, although there was plenty of need for it. Portrait paintings of the period seldom if ever showed their subjects smiling. Social historians credit this to the fact that a smiling visage was not considered proper for formal portraits. Equally to blame was the fact that most early nineteenth-century Americans were missing one or more teeth. Poor diet and the complete ignorance of dental hygiene wreaked havoc in the mouth of just about every citizen. Tooth decay, and its accompanying pain, was a regular feature of life. Its only relief lay in the extraction of an offending tooth, usually by a heavy-handed blacksmith whose clamping tools were the only ones suitable to the task.

Until the War of 1812, American society as a whole seemed content with life as it was, even with all its physical hardships and dangers. This was attributable in part to the strict policy of neutrality that had been implemented by Thomas Jefferson and carried on by his presidential successor, James Madison, in the face of the continuing Anglo-French struggle in Europe. With a few isolated exceptions, Americans showed little interest in the advances that had been made in science, industry and technology in Europe. Napoleon had reinvigorated scientific research on the Continent by giving it the imprimatur and financial backing of the French government. In reaction, Great Britain had redoubled its support of scientific and technological endeavor. The results were a repeated series of breakthroughs on both sides of the English Channel in chemistry, physics and biology which, though often achieved for war-making purposes, were applicable as well to the enhancement of human life and living conditions. But the United States, increasingly estranged from England and disillusioned by the unexpectedly brutal despotism of post-Revolutionary France, made little effort to import the new knowledge.

The War of 1812 shook America out of its isolationist lethargy. Although a war fought primarily over international maritime issues, most of it was waged not at sea but on American soil and internal waterways. The war had been abuilding for almost a decade. Between 1804 and 1807 the struggle for control over Europe between Napoleonic France and England had increasingly interfered with young America's most profitable organized industry: exports, mostly agricultural, and their system of delivery to foreign ports by merchant ships. While the country's domestic industrial framework had grown at a snail's pace in the thirty years following the War of Independence, its foreign shipping industry, having gotten a generous head start during the colonial period, had boomed.

Inland, the production of tobacco, cotton, grains and other agricultural staples remained a slow, tedious and expensive affair. Getting such produce to the Atlantic ports over the country's primitive roads consumed further time, money and labor. Once at the ports, however, the process became much more efficient. Well practiced in the techniques of the export trade, merchant marine companies were able to load their sailing ships quickly and send them on their way to foreign ports. Because of this intensive export activity, the nation's port cities and their shipbuilding adjuncts had thrived. In contrast, the cities of the interior—in reality still only villages and towns based on an agricultural economy—continued to languish.

By 1805 the maritime shipping industry was the largest and most economically productive in the land. As well, it had become the government's principal instrument in dealing with overseas nations, the matrix of the country's private investment-banking system, and the lens through which foreign peoples viewed and were attracted to the United States. The increasing procession of American merchant ships sailing into the harbors of northern and southern Europe, their crews regaling the local populace with stories of the money to be made and opportunities to be had in America, did more than anything else to put the United States on the map in the collective consciousness of Europe.

Between 1804 and 1807, however, much of the United States' seagoing freedom—and as a consequence much of its burgeoning export economy—was severely compromised by the Anglo-French wars. Jefferson had declared America's neutrality in the conflict. In the meantime, American export trade with England and France rose sharply as both countries found greater and greater need for foodstuffs and other raw materials for their armies. Yet each took a dim view of the fact that the United States was supplying the other, as well as itself. As a result, first Britain, then France, began to intercept and seize American merchant ships voyaging to each other's ports. These events were compounded by the English policy of forcing captured American merchant seamen to serve in the British Navy.

British actions against American shipping prompted a demand
for counteraction—even war—against England in the United
States. But Jefferson, clinging to his traditional humanistic principles, was determined to avoid war and maintain America's neutrality. Pursuing a policy he called "peaceful coercion," he
persuaded Congress in December of 1807 to impose a strict embargo on all American exports, not only to Britain and France but
to every foreign market within their respective domains. Jefferson
believed that the Embargo Act would have a twofold effect. First,
with American ships prevented from going to sea, the British and
French would no longer be able to seize them. Second, by being
deprived of American goods, even by way of third countries, the
two warring nations would eventually agree to provide safe passage to the merchant vessels of the neutral United States. Jefferson also contemplated a third consequence: that the embargo
would expedite the conclusion of the Anglo-French wars.

As it turned out, the Embargo Act did nothing to affect the
hostilities in Europe. And though it brought an effective end to
the seizures of American ships, it also gravely eroded America's
maritime commerce, theretofore the economic lifeblood of the nation. The long-term result, however, was inadvertently salutary.
The major maritime companies had amassed huge profits from the
export trade. Unable to continue reinvesting their capital toward
the expansion of their fleets and warehouses, the shipping barons
began to look to other areas of industrial enterprise in which to
sink their funds.

Because of their extensive contacts with England and northern
Europe, the leaders of the maritime industry were better acquainted than anyone else in America with the rapid progress of
the Industrial Revolution abroad. When Jefferson's embargo cut
off the return trade of finished industrial products from England
to America, and when the maritime tycoons saw how ill-equipped
the United States was to supply itself with its own advanced industrial products, they perceived their opportunity and began to
funnel large portions of their capital into land-based industry.
Samuel Slater's spinning machinery, Eli Whitney's utilization of
interchangeable parts, and Robert Fulton's successful experiment
in steam power had provided the collective impetus for the development of a more varied domestic industrial complex. In the face
of the still-influential Jeffersonian design for the nation, however,

that impetus had gained little momentum up to the time of the Embargo of 1807. Now, unwittingly, Jefferson the agrarian had let the beast of industrialism out of the cage. Despite his repeal of the Embargo Act in 1809 under strong pressure from Congress and the nation's maritime interests, he would never be able to recapture it.

In repealing the Embargo Act, Jefferson replaced it with the Non-Intercourse Act, which reopened foreign trade with all nations except Britain and France. Shortly thereafter, James Madison succeeded Jefferson as President. In 1810, duped by Napoleon, Madison, under powers granted to him by the Non-Intercourse Act, allowed maritime trade with France to recommence but retained the ban on commerce with England. This provoked a naval blockade of American ports by Britain in 1811 and a resumption of the seizure of American vessels sailing for foreign ports.

In the meantime, the westward expansion of America's continental territories had provoked the bitter resistance of the Indians. England, which had retained Canada as its remaining North American colony following the American Revolution, feared that the expansionist movement in the United States would spill over into Canada. As a consequence, the British, through their Canadian outposts, supplied arms to the Indians in the United States' western territories and encouraged them to fight against white settlement. Under the leadership of the tribal chief Tecumseh, Indians began to terrorize white settlers in the Indiana territory during the summer of 1811. In reaction, General William Henry Harrison, the governor of the territory, led a force of a thousand frontier soldiers to subdue Tecumseh's well-armed Indian guerrillas. The resulting clash, known as the Battle of Tippecanoe, was won by Harrison's troops but at great cost in casualties. Because Tecumseh's Indian fighters had been armed and supplied by the British, when the news of the battle spread through the United States it further incited anti-British sentiment. James Madison in Washington was still trying to work out a diplomatic détente with England, in the spirit of Jefferson before him. War fever rose to a steep pitch, however, incited particularly by a number of frontier politicians, elected to Congress in 1810, who felt their own constituencies threatened by the British arming of the Indians.

Led by Henry Clay of Kentucky and John C. Calhoun of

South Carolina, both riveting orators, the new Congress agitated for war against England. Midway through 1812, with his own reelection campaign in prospect and confronted by an increasingly impatient and bellicose Congress, Madison all but abandoned his diplomatic efforts and recommended a declaration of war. Congress endorsed the recommendation in short order, and on June 19, 1812, the United States and England were once again locked in combat.

To many Americans at the time, going to war seemed a hasty and improvident decision. Despite its large merchant marine, the United States had a tiny armed navy as compared to Britain's, and its standing army was small, poorly administered and ill-equipped in contrast to England's considerable forces in Canada. The American High Command, such as it was, decided to attack those troops before they could be reinforced from England. The result was a debacle. The British soundly repelled three separate American attempts to invade Canada shortly after war was declared. Soon thereafter Madison put out peace feelers to London. They were summarily rejected. For the first time, the United States realized that it was in a war that could well destroy everything achieved by the Revolution—could even return America to England's imperial fold—if something wasn't done to improve the country's ability to wage war.

At first little *was* done. As in the War of Independence thirty-five years earlier, there grew a strong and abiding domestic opposition to the war, especially within the New England and central seaboard states. Instead of the loyalist Tories of 1776, the War of 1812's domestic opponents were the northern political heirs of Alexander Hamilton, slain eight years earlier in a duel with Aaron Burr near New York. The refusal of the Federalist segments of American society to support the war led ultimately to the downfall of the Federalist party, but Federalist resistance did not prevent many individual Federalists from profiting from the conflict. The British Navy reinforced and enlarged its blockade of the American coast in 1813, thereby shutting off the importation of vital manufactured goods from neutral nations and creating increased scarcities. In reaction, northern Federalist entrepreneurs, many of them already rich as a result of their prewar maritime holdings, decided at last to deploy their funds to expand and improve the country's domestic manufacturing facilities. Their motives may have been partly altruistic—to relieve the scarcities caused by the British blockade—but by the time they began operations, the demand for their products was so intense that they could charge exorbitant prices and get them.

The establishment of the first large-scale American manufacturing enterprise took place in coastal New England. The reasons were several. First, New England was the heartland of the Federalist party, and the Federalists had long subscribed to Hamilton's founding imperatives about the need for America to develop a vigorous and diverse industrial capacity of its own. The country's commercial helplessness in the face of the British blockade had proved the correctness of Hamilton's vision and the fallibility of twenty-five years of Jefferson-inspired agrarian opposition.

Another reason was that New England, particularly in the areas of its major port cities, held the major concentrations of money. The Embargo Act of 1807 had already resulted in the diversion of funds earned from overseas shipping into small-scale manufacturing enterprises. Now, in 1813, with shipping once more shut down because of the British blockade, greater amounts of money were available for more ambitious manufacturing pursuits.

Still another reason derived from New England's relative proximity to Britain, where industry and industrial innovation were still expanding at an unprecedented pace. A little over twenty years before, Samuel Slater had been the first to transport England's industrial secrets, and he had made his fortune in New England. In the years after his arrival many other English factory hands, experienced in the advanced machine-manufacturing methods of their native country, and carrying secrets of their own, had followed in his wake. The majority of them had settled in New England and made their expertise available there.

Yet another reason had to do with New England's geography and climate. Throughout New England a series of strong-current rivers flowed from the interior mountains and uplands to the sea. These streams had provided a natural source of waterpower to run the small threshing mills of colonial times, and they had proved sufficiently potent to propel the waterwheels that powered Slater's later and larger spinning mills. Although many factories in England had already converted to steam power, the British had, before steam, devised an advanced system of river dams and millraces by which to power their earlier factories. Despite Robert Fulton's continuing experiments with steam power in the United States,* the steam engine as a source of factory power was still a dream in America. Even though the existence of coal in large quantity had been discovered in Pennsylvania, no way had yet been found to mine it efficiently and economically.

So New England's abundance of natural waterpower, and its enhancement through the construction of dams, weirs and races, made the region highly conducive to the establishment of larger and larger factories. The ultimate component of the formula, though, was New England's cold climate. The three basic necessities of life in any northerly region were food, shelter and clothing—warm clothing. For their food and shelter needs, New Englanders had always been able to supply themselves from their indigenous farms and forests. However, for the raw materials of their clothing—spun and woven cottons and woolens—they had been dependent on imports from England, as had the rest of the country. Between 1795 and 1805, Slater's Rhode Island and Massachusetts mills had eased some of that dependence. But because the population of New England, as well as that of the rest of the country, was expanding so rapidly, the supply of domestically spun clothing materials could not keep pace with demand and the nation's dependence on English textiles grew even more intense. The dependence was particularly dire in New England and the central states, where the icy winter climate put a premium on woolen goods. Although Slater had established cotton-textile manufacture, the mass production of wool cloth remained the province of British industry.

The 1807 embargo had prompted New England industrialist-entrepreneurs to establish several small wool-weaving mills. But it was not until the English blockade of 1813–1814 that the need presented itself for the establishment of a much-expanded, self-sufficient textile industry. Once committed to such an industry, the New Englanders poured their hearts and souls into it, as well

*In what was the first case of the export of American technological know-how, the Scottish engineer and inventor Henry Bell launched Great Britain's first steamboat, the *Comet*, on the Clyde River in 1812. By that time Fulton had several passenger steamboats plying the Hudson and other rivers in America, and was working on the development of an oceangoing steamer. Bell's British steamboat was copied largely from Fulton's.

as their money and organizational ingenuity. The first collective American effort at industrial problem-solving, its singular success would propel the United States toward the beginnings of industrial independence. It would be a form of independence as significant for the country as the political independence it had won three decades earlier.

CHAPTER 5

THE MOMENTUM BUILDS

The pioneering figures behind the establishment of the expanded factory system in New England during the War of 1812 were not only inventors and engineers but business organizers and financiers. Foremost among them was Francis Cabot Lowell, a wealthy Boston sea merchant who had traveled to England in 1810 to try to mediate an end to a succession of trade stoppages between Britain and the United States. While there, he toured the textile factories of the Midlands. When war broke out in 1812 and his shipping business began to dwindle, Lowell decided to follow the example of other wealthy New England maritime merchants and diversify into textile manufacture. Having seen at first hand the operation of the English system, however, he resolved to enter the industry not as an experimental sideline, as his colleagues were doing, but in full force. Accordingly, he acquired several rural land sites along the Charles and Merrimack rivers, not far from Boston Harbor, and engaged a man named Paul Moody to design and oversee the building of a complex of mills.

In many respects Moody played as vital a role as Lowell in what was to become a peculiarly American and progressive version of the British factory system. Moody was a self-taught engineer and inventor who had worked briefly in one of Samuel Slater's early spinning mills. In contemplating his designs for the Lowell factories, Moody realized that there was a dearth of skilled labor in Massachusetts capable of operating the complicated Arkwright-Slater power looms. Consequently he redesigned much of the machinery, simplifying its operation wherever he could in order to make it easier and quicker to train neophyte workers.

Moody's concept of simplification inspired a further idea. Lowell's original plan had called for the construction of several small factories at various riverside sites around Boston in which separate stages in the fabrication of cloth would be carried out. This was how the English system functioned—the system Lowell had observed in 1810 and set out to emulate. Why not, suggested Moody, erect a single larger plant in which all phases of manufacture could be combined under one roof? At first Lowell was skeptical, reluctant to tamper with the tried-and-true British system. But when Moody demonstrated how it could be done by running a variety of different machines from the same waterpower source, and when he showed him how costs could be reduced by eliminating the need to transport goods in various stages of completion from mill to mill, Lowell consented. Hence, choosing one of Lowell's sites along the banks of the Charles River near the village of Waltham, a few miles west of Boston, Moody designed and erected a single factory during the first two years of the War of 1812. By the end of 1814, under the name of the Boston Manufacturing Company, the factory started operating. By virtue of its simplified machinery and its concentration of all the processes of manufacture in one central plant, it represented a twofold advance on the traditional methods of mechanized textile manufacture.

The Waltham factory's opening coincided with the end of the war.* Although Britain had inflicted heavy damages, including the burning of the nation's capital, it had finally grown tired of the fight and agreed to a peace treaty. By 1815, once the British blockade of American ports had been lifted and cotton from the South was again easily shippable to New England, the Waltham plant began to prosper. It also became an object of marvel and resentment among those who lived in the region. Admirers marveled at it because no one before had created such an efficient method of machine manufacture. Until then, even in England, the factory system had developed merely as an extension of the old cottage industry methods. Each stage of the manufacturing pro-

---

*The American national anthem, "The Star Spangled Banner," had its origin in the War of 1812. Although the words were written by Francis Scott Key, a Baltimore lawyer, the anthem itself came from England. The music had been composed by a Londoner, John Stafford Smith, as a drinking song.

cess had been carried out by specialized workers at separate sites, originally with manually operated tools in scattered homes and workshops, then with water-powered machinery in more concentrated but still separate spinning, weaving, dyeing and printing shops. At Waltham, observers could watch raw cotton go into one end of the factory and finished cotton cloth, ready for market, emerge a short while later from the other end.

Less sanguine in their reaction to the factory, and less awed, were many of the skilled home-and-workshop handcraftsmen who worked in the Boston region. In their view, the new mass-production process sounded the death-knell of their specialized livelihoods. Francis Lowell and Paul Moody had already proclaimed that the Waltham plant marked the advent of a revolution in manufacturing, not just in textiles but in many other product areas as well. In addition to releasing the United States from its dependence on foreign goods, Moody asserted, one of the most important benefits of the revolution would derive from its democratization of labor. Until then, the native American manufacture of finished products had been the monopoly of the nation's "labor elite," the skilled specialists who were for the most part the heirs of the educated, colonial-period, closed-shop craft families and guilds. Now, Moody said, the opportunity to work and earn a decent wage would be open to every American, no matter his station in life.

What compelled Moody to discourse so avidly on the labor implications of Waltham constituted a third component of the revolution he and Lowell had inspired. In England, the rise of the factory system in the Midlands in the early 1700s had come at a time when the island was swelling with an uneducated, barely literate, impoverished underclass. Indeed, it was that underclass that expedited the spread of the factory system, since it functioned as the principal pool of cheap labor. As British machine industry developed during the 1700s, most of its manufactures were tagged for export, with the remainder directed to the country's relatively small upper-class domestic market. So poorly paid was the expanding factory labor force that it hardly constituted a market in itself; few English mill workers could afford to buy the products they manufactured. What evolved in England, then, was a permanent "factory class" which lived barely above the poverty level in the squalid manufacturing towns and cities that had grown up and sprawled out around the major industrial centers. By the early 1800s this class had perpetuated itself many times over. An American visiting the Midlands just before the War of 1812 would more likely be profoundly depressed by the conditions of the factory cities than impressed by the efficiency and productivity of the factories themselves.

Francis Lowell had been such a visitor. When he returned to Boston in 1811 with the idea of starting his own water-powered textile factories in the fashion of the English system, he was determined that the one aspect he would not emulate was that system's treatment of its labor force. It was this determination that had attracted Lowell to Paul Moody. Moody had seen the pioneering Rhode Island spinning mills of Samuel Slater succeed partly as a result of Slater's English-style labor practices, which impressed entire families into the mills' work force and, paying them pittances, housed them in shacks adjoining the mills. In such a way had the grimy slum cities of Midlands England sprouted up, and Moody foresaw the same fate for all the riverside areas of New England if Slater continued to copy the British. When Slater had resisted Moody's entreaties to pursue a different course in 1809, Moody quit his association with Slater's mills. Francis Lowell found a like-minded spirit in Moody. As the Waltham factory was being built in 1813, both agreed on the need for a labor policy different from the one entombed in British tradition. Because of the practical exigencies of the day, moreover, their philosophical agreement was sharpened by pragmatic concerns.

In his "Report on Manufactures" in 1791, Alexander Hamilton had cautioned that the abundance of land in America might prove an obstacle to the development of an adequate industrial foundation in the nation. Most post-Revolution Americans had come out of an agrarian past, he said, and as more and more land became available, they would tend to be drawn to it rather than to industrial crafts. By 1812 it was clear that Hamilton had been largely right, even with respect to the Northeast. As more land had opened up throughout the region, native citizens and new immigrants alike had settled it. Even more than seafaring, farming and tinkering were the dominant private cash enterprises of New England in 1812.

In scouting the Boston region in 1813 for sources of trainable native labor for their Waltham factory, Lowell and Moody encountered few choices. Most able-bodied young men not otherwise employed were involved in wartime pursuits. Older men engaged in the workshop handcrafts were stubbornly resistant to the idea of laying aside their tools to operate the newfangled textile machines. Only farmers were left, but they, too, declined to trade their open-air existence for life in a factory.

It was then that Moody had another idea. Before reverting to the English practice of conscripting whole families to work in their spinning mills, Samuel Slater and Moses Brown, as an experiment in their first mill at Pawtucket, had trained children and put them to work at the machines. Because the wooden machinery was light in weight, as was the raw cotton that went into them and the spun cloth that emerged, the experiment was successful insofar as it proved that the muscle power of grown men was not required for the efficient functioning of a textile mill. Although Moody morally disapproved of the idea of using children under the age of twelve, which is what most of the Slater-Brown workers were, he saw nothing reprehensible about training older women to work at Waltham. Since the eligible male work force in the Boston area was averse to factory work or otherwise employed, female labor appeared to be a sensible solution to the problem.*

But not just any female labor. The demand for home spinning and weaving, done by farm women under the "putting-out," or piecework, system, had practically been erased by the growth of mechanized mills in the twenty years between 1792 and 1812. Women living on farms in the region had thereby lost the only opportunity they had had to supplement family income. It was Lowell's idea to recruit some of these women from farm families near Boston to work at the Waltham factory. Not the wives and mothers, since their labor was still needed on the farms, but those among the daughters of a family who had reached a near-adult age.

And so was launched the "Waltham" or "Lowell System," as it came to be known—centralized factory manufacture carried out largely by young women who worked in comparatively clean sur-

---

*By "eligible male work force" I mean those workers who would have been acceptable to Moody and Lowell. The two men, along with Lowell's financial partners, Nathan Appleton and Patrick Jackson, were religious men with strict moral and social standards. The population of the Boston area contained many "ineligible" males when gauged by those standards—men who came from the wrong social, ethnic and religious milieu, and those who failed to measure up in other ways.

roundings and were monkishly protected by a paternalistic employer. For Waltham, Lowell and his associates recruited their female workers from only the most respectable rural families. They cloistered them in special boarding houses built for that purpose and placed them under the supervision of responsible older women. For a girl's family, the arrangement was ideal. She was hired for just two or three years at a time in her life when she was neither child nor adult, and her wages were applied either toward her dowry or to the family coffers. For Lowell and his associates the arrangement was equally satisfactory, for it helped them avoid the formation of a permanent factory class. By employing the young women temporarily, then returning them to their home farms and villages to marry, and by replacing them with other young women on an equally temporary basis, the Lowell System established a revolving labor force that never had time to become mired in its industrial surroundings. Thus, at least in the early stages of America's manufacturing revolution, factories did not spawn the ugly urban squalor that was a principal feature of England's industrial belt. Only much later, and to a lesser extent, would the introduction of heavy coal- and steam-powered industry begin noticeably to scar the American landscape.

Now, for the first time, one could sense a telescoping of time in the United States. In 1822, associates of Francis Lowell, who by that time had died, built a second and much larger factory near a village on the banks of the Merrimack River north of Boston. By then dozens of other unified textile mills had been erected, both in the Boston region and farther afield, and water-powered machine factories specializing in other forms of manufacture dotted the Northeast. Aside from the American System style in which the plants operated, what further distinguished them from their older English and European counterparts were their remoteness and cleanliness.* During the 1820s and 1830s, several European travel writers, accustomed to the Dickensian grime of the Anglo-European manufacturing centers, took pains to remark on the picturesqueness of the American industrial scene. Even Charles Dickens himself, noted for his anti-Americanism, had his eyes opened

*The Lowell System soon came to be called the New England System. Then, when merged with the "Whitney System" of uniform-parts manufacture, the entire concept became known as the American System.

while traveling through the United States in 1842. When he compared the American industrial milieu to that of England, he wrote that it was as "between the Good and Evil, the living light and the deepest shadow."

The relatively pristine quality of American machine industry during its first stages was due largely to the fact that coal-fired steam power had yet to appear as the driving force of the country's industrial complex. This was caused more by lack of coal than by any backwardness in steam-engine technology. Robert Fulton and his chief rival, John Stevens, as well as others, had clearly caught up with the technological intricacies of British steam engineering. But without coal, steam power for factories, although greatly more productive than waterpower, was simply too expensive because wood was still the only steam fuel available in America. It had been the discovery of coal in England, at a time when that country's forests were fast dwindling, that had made steam the standard industrial power source there. Operators of the expanding fleet of steamboats in the United States had learned well the wood–coal equation when, in 1815, they imported a shipload of British coal. A bushel of coal, they discovered, would sustain a large steam engine for one hour; for the same amount of time, the identical engine required a full cord of hardwood. In England a bushel of coal could be extracted from the ground in a few minutes by a single miner. The amassing of a cord of firewood, on the other hand, required the intensive labor of at least a dozen men, using hatchets and axes, over several hours.

The economics were simple. And then there was the matter of storage. The amount of coal it took to fuel a steamboat-sized engine for a full day could be stored in a small bin, whereas the equivalent amount of firewood required the space of a large shed. It was for this reason that the steamboat in America remained for so long a river and coastal craft exclusively. Although Fulton, just before he died in 1815, had seen to the launching of an oceangoing steamboat, true sea-voyaging by steamboat remained an impracticality. Riverboats were able to pause every hundred miles or so to replenish their firewood stocks. But an American steamboat trying to cross the Atlantic, or even make the West Indies, would run out of fuel in a day. It was not until 1819 that the *Savannah*, a huge, fully sail-rigged ship equipped with what might have been

termed an auxiliary steam engine and propulsion paddles, succeeded in traveling the Atlantic from Georgia to Liverpool. The
Savannah carried no passengers, however; no one wished to risk
such a voyage.*

Coal, then, was the key to the broader application of steam
power in the United States, and thus to the expansion and diversification of the country's virgin mechanized industry in the
1820s. Coal had been discovered in small quantities along Virginia's James River as early as 1750, but the means of extracting it
in any significant quantity had remained beyond the grasp of
American ingenuity. Coal mining was a filthy, dangerous and
claustrophobic form of manual labor, and few early Americans
saw any point in it.

It was only when enormous coal deposits were found in Pennsylvania at the beginning of the 1800s that the country's proto-indus-
trialists began to address the problem of mining it in quantity. But
by 1820, despite the fact that steam power was technologically
advanced enough to be applied to a variety of industrial pursuits
beyond water transport and was lacking only a cheap and efficient
source of fuel, the problem of mining coal in quantity remained
unsolved. The problem was still primarily one of labor. Not until the
decade of the 1830s, when the United States experienced its first
massive wave of immigration, would willing and abundant mining
labor become more readily available. Many of the immigrants were
desperate lower-class refugees from the famines in Ireland and the
political turmoil in Europe, particularly the central European states.
They would prove to be willing to work anywhere, even in the lung-
choking coalfields of Pennsylvania and those more recently discovered in Ohio, Kentucky and West Virginia.

In the meantime, northeastern America gathered momentum in a
number of technological and industrial fields other than textiles
during the decade following the conclusion of the War of 1812.
The surge was encouraged by the election of James Monroe as
President in 1816, and by the rising power of Henry Clay and
John C. Calhoun in Congress. All three were Southerners who

---

*Charcoal, a wood-derivative fuel obtained by charring chunks of wood in an airless
kiln until they were burned through but still solid, gradually replaced firewood for the
fueling of many steamboats and made the *Savannah*'s voyage possible. But because charring
required its own slow industrial process, the fuel was even more expensive, albeit less
space-consuming, than plain firewood.

had been weaned on Jeffersonian agrarianism and anti-Federalism. The war had changed their outlook considerably, however. Although defeats in the 1816 elections marked the end of the Federalist party as a significant political factor in American life, Monroe, Calhoun and Clay merged their own regional chauvinism with the industrialism that had for so long been a principal feature of northern Federalist philosophy. The result was an outbreak, originating in Washington but spreading rapidly throughout the country, of intensive American nationalism.

Shortly after his inauguration in 1817, Monroe toured the Northeast. He actively promoted the intensification and expansion of industrial enterprise "for the purpose of raising the United States to a level of parity with the great states of Europe," and he promised "the systematic and fostering care of the government" to all who joined in the expansion of industry and the improvement of the country's still-primitive transportation and communications networks. In Washington, Clay and Calhoun had already engineered a series of tariff-penalties against the import of key foreign manufactures. Along with Monroe, they expanded this protection of infant American industry in 1818 by sponsoring an even more wide-ranging tariff act. The message was clear. No longer would there be any philosophical disputes about the direction the United States should take as a nation and society. To be sure, agriculture would remain the pedestal upon which the national statue was to be built. But the statue itself would be manufacture.

No single citizen responded to Monroe's policy with greater enthusiasm and energy than did DeWitt Clinton, a forward-looking New York politician who held a variety of high public offices locally and nationally between 1798 and 1815. Clinton had been mayor of New York City in 1806 when Robert Fulton returned from France to begin work on his Hudson River steamboat. Fulton's success, and the subsequent establishment of regular and frequent steam traffic between New York and Albany, had improved New York's economy remarkably. As the city's mayor, Clinton was effusively grateful to Fulton, and the two men had become friends.

In 1808, Fulton, recalling his struggling-artist days in England's canal country, had a new idea. Western New York was rapidly being settled, as to a lesser extent were the southern shores of the Great Lakes in Pennsylvania, Ohio, Indiana and

Michigan. Most of the canals that had been dug in the United States up to that time had been commercial failures because of their builders' lack of engineering know-how. Fulton had accumulated a great amount of canal lore while in Europe. That, coupled with his expertise in steamboat technology, prompted him to propose the building of a long canal from the Hudson River at Albany to Lake Erie. Not only would such a project open up the port trade of New York City to the western territories, thereby further enhancing its economy, but it would also provide a lucrative new market for Fulton's steamboat lines.

Clinton was again mayor of New York in 1810. Earlier in his career as a New York State legislator, he had sponsored such laws as those that relieved debtors from prison terms, abolished slavery in the state, and established the pioneering statewide public school system. Although politically a Republican, Clinton had proved himself far more daring and progressive than many Federalists. Most New Yorkers greeted Fulton's canal idea with the same bemused skepticism they had earlier displayed when he announced his first steamboat. Not Clinton, though. Clinton, already a steam enthusiast, became an intrepid champion and promoter of the canal when he resumed the city's mayoralty in 1810.

The War of 1812 effectively barred further development of the idea for a time. During the war, however, while he was busy enlarging his steamboat holdings, Fulton sketched plans for his proposed Hudson-to-Lake Erie canal. The war, in fact, made the need for such a canal seem more obvious. Much of the important fighting took place in the Great Lakes area, and the federal authorities in Washington began to realize how much easier it would have been to supply and communicate with the American forces in the region had there been a canal already in place.

Fulton died early in 1815, almost coincidentally with the formal end of the war. Later that year, Clinton resigned as mayor of New York to pursue the presidency. He had made a run at incumbent James Madison in the 1812 campaign for the presidency and had lost, but he remained popular in the Northeast and was eager for another try, this time against the Southerner James Monroe. Although the Madison-backed Monroe easily defeated Clinton, among other aspirants, Clinton's strong advocacy of the importance of improving the country's internal industry and transport facilities did much to bring Monroe around to the same persuasion. When Monroe, in his 1817 inaugural address, announced his administration's commitment to immediate internal improvements, and when he later toured the Northeast urging the expansion of the nation's industry, his statements were credited in large part to Clinton's influence. With his prestige thus enhanced, Clinton ran for the governorship of Federalist-dominated New York and was elected with ease.

Clinton based his campaign for the governorship on the revival of the idea of a canal between the Hudson and Lake Erie. When Robert Fulton had first hatched the notion eight years before, the 360-mile distance made its realization seem inconceivable to the average citizen. But the nationalistic spark that Monroe, Clay and Calhoun lit in the country abolished most doubts, at least in New York. If the United States was to cease being a commercial backwater on the international scene, the citizenry as a whole would have to transform its complacency, bred by its geographical remoteness, into a more aggressive enterprise. This was the message implicit in the new Monroe administration's pronouncements. New York, physically the largest state in the nation, yet less advanced in its economic base than many of the smaller states, decided under Clinton's inspiration to take the lead. Even before Clinton assumed the governorship in 1817, the state legislature passed a bill authorizing the raising of funds for the construction of a canal through private investment, to be guaranteed by the state government.

It took eight torturous years to build "Clinton's Ditch," or the Great Western Canal, as the Erie Canal was first officially called.* Planned to be more than a yard in depth and twenty-four feet wide, the canal was started on July 4, 1817. Digging began approximately halfway along its intended course near what is now Rome, New York, and it was first dug in two sections that extended eastward and westward in opposite directions. Later in its construction, as more labor became available, two more sections— one from Fort Niagara on Lake Erie, the other from the Hudson near Albany—were started to link up with the first two. Eventu-

---

*Actually, this would be just the first of three Erie Canals. In 1835, when it was decided to widen and otherwise improve the canal, many new stretches were dug and original sections abandoned. That reconstruction was completed in 1862. The same thing occurred again between 1905 and 1918.

ally, three thousand "mechanics"—a nineteenth-century term for day laborers—worked on the project, most of them recent Irish immigrants.* Their pay was 26 cents a day plus a daily tot of whiskey. They welcomed the whiskey, since the work, much of it taking them through mosquito-infested marshes in alternatingly humid and frigid dawn-to-dusk weather, was backbreaking. The canal bed was dug almost entirely by hand. The tedious pick-and-shovel work came to a stop only in winter, when the ground froze to depths of six feet and more. It was a fairly straightforward engineering job for its day, and except for the special construction of locks designed to carry the eventual canal traffic across unavoidable land elevations, most of the canal's course was improvised as it progressed.

When it was formally opened to traffic in 1825, the Erie Canal was an almost instant financial success, its system of tolls and absence of any competition ensuring its prosperity. But its opening had considerably more far-reaching commercial and psychological effects on the nation. By providing New York City with a direct link to the Great Lakes region and the developing territories beyond, it secured the city's future as the country's most important financial and commercial center. Its success also generated a near-mania of canal building in the rest of the nation. As well, it launched an era of intense commercial competition between New York and the other northeastern and mid-Atlantic states as the latter sought to recover from the loss of their waterborne trade. It also marked the true beginning of large-scale private-citizen investment in American industry—the fuel that would feed the engine of the country's rapid growth and make the term *Wall Street* the symbol of an aggressive, uniquely American version of capitalism.

But most significant of all was the fact that the opening of the Erie Canal, dubbed for a time the Eighth Wonder of the World, infused the collective American spirit with an expanded sense of what the country and its people were capable of. Although for the most part the product of mass hand-labor—not to mention the fact that it was largely imported labor—the canal was nevertheless

---

*The first great wave of Irish immigration to the United States in the nineteenth century had its beginnings in the building of the Erie Canal. Manual laborers were recruited in great numbers in Ireland to work on the canal. Once it was finished, rather than return to Ireland, most brought their families to the United States.

a monument to the innate daring, industry and productivity of an America operating under the inspiration and imperatives of the new postwar nationalistic impulses. The connection was quickly made: The future personal interest of every citizen was inexorably tied to the advancement of the national interest. National prosperity meant greater opportunity for individual prosperity. And inherent in the promotion of the national interest, as the Erie Canal had proved, were the determined acceleration and expansion of industry, invention, commerce and productivity.

CHAPTER 6

CHANGING PERCEPTIONS

The combination of the Monroe administration's increasingly avid nationalism and the opening of the Erie Canal had, by 1825, sharply changed Americans' perceptions of themselves and their country. The change was abetted by the rapid expansion of newspapers during the 1820s. In fact, newspapers were fast on their way to becoming, collectively, an unconscious voice of the government as they vied with one another to extol and promote the "American system" of political values and economic aspirations embodied in the policies of the Monroe and Adams administrations. The dissemination of hard factual news was not significantly improved by the growth of the newspaper industry, however. The real effect of the growth was in the proliferation of editorial opinion that at once celebrated the hardy virtues of the newly emerging American way, promoted the benefits—earthly and divine—of the Christian work ethic, and exhorted local populaces to greater effort in economic pursuits.

This journalistic nationalism—commercial boosterism, if you will—became widely contagious. In the late 1820s, as villages and towns and even small cities began to spring up beyond the Appalachians, every community of any size had at least one daily or weekly paper devoted to promoting further settlement and commercial development. The American newspaper became a kind of local Rotary bulletin, expounding the unique advantages of its particular locality and, when sent back east, enticing immigration with reports of bargains in land and opportunities in commerce.

In this manner, the American newspaper became a model for

81

the rest of the small nation's expanding industrial potential. The burgeoning newspaper industry symbolized the very basic law of supply and demand in action. The more settlers a particular paper could attract to a region, the more readers there would be for the paper, and thus the more profits and prosperity for the paper's owner.

The press played as vital a role in the great westward expansion as the Conestoga wagon, a weighty but agile boat-shaped vehicle devised prior to the Revolution by German-immigrant settlers in Pennsylvania's Lancaster County. Neither the wagon nor the newspaper was a new invention; both had long been extant in Europe. But just as the Pennsylvania Germans had adopted the conventional European wagon to a uniquely New World use (the Conestoga was the forerunner of the covered wagon or "prairie schooner" which would become the standard means of travel during later migrations beyond the Mississippi River), so, too, did early American newspaper proprietors improvise on the traditional functions of the European press.

Not that all newspapers of the period took the form of local-interest heralds. Indeed, before the Revolution several colonial newspaper founders had done an even more radical turn on European press customs. Since their inception, newspapers in Europe had by tradition been closely controlled instruments of the various ruling aristocracies; there was no such thing as a privately owned paper, and printing presses were all but barred from private hands. The "free press" provisions of the American Constitution, however, guaranteed what had become an innovation in colonial America: the right privately to publish individual comment and criticism about people and institutions without interference by the government. Thus, rather than evolving as direct instruments of the new government, several metropolitan tabloids after the Revolution became organs of the different political parties engaged in the conduct of government. Yet they, too, though in a more sophisticated fashion than their frontier counterparts, preached the virtues of honest industry, hard work and technological progress as the keys to advancing the economic fortunes of the United States in the 1820s.

And well they might have, if for no other reason than that the putting out of a regularly scheduled newspaper—even one of no more than four pages—required a large and sweaty measure of individual industry. The setting of type was a tedious task, the hand-printing process even more laborious and messy. In many cases it was the proprietor-editors themselves who carried out these jobs, since few papers were profitable enough to employ their own compositors and pressmen. Tied to an archaic method of producing their own product, they heralded the development of every new device whose purpose was to ease and expedite the manufacture of products in other industries, in the hope that the sudden surge of American inventiveness would spill over to their own industry and thereby ease its onerous tasks.

It was the newspaper industry, then, that most vigorously championed mechanical invention and innovation. Collectively in the United States of the 1820s, newspapers played the role that Francis Bacon had assumed in England two centuries earlier—urging the study and application of abstract science to the practical betterment of the national populace. The only major difference was that in the United States of the 1820s, science and scientific research were still struggling to escape the yoke of religious stricture, whereas in Great Britain and Europe they were much more free to venture farther afield.

As a consequence, scientific expertise in itself had little to do with the American upsurge in mechanical innovation in the 1820s. The trend's inspiration was instead a religio-social fervor fueled primarily by the nation's press. It was religious because it derived from the ordinary American's observance of the correlation between earthly work and divine virtue. And it was social because the nation had become convinced by its preachers, politicians and editorialists that the kind of work that resulted in easing the individual's daily labor burden was in itself a higher form of work, the greater to be rewarded on both the divine and the earthly planes.

Any notion that America's general lack of scientific knowledge should impede technical invention had already been laid to rest by the achievements of such as Whitney, Fulton and Lowell. There had not been a trained scientist among them; rather a lawyer, an artist and a sea merchant. Hence the mechanical tinkerer—the insatiably curious, pragmatic, self-taught, backyard amateur formed in the Franklin mold—and the religion-oriented economic opportunist in the tradition of Livingston, Lowell and Clinton, became the progenitors of the great garden of invention and innovation that began to rise in the late 1820s and blossomed into full flower a decade hence. A hundred years later the eminent British philosopher Alfred North Whitehead would observe that the greatest invention of the nineteenth century was the *method of invention* established in America in the early part of the century. That method, which made it possible for anyone with a practical idea to be heard, no matter his lack of scientific or technological credentials, would, not long after, transform the United States into the world's foremost symbol of mass progress.

During the 1820s the technological initiative remained on the other side of the Atlantic nevertheless. In the decade before, the French scientist François Appert had discovered a method of preserving food over long periods in heat-sealed jars. Scottish engineer George Stephenson had built the first successful steam rail locomotive. John McAdam had found a way to improve England's rutty carriage roads, and thereby increase the ease and pace of personal travel, by surfacing them with fine-crushed stone. René Laënnec in France had invented the stethoscope, opening a whole new chapter in the still-primitive art of diagnostic medicine. And in Britain a stonemason, Joseph Aspdin, developed a process for making a much improved bonding material—Portland cement—that would revolutionize building construction.

Recently—in fact, in the year of the Erie Canal's completion—England had built and put into operation the first passenger railroad, operated by Stephenson's coal-fired steam locomotive. And in France, in 1827, the optics specialist Joseph Niepce made the first crude camera photograph the world had ever seen. Others in Europe had been busy discovering a host of new chemical elements, as well as expanding and refining the principles and laws of the abstract sciences.

Notwithstanding the progress in Europe, the United States, in the person of a few enterprising individuals, showed unmistakable signs of a determined intent to catch up. Even as steam railroads proliferated abroad in the late 1820s, cable and horse-drawn railways were being constructed in Massachusetts, Pennsylvania and elsewhere for cargo hauling, usually from an interior mine or quarry to a river- or canal-side shipping point. New Jersey engineer John C. Stevens, who had been the late Robert Fulton's chief rival in American steamboat technology, was by then only a few years behind Stephenson of Scotland in developing the steam-powered rail locomotive. Indeed, it was as a result of England's railroad technology that the first great flurry of heavy mechanical invention and innovation occurred in America, beginning in 1830.

Railroad evolution also provided the impetus for the development of what since has become the most singular hallmark of the American capitalistic system: the huge, publicly owned corporation. The Erie Canal had been a public-works project, private investment in it guaranteed by the state of New York. With the spread of private railroads across America in the 1830s, the template for American corporate capitalism—the investment of risk capital on a huge scale—was shaped and cast.

In 1830 the United States had but twenty-three miles of railroad track, all of it short-haul adjuncts of the several canal-building companies that had sprung up in various states in the hope of emulating the success of the Erie Canal. The canal builders had realized that the development of long-distance railroads in America, on the emerging European model, would pose a direct threat to their future interests. Many among them set out to block commercial railroad development, even going so far as to lobby and petition state legislatures and the federal Congress to outlaw the newfangled machines as too dangerous and, with their sooty effluvia, too dirty. They were joined by the operators of steamboat companies who were more than willing to testify about the filth the locomotives would spew over the land, not to mention the infernal racket they would make. These drawbacks were forgivable along the wide waterways on which steamboats navigated, since there was plenty of distance between ship and shore, but they were a dire threat to human health and sanity when transposed to land.

The protests fell on deaf ears for the most part, so a few of the more forward-looking canal and steamboat entrepreneurs, deciding "if you can't beat 'em, join 'em," rushed to grab a slice of the not-yet-existent railroad industry. They did so, in the late 1820s, by securing charters for railroad rights-of-way, usually running parallel to their canals.

But still required was the technology, and a complicated technology it proved to be for America's barely sophisticated heavy-iron industry. During the previous twenty years of building waterborne steam engines, the industry had taken a significant stride forward from the time when all it could do was smelt and mold crude soft iron for armaments and munitions. But the much more complex steam-locomotive metallurgy and engineering required a quantum leap forward, both in the techniques of molding and shaping to finer mechanical tolerances and in the methods of producing stronger and more fracture-resistant metals.

The steamboat engine drove one or more lightweight paddle wheels against the modest resistance of water. The steam locomotive engine, on the other hand, was required to propel its leaden self, so to speak, through a series of rotating shafts, cams and iron wheels against the unyielding friction of two rails, and to do so with a heavy haul behind it, often uphill. These requirements demanded a tremendous increase in power over the standard steamboat engine's output, and thus a tremendous increase in steam pressure, which in turn entailed larger and thicker boilers and even more weight to be propelled.

As with Fulton's steamboat engine, the first American railroad entrepreneurs sought to solve the problem by importing a British-made locomotive. The Delaware and Hudson Canal Co., a New York company that had dug a ditch between the two rivers in order to transport coal in bulk from the recently opened northeastern Pennsylvania coalfields to New York City and other communities along the Hudson River, acquired a heavy English locomotive called the *Stourbridge Lion* in 1829. The six-ton machine proved much too heavy and, with its fixed wheels, too inflexible for the soft-iron American track. This left early American railroad developers with the option of buying unimaginable lengths of British track to accommodate the adipose British locomotives, an expensive and time-consuming prospect at best, or of developing their own locomotives to use on cheap, if relatively soft, native track forgings. They opted for the latter course, and the magnificently crafted *Stourbridge Lion* became instantly obsolete except for what it could teach American forgers and steam engineers to avoid. One of those engineers was a young man who had driven the *Lion* in its first trials along a short stretch of Delaware and Hudson experimental track near Scranton. Horatio Allen, only twenty-seven, boasted that he could build a much lighter and more efficient locomotive.*

When Allen brought his boast to his Delaware and Hudson employers, they rebuffed him. As a result he quit the D & H and sought alternate financing in New York. A New York banker

---

*John Stevens's first American locomotive, built in 1825 on his estate in Hoboken, New Jersey (now the site of the Stevens Institute of Technology), never actually operated beyond the walls of the estate. Stevens had built it merely to prove to the canal companies and other doubters that it could be done, and he hoped to use it to start his own commercial railroad company. But he was seventy-six when he finished it, and his poor health prevented him from pursuing his goal.

soon put him in touch with the recently formed South Carolina Canal Company. The South Carolinians responded to Allen's claims with guarded enthusiasm, formed a railroad-development subsidiary, and awarded him a modest stipend to develop a steam locomotive. Working in an iron forge in the South Carolina capital of Charleston and closely watched by the officers of the canal company, Allen managed within eight months to produce a functioning wood-fueled steam locomotive of less than four tons. Late in 1830 the engine made its first run on freshly laid American-forged rails, the initial stretch of the rail line that would eventually connect Charleston to Hamburg, South Carolina—a distance of thirty miles, most of it flat.

In the meantime the Baltimore and Ohio Canal Company, created a few years before by a group of Baltimore merchants to dig a Maryland version of the Erie Canal, had also become interested in the railroad prospect. The company formed a railroad division and commissioned New York artist-inventor Peter Cooper to produce a workable steam locomotive. Using funds furnished by the B & O, Cooper, an aggressive, somewhat arrogant mechanical prodigy in his mid-thirties, established an ironworks in Baltimore in 1828 and proceeded to design and build a locomotive smaller, yet more powerful, than Allen's. He christened it the *Tom Thumb*, a name calculated to convey its superiority to Allen's more ponderous engine. The B & O right-of-way into the Ohio Valley would entail many a curve and upgrade to negotiate the Appalachian barrier successfully, and the more agile the locomotive the better.

In effect, Cooper and Allen were in a footrace to produce a prototype locomotive that would set the standard for the tyro railroad industry and would, depending on who won, make one or the other rich. Inasmuch as Allen's South Carolina locomotive, named *The Best Friend of Charleston*, was the first to operate over American-forged rail, he seemed to have won. But when Cooper's lighter, more compact and essentially cheaper *Tom Thumb* made its debut a few months later, Cooper snatched the victory away from Allen. Cooper would go on to become one of the richest and most celebrated men in mid-nineteenth-century America.

Peter Cooper's engine launched the American railroad industry—nay, catapulted it—into dominance of American commercial life for the next fifty years. By 1860, it has been estimated, 40 percent of the population of the country was in one way or another dependent on the boom in railroading for its livelihood. Up to that time more was accomplished in the areas of railroad invention, innovation and expansion than in any other single industry in America. Indeed, just about every other field of endeavor, from dirty-hand pursuits like agriculture and mining to such "white collar" occupations as banking and law, owed its prosperity to railroading.

During the 1830s alone, as railroad fever grew, the nation's original twenty-three miles of track lengthened into nearly three thousand. John B. Jervis improved on Cooper's original locomotive by inventing a wheel mechanism that, much like wagon wheels, swiveled beneath the front end of the engine and thus permitted curved track—an essential if railroads were to traverse the mountainous regions of the East. Cooper's stubby *Tom Thumb* had been dubbed "the teakettle on a wagon" because it consisted of nothing more than a boiler and smokestack on four large, rigidly fixed wagon-type wheels driven by iron rods connected by geared camshafts to the engine's piston. With Jervis's invention, locomotives began to stretch out, with separate fixed drive wheels in the rear and the guide wheels mounted on a swiveling "truck" in front. This arrangement accommodated larger boilers, which in turn increased the pulling power of the locomotive.

Other vital innovations in the early 1830s were the introduction of the T-shaped rail by Robert Stevens, John Stevens's son, and the invention by Horatio Allen of a cutoff valve for the locomotive steam boiler. Both increased the safety of primitive railroading in America by reducing derailments and boiler explosions, still common hazards in England.

The Baltimore and Ohio was the first long-distance railroad to operate in the United States, completing a line from Baltimore to Washington in 1835, and its success further stoked the already well-fueled fires of railroad mania in the East. But the tremendous surge of private investment in various rail projects during the following two years led to the country's first real economic depression, precipitated by the Panic of 1837.

The panic had several major causes, but the predominant one was the wild speculation in public lands that accompanied railroad investment in the early 1830s. Typically, people bought up lands from the government along anticipated railroad rights-of-way in the hope of making generous profits when the railroad companies later came along to acquire the land. The trouble was that much more land was purchased than would ever be needed by the rail-roads. When definite rights-of-way were finally settled upon, a few landowners profited but most were left with practically worthless expanses. Having sunk their savings into their pur-chases, and having further financed them through state bank notes and other forms of credit, many speculators were unable to pay off the banks. The banks themselves in turn were unable to satisfy their liabilities, many of which were to the federal government in the form of government demand deposits. The situation was exac-erbated by the government itself in 1836 when it sought to regu-late land sales by issuing the Specie Circular, which among other things limited the means of purchasing government-sold land to payments in gold and silver.* Paper money, until then the chief currency of land speculation and, because of its easy availability, the cause of the nation's spiraling inflation, would no longer be accepted.

The Specie Circular, which declared paper money essentially valueless, dropped the bottom out of the inflated economy. Prices plummeted in every commodity, including land. The state banks had done most of their lending to land speculators in paper money and now had to struggle to collect what were, for all practical purposes, worthless debts. In the spring of 1837 banks in New York, Philadelphia, Boston and Baltimore began to fail. The new President, Martin Van Buren, would find his administration haunted by the subsequent four-year-long depression and would devote much of his energy to trying to develop an independent national banking system that would not have to rely on state and private banks for the preservation and management of the federal treasury.

The Panic of 1837 slowed but did not materially deter private railroad development. In addition to the Baltimore and Ohio, in the late 1830s several other companies completed the construction of short lines in various states and began to contemplate more dis-tant destinations. The most ambitious of these was formed by a

---

*Since the time of the establishment of the federal government in 1790, various land acts had been introduced to enable citizens and settlers to purchase pieces of the vast tracts that had come into the public domain as a result of independence. These acts were de-signed primarily to generate operating revenues for the government. Along with customs duties, land sales had been the principal source of federal revenues. The land acts, how-ever, encouraged speculators at the expense of legitimate settlers, and in 1836 the admin-istration of President Andrew Jackson decided to try to stem the tide of government-aided speculation.

group of wealthy Boston merchants who proposed to lay a swath of track across Massachusetts and over the Berkshire Mountains to the Hudson River at Albany. In the preceding ten years the Erie Canal had transformed New York City into the nation's premier seaport and turned Boston, formerly the busiest and most prosperous international port, into a comparative backwater. The Bostonians saw in their proposed railroad a way to recover much of the foreign trade lost to New York. By being able to ship foreign freight quickly overland to the region where the Erie Canal commenced, and to bring freight from the nation's interior back to Boston by the same route, they hoped to recover much of the trade that theretofore had been routed down the Hudson River for transshipment through the port of New York.

The Boston railroaders called their company the Western Railroad Corporation and carved out their line between 1835 and 1842. The opening of the nearly two-hundred-mile-long Western (later known as the Boston and Albany) Railroad was viewed as an achievement almost as miraculous as that of the Erie Canal, especially since its tracks managed to surmount the forbidding Berkshires. And it gave reality to what, until then, had been only a grandiose notion: the idea of building railroads that would span the entire continent.

The success of the Boston and Albany spawned a host of other medium- and long-distance lines. Among the first to be completed was the New York and Harlem (later, after a number of consolidations, the New York Central) Railroad, which traveled the east bank of the Hudson from New York to Albany, connected with the Boston and Albany, and then later struck out westward across New York State on a route that ran close and parallel to the Erie Canal. The canal, operated by New York, had proved a bountiful revenue producer for the state. Suddenly there was about to arrive faster and more efficient, if not cheaper, private rail competition. The state's ruling politicians were not the only ones alarmed; so were operators of the Hudson freight and barge steamers who had held a monopoly on cargo commerce between New York City and the canal for two decades.

Foremost in influence among New York's political establishment was Martin Van Buren—formerly the governor of the state and still its most powerful backroom political boss, formerly a United States senator, formerly a Secretary of State, formerly a Vice-President, and most recently President of the United States.

The diminutive Van Buren, a Democrat, had been defeated in his run for a second term in the White House by William Henry Harrison in 1840, and he had been rebuffed in two further bids to regain the nomination in 1844 and 1848. Now, in February of 1849, from his presidential retirement home near the village of Kinderhook, New York, he penned a testy letter to the newly inaugurated President, Zachary Taylor:

> Dear Mr. President:
> The canal system of this country is being threatened by the spread of a new form of transportation known as "railroads."

After setting down a long litany of just how the advent of railroads threatened to destroy the canal system (he didn't mention the Erie Canal specifically) and leave countless citizens "destitute," Van Buren went on:

> For the above-mentioned reasons, the government should create an Interstate Commerce Commission to protect the American people from "railroads" and to preserve the canals. . . . As you know, Mr. President, "railroad" carriages are pulled at the enormous speed of 15 miles per hour by "engines," which in addition to endangering life and limb of passengers, roar and snort their way through the countryside, setting fire to crops, scaring the livestock, and frightening women and children. The Almighty certainly never intended that people should travel at such breakneck speed.*

Van Buren—like DeWitt Clinton, his immediate predecessor as governor of New York—had been one of the leading proponents of the building of the Erie Canal and was acutely aware of the prosperity it had bestowed upon the state. In 1849, as a retired American President and the "Lord of Kinderhook," he was the *éminence grise* of the upstate New York political hierarchy.

---

*As reprinted in the *Chatham Courier*, Chatham, New York, April 7, 1982. Van Buren's recommendation for an Interstate Commerce Commission showed prescience on his part: Such a commission, to protect Americans from railroad company abuses, was created about forty years later. (The authenticity of the Van Buren letter has been questioned by some scholars, who contend it was forged by a group of Hudson River steamboat entrepreneurs anxious to prevent completion of the New York and Harlem Railroad.)

(Kinderhook is a few miles south of Albany.) No doubt, if his letter was genuine, he wrote it at the instigation of his political cronies in the state government and Erie Canal Commission who felt threatened by the spreading railroad network. But his anti-railroad sentiments may also have arisen from his personal experience. The Boston and Albany line "roared and snorted" through the village of Chatham, just a few miles east of Van Buren's Kinderhook estate. And a stone's throw to the west, at the foot of the bluffs overlooking the Hudson, track was being laid for the main New York–Albany line of the soon-to-be New York Central.

American perceptions were surely changing. But not all American perceptions.

CHAPTER 7

INVENTION MOVES WESTWARD

The arrival of the steam-powered railroad in the United States of the 1840s marked the start of a revolution not only in transportation but in scores of corollary industrial enterprises as well. Since the beginning of time the long-distance transport of people and goods had been limited by the vagaries of wind and current, and by the plodding undurability of animals. Suddenly, within the span of ten years, both the pace of long-distance movement and its capacity quintupled. A primitive American freight or passenger train could haul five times as much as a canal barge pulled by a team of horses or oxen, and at five times the speed. Similarly, a train from Boston to Albany could reach its destination in less than fifteen hours in fair weather, whereas it took a steamer nearly five days to make the water journey around what was then known as The Cape—the sea route to New York harbor, then up the Hudson. Sail-rigged packet boats and cargo "coasters" were, of course, much slower.

Although wood-fueled steamboat transport had spread widely over America's inland waterways by the early 1840s, the country's oceangoing mariners continued to lag in adapting to steam power. Great Britain, on the other hand, had been quick to convert to a steam-powered merchant marine—this again due principally to the fact that coal was in increasingly plentiful supply in Britain. In America, though coal was just beginning to be mined in the hills of Appalachia, the techniques of producing it in quantity had not yet been fully mastered. Most of the coal that *was* brought out of the ground was reserved for the furnaces of the new ironworks that had sprung up near the coalfields to service the fast-expanding railroad industry. Thus, despite the fact that the introduction of steam navigation had been basically an American achievement, the British, and not much later the French and Germans, stole a beat on the United States when it came to the most lucrative aspect of water transport: international trade.

Another irony sprang from the fact that while the rapid construction of railroads depended on coal for iron making, there was still not enough coal available to fuel the locomotives. Also, the first major commercial railroads built—the B & O, the Western, the New York and Harlem—were located far from the known bulk sources of coal. As a consequence, railroading in America, like steamboating, began as a woodburning enterprise. Fuel for the locomotives could be obtained only by felling and chopping up trees along the rights-of-way.

This practice, which continued well into the latter part of the century as the railroads wove a spider-web of rights-of-way up, down and across the country, produced the first instance of wide-scale ecological despoliation by industry in the United States. Europeans like Charles Dickens and Alexis de Tocqueville who traveled through America in the 1830s and early 1840s had extolled the tidiness of the country's modest industrial centers. Those who came after them in the forties and fifties were hard put to understand what their predecessors had found so remarkable. As heavy industry spread along with the railroads, the pristine pastoral ideals embodied by the Lowell System began to vanish.

With their indiscriminate ravaging of the landscape—an item Martin Van Buren might have added to his list of reasons for opposing them—the railroads set the example for the industries that followed in their trail, supporting or depending on them. Once-neat villages and towns through which the railroads passed became eyesores almost overnight; factory districts sprawled around them and attracted itinerant lower-class laborers, many of them newly arrived from Europe and with little interest in visual aesthetics. America was beginning to realize one of the basic costs of technological progress. Those Americans who cared about retaining the country's colonial aura were increasingly outnumbered by hungry immigrants who were concerned only about work and economic opportunity, whose sensibilities had been conditioned by the squalor of Europe's industrial centers. To most of them, squalor was the price a people had to pay for a full belly.

Immigration between 1820 and 1850 was formidable; no nation in history had experienced anything like it before. Although the United States had enacted an immigration law in 1819, its purpose was not to regulate the inflow of immigrants but to protect them from the overcrowding and sanitation hazards of the Atlantic crossing. Thus, to a degree, everyone was welcome, although northern Europeans were preferred for their experience and industry. In the thirty years between 1820 and 1850, the number of immigrants who came into the country was almost equal to the nation's total population at the end of the Revolution: 2.5 million. Most of that number were adults; Europeans tended to have small families, and usually only the male adults emigrated, bringing their families over years later.

By 1850 the nation's population stood at about 23 million.* But because native Americans were given to having large families (it has been estimated by the Census Bureau that in 1850, eight out of every ten native-born Americans were either women or children), the native male labor pool consisted of only about 4 million, and many of these were the first-generation offspring of immigrants. Contrast this to the 2.5 million immigrants who came into the country between 1820 and 1850, of which approximately 1.5 million were able-bodied males with experience in European factories and eager to find employment. It was this work force that more and more frequently got the jobs, particularly in the expanding industrial Northeast and in those central and western sectors of the country that were rapidly being developed industrially by the extension of, first, the canals and then the railroad systems.

The country was on the move, and many of the key movers were those who were fresh from the industrial ghettoes of Britain and northern Europe, or from the unproductive landscapes of Ireland and southern Europe. As they spread through the country, extending a railroad here, erecting a factory there, they began inevitably to reproduce the visual ugliness that had become the standard in much of Europe.

Eli Whitney's cotton gin, the complex Slater looms of Waltham,

*Which is to say, the nation's white population. Neither Negroes nor Indians were included in early American censuses.

and Fulton's introduction of the working steam engine had, over a period of less than fifteen years, unleashed an obsessive fascination with the machine in America. But it took another twenty-five years and the birth of the railroad industry for any further significant breakthroughs to occur in the invention of large-scale labor-saving devices. Although wood burned hot enough to run steam engines, its heat was not sufficient to refine iron ore into anything but the crudest, softest metal. Soft bituminous coal, discovered in southwestern Pennsylvania and western Virginia, improved matters a bit, but not enough for the needs of the railroads with their great physical stresses and pressures. All of the hard iron used in the early American railroads had to be imported from mills in England, and its steep cost soon sent the railroaders and iron forgers in search of a means to fashion railroad-tough native iron. The key was anthracite.

Iron making on a large scale was a relatively simple process, albeit a labor-intensive one, as was the shaping of iron into specific forms. Since ancient times, iron ore—a rock-mineral substance with certain chemical properties that permitted it to be transformed under heat from a granular to a liquid to a solid state—had been heated, solidified and then pounded with hammers into specific shapes to make what is known as "wrought iron"; or melted under much greater temperatures in a crucible, then poured into shaped molds and allowed to cool and harden into what is called "cast iron."

Whether wrought or cast, such solid iron was brittle because it had a carbon content of about four percent. The lower the percentage of carbon, the stronger and more resilient and durable iron becomes. Today a popular demonstration of the martial art of karate is for an expert to shatter a stack of wood boards with a single slashing blow. Although there were no known karate practitioners in the America of the 1830s, had there been one he might have done the same to a ten-pound, inch-thick bar of native crude iron. In the 1820s and 1830s, cast iron was not much stronger than hardwood; in fact, many early railroad tracks were made of wood. Harder iron required higher smelting temperatures obtainable only by the burning of anthracite coal in closed furnaces, as was done in England.

Anthracite had been discovered in eastern Pennsylvania as early as 1770, but because its hardness made mining it difficult as compared to the softer and more abundant bituminous of western Pennsylvania, it was largely neglected until the 1830s. Then, as the demand for tougher railroad iron rose, more and more miners went after it. And as more and more anthracite was mined, established iron foundries in the bituminous coal-burning Pittsburgh region were enlarged to utilize it. To solve the problem of getting the coal quickly and in bulk to Pittsburgh, still another railroad was chartered—the line that would eventually become known as the Pennsylvania Railroad and stretch from New York through Philadelphia and Pittsburgh to Chicago.

Railroads, mining and iron manufacture—the railroads depended on the latter two for their growth, while the growth of the mining and iron industries was stimulated by the sudden high-demand market the railroads represented. It was in this fashion that the three separate industries combined to form the nation's first massive industrial monolith. It was a monolith that later, when steel, petroleum and electricity were added to the equation, would pave the road to the American colossus.

But for the time being, the road, to extend the metaphor, remained primitive and rutted. Life in Britain and on the European continent was still considerably more advanced in the 1830s than it was in the United States. The only difference was that fewer people, comparatively, got to enjoy the fruits of Europe's greater progress than benefited from the lesser progress in America. A modest measure of social and economic democracy had taken hold in America in the fifty years since the nation's founding, much more so than in Europe. Although it was imperfect, still explicitly excluding nonwhites and, in the South, intensifying the practice of slavery, it provided economic opportunity to enough people to make democracy a self-regenerating, self-expanding system. The notions of competition, free enterprise, individual initiative and personal industry were seen to provide the potential for significant real-life rewards, and theoretically no one—at least no white person or, to be more accurate, no white man—was barred by tradition or cultural mores from pursuing those rewards. The system continued to demonstrate that anyone could get rich, provided he had the determination, ingenuity, skills and a dash of luck. During the forty years between 1790 and 1830, the U.S. Patent Office had received about fifteen thousand patent applications. That many and more were submitted in the single decade of 1830–

1840, and thereafter patent applications roughly doubled with each succeeding decade of the nineteenth century.

The most significant patent granted in the early 1830s—significant both in its cultural benefits to the nation and in its personal rewards to the man behind it—was for the "mechanical reaper." Notwithstanding the intensifying concentration on cloth manufacture and heavy industries during the period, America, with its constantly expanding frontiers and fast-spreading, food-requiring population, remained at heart an agricultural nation. North and south, farming had spread as far west as the Mississippi River and, in some areas, beyond. The upper Mississippi Valley and the broad, flat prairies that bordered it were proving particularly hospitable to the growing of staple grains. With the addition to the country of such vast, fertile expanses, farming was rapidly being transformed from a local subsistence enterprise into a broader commercial one. Thousands of settlers, many of them fresh from Europe, poured into the region to establish large farms specializing in the cultivation of wheat and corn, and they soon began to use the Mississippi waterway system to ship their commodities to New Orleans for transshipment to eastern American ports or abroad. The only impediment to greater productivity, and therefore to greater commercial success, lay in the scarcity of farm workers to hand-harvest the crops. It was to this problem that Cyrus Hall McCormick addressed himself while still in his teens.

McCormick was born in the hills of southwestern Virginia. His father, Robert McCormick, was a mechanic as well as a farmer, and young Cyrus grew up watching him try repeatedly, without success, to devise a workable grain-harvesting machine. Cyrus, learning from the elder McCormick's mistakes, began to experiment with his own labor-saving implements in 1828. In 1831 he fabricated and patented a special hillside plow, but it was his invention of a year later that brought him his enduring riches and fame.

The invention took the form of a simple channeled iron bar mounted low and laterally between and behind a pair of wheels. Set into the channel was a row of sharpened, triangular metal teeth, each joined horizontally to its neighbor through a wooden "spine." The spine itself was attached at its two ends, through a series of gears, pulleys and belts, to the wheels. When the wheels rotated as they were pulled by a draft animal, they imparted a force to the spine that caused it, and its attached teeth, to slide laterally back and forth within the channel. McCormick then added a second channel with a slightly overlapping spine of teeth that operated reciprocally to the first. The result was a clean lateral shearing action along the entire length of the anchor bar.

With this crude device, McCormick set in motion the complete transformation of agriculture. Since ancient times, grain and grass had been cut by hand with scythes and sickles, while other crops were hand-cultivated and harvested. Farmers had dreamed for centuries of a machine that would do some of this backbreaking work for them. Now it existed. McCormick called his contraption a mechanical reaper and quickly patented it.

But that was just the beginning of Cyrus McCormick's rags-to-riches saga. A secure and exclusive patent provided him with the time to improve and refine his machine, replacing the soft iron teeth with harder and sharper teeth fashioned out of steel acquired from England,* making the cutting action more precise, and adding metal guards to protect the reciprocating teeth from field stones. Then, late in the 1830s, McCormick set up a shop on his father's Virginia farm and began to hand-manufacture his improved reaper for commercial sale locally. At first his sales were practically nil—the farms in his region were small, mostly of the subsistence variety and with few large plantings of grains. But then, in the early 1840s, as word of the machine spread to the Mississippi Valley states and the Great Plains territories beyond, orders began to trickle into his Virginia shop.

McCormick, as it would turn out, was not only an adept inventor and manufacturer; he also became the country's first genuine marketing pioneer. Encouraged by orders from the West, he decided that that was where his reaper's most lucrative future market was. Accordingly, he toured the region with a demonstration model during the fall harvest season of 1845. Within a few weeks, orders for it skyrocketed. So impressed was the first mayor of Chicago by McCormick, his machine and his unusual (for then) personal marketing technique, that he persuaded the Virginian to

---

*Steel is an iron alloy with the least possible carbon content. Although steel had been in existence for some time, its manufacture was a tedious process and it could be produced only in small amounts. A method of fabricating steel quickly, cheaply and in quantity had not yet been discovered, although with the advent of the railroad age in the 1830s many iron makers were desperately trying to find the secret.

move his manufacturing operations to the rapidly growing town
on the southwestern shore of Lake Michigan.

This was western municipal boosterism at its most sophisticated. Chicago, nothing more than a frontier trading post a few
decades before, had only recently begun to be settled. Because of
its location at the threshold of the Mississippi Valley and the
Great Plains, practically every migrant heading for the region
passed through. Many stayed. A village of not more than a few
hundred souls in 1830, its population had grown to four thousand
by 1837, when it was incorporated, and was thrice that when
Cyrus McCormick arrived in 1845.

Chicago was the fastest growing community in the nation in
the 1840s. To accommodate the swelling population, early self-
taught carpenters, with few links to conventional building traditions, developed a faster and cheaper way to construct dwellings.
The traditional construction method was the heavy-timber post-
and-beam frame clad with logs, thick planks or even thicker ma-
sonry—the log house, the plank house, the stone or brick house.
Such construction, because the timbers had to be hand-cut and
chiseled to fit snugly, was slow and demanded a high degree of
craftsmanship. The Chicago settlement of the 1830s had few such
practiced carpenters, however. What it did have were several
"mechanics," recently arrived from New England, who were familiar with the pedal-powered circular metal saw that had been
copied from similar English devices by David Melville in Massachusetts and introduced by him there in 1815. The circular saw
had been rapidly put to use in the rough-cutting of heavy construction timbers in the East, but no one had yet thought of using
it for more precise techniques of building framing.

The early settlers of Chicago, besides lacking experienced carpenters and joiners, were confronted by another problem. The
farther west toward the Plains one traveled, the sparser the native
forests became. And even where woodlots were found, their trees
were usually of the thin and spindly variety; rare were the thick,
dense maple, ash, oak, fir and pine of the mountainous East. Out
of these twin scarcities emerged the Chicago "balloon" or "stick-
frame" method of construction. Slender logs were sawn into narrow stick-like lengths. The sticks (early versions of today's two-
by-four stud) were erected vertically a foot or more apart around
the perimeter of the intended building and fastened by iron nails

to thin horizontal sills and plates, also sawn from local logs. Then more of these thin studs were nailed and extended at an angle from the opposite topmost horizontal plates to meet at a ridge and form the frame of the structure's roof. The perpendicular perimeter studs were then sheathed outside by thin-sawn siding and inside by lath and plaster, with the hollow spaces between often filled with horsehair, shredded newspapers and other such materials designed to serve as insulation.

The first observers of this new construction method belittled it, predicting that the violent winds Chicago was fast becoming famous for would wreak havoc on such fragile-looking structures. "They will vanish into the sky, like balloons," cracked one local newspaper editorialist, thus unintentionally giving the method its original name. But Chicago's first such balloon structure—a small church—did not levitate as predicted when a violent storm struck the settlement in 1834. Thereafter the balloon frame became the town's standard method of house building. Because it was fast and cheap—two carpenters could erect a finished house shell in a week—frame houses, indeed whole neighborhoods of them, sprouted within months inside the corporate limits of Chicago during the late 1830s.

This was one of the main reasons a great number of Plains-bound settlers, at first just passing through, decided to stay or return. Once convinced of the structural integrity and durability of the new construction, the town fathers used the idea of cheap frame houses to lure settlers. Why venture beyond into the bleak prairie, where you would have to spend years building a home— went the sales pitch—when you can have your own home right here in Chicago, almost overnight and at little cost? Why risk the rough and uncivilized unknown when you can start enjoying a civilized life immediately in our growing metropolis?

The mayor of Chicago, the town's leading booster, even invested his own money in what was to be the country's first organized housing development. In 1839 he commissioned a gang of carpenters to erect a square block of frame houses on land he owned in what is today the city's Near North Side, a short distance from the lakefront. Most of the houses were rented before they were completed, and with his profits he started other housing blocks. By 1845 he was a rich man, and when he encountered Cyrus McCormick and his reaper in the fall of that year, the most persuasive element of his argument that McCormick should move his manufacturing operation to Chicago was his offer to back the inventor personally with an investment of $50,000.

The mayor was no fool. He knew that McCormick's machine, and the other advanced farm machinery the young Virginia pioneer was in the process of designing, would find an immediate and growing market among the Plains farmers, and that in turn the reaper would attract still greater numbers of farmers to the region. His investment was a sure thing.

But he was twice no fool. The reaper's quick success, and the fact that it was manufactured in Chicago, would mean a rapid influx of industrial workers to man an ever-expanding McCormick plant. This would create a rising demand for cheap housing near the plant, housing that the mayor intended to supply. The mayor's vision was accurate in all respects. After McCormick set up his reaper business in Chicago and conducted further demonstrations, orders multiplied at a dizzying rate—this despite the fact that his exclusive patent on the machine would expire in 1848 and he would thereafter be confronted by a swarm of competitors.

It was in this regard that McCormick proved his mettle not only as an inventor but as a creative business pioneer. In order to blunt the impact of the dozen competitors who started to make their own versions of his machine in the late 1840s, he instituted a policy—unheard of until that time—under which he guaranteed the McCormick reaper, offered it to farmers on approval, and even agreed to finance its purchase on a credit and deferred-payment basis. The strategy worked, and both McCormick and increasing numbers of farmers benefited from it. McCormick managed to keep the lion's share of the constantly expanding market—in 1854 he would sell more than a thousand machines—and farmers were able to harvest vastly greater quantities of grain than ever before. The greater harvests soon brought huge grinding mills into the northern and central Plains around which further towns and cities grew, shortly to be serviced by the expanding network of railroads.

Along with the railroad, Cyrus McCormick's reaper did more than any other mechanical invention to accelerate the development of the western United States in the mid-nineteenth century. Too, it sharpened the American people's expansionist, colossus-building impulses, which had only recently been expressed by

"Manifest Destiny." The phrase was coined in 1845 by a magazine editorialist, John O'Sullivan, in reaction to the United States'
quarrels with foreign governments over territorial rights in Texas
and the Far West. The United States was about to go to war with
Mexico over control of Texas and the Southwest in general, and it
was engaged simultaneously in a territorial dispute with England
in regard to the Northwest—the vast Oregon Territory, as it was
then known. In his journal *The United Magazine and Democratic Review*, O'Sullivan wrote that foreign governments were interfering
with America's territorial ambitions beyond the Mississippi in
order to block "the fulfillment of our manifest destiny to over-
spread the continent allotted by Providence for the free development of our yearly multiplying millions." Manifest Destiny
quickly became the rallying cry of the recently elected expansionist administration of President James Polk, and the moral jus-
tification for the war against Mexico. If the United States had
been hesitant before 1845 about extending its hegemony to the
continent's Pacific shores, thereafter it was militantly determined
to do so.

That determination was sharpened by the discovery of the rich
fertility of the land that stretched beyond the Mississippi frontier
to the Pacific. And it was turned into national gospel when vast
lodes of gold were unearthed in California in 1849. But along with
the development of railroad technology, Cyrus McCormick's
reaper had lit the original spark of the expansionist impulse.

McCormick's contribution was not limited to that, however.
Of equal importance were the new business, marketing, organizational and managerial methods he introduced to the country. Until McCormick, the American business complex operated for the
most part on the single-proprietor formula; that is, small businesses created and tightly controlled by their founders, who usually remained their chief and only managers for life. Often when
the founder-manager died, the fortunes of a business, bequeathed
to his heirs, either died with him or were dissipated through mismanagement.*

*There were exceptions to this rule, of course. One was a small printing company
established in New York in 1802 by John Wiley. The Wiley print shop was among the first
to publish the books of early American writers such as James Fenimore Cooper and Washington Irving. When the founding Wiley died, he passed the business on to his sons. It has
since gone through five generations of Wileys and is today, with the help of a certain
measure of nonfamily management, one of the larger and more successful publishing organizations in the United States.

McCormick, on the other hand, hired outside submanagers, foremen and even marketing planners and promotional specialists to help him run his burgeoning business, while he acted as its overall chief executive. He also employed and trained mechanical engineers to work on improvements to the reaper and its manufacture, and on the creation of other suitable machinery the company could manufacture. And he almost singlehandedly established the practice of retail installment credit—a practice that has played no small role in America's remarkable material growth. Although he would ensure that the company remained within his family's control after his death in 1884, he established the standard for operating a large business. This standard, frequently copied, became the template upon which later American management methods were formed. These methods had as much to do with turning the United States into the rich industrial and technological colossus it is today as did the nation's abundance of natural resources, its territorial breadth, its fast-multiplying population, its educational system and its mechanical inventiveness.

CHAPTER 8

MAGIC IN A WIRE

Because the emphasis in the 1830s was on progress in the heavy industries—mining, iron making, railroad construction and labor-reducing machinery—what turned out to be the most mysterious and far-reaching invention of all in early America appeared out of the blue, leaving the nation initially both awestruck and derisively skeptical. Given the fact that mass formal education was still a thing of the future, and that there was thus no uniformly trained corps of mechanical and scientific specialists in the country as yet, it was not surprising that the invention sprang from the mind of a man who, like Robert Fulton a generation before him, had set out in life to be an artist. Unlike Fulton, however, the man had achieved singular success and celebrity in the world of paints and canvas by the time he introduced his startling device to the world.

The man was Samuel Morse, and his invention was the electric telegraph—a device that revolutionized communications and led the way to the shrinking of the world into what would be called, a hundred years later, the "global village." Morse's discovery, however, did not explode full-blown from his ingenious brain alone. It was, rather, a serendipitous product of the kind of process that had shaped almost every other chapter in the story of human and scientific progress. Morse simply happened to be in the right place at the right time.

Samuel F. B. Morse was born in 1791 in Charlestown, Massachusetts, just outside Boston. The son of a geographer-mapmaker and Congregational clergyman, he was graduated from Yale in 1810, three years after Fulton's first steamboat voyage and at a time when his fellow Yale alumnus Eli Whitney was pioneering the idea of precision mass manufacture in the United States. Despite his scientifically minded father and his exposure to the mechanical pulse of the early-1800s Northeast, Morse's dominant ambition was to become a painter of portraits and historical events. After his graduation, he went to England to study and did not return to Boston until 1815. Boston was already liberally peopled by portraitists, however, and after working for three years there with little commercial success, he moved to Charleston, South Carolina. In Charleston, Morse began to receive commissions from the South's wealthy plantation owners and cotton merchants, and in 1823 he brought his rising reputation to New York. In New York he became acquainted with many among the city's intellectual and artistic elite. His repute as a painter was secured in 1825 when he was commissioned by the federal government to execute two portraits of the Revolutionary hero Lafayette. Thereafter he became a leader of the New York intellectual establishment and one of the city's most visible social figures.

Morse returned to England in 1829 to fulfill several portrait commissions. Remaining in London for three years, he renewed his earlier friendship with the popular expatriate American writer James Fenimore Cooper, whom he had first met in New York. He also became well-acquainted with America's other most notable author, Washington Irving, who was serving in the United States legation in London. The three spent much of their free time together observing the industrial and scientific progress of England and discussing its implications for their homeland.

By the time Morse was ready to return to the United States in 1832, he had grown bored with portrait painting. He had developed instead a fascination with England's growing railway system. The practicability of railroads was in the process of becoming established in America in the wake of Peter Cooper's *Tom Thumb*, and Morse sensed that once an American railroad network was in place, it would be plagued—infinitely more so because of the much greater expanse of the nation—by the same problem that hindered the operation of the British system. The problem was how to keep constant track of the whereabouts of the system's trains. England's railroads had been built, as America's would be at the beginning, according to a single-track system. Trains traveled in both directions over just one track and relied on a complicated method of human "lookouts" and signals to avoid accidents. Already the method had proved faulty. Several disastrous head-on collisions had occurred along British rail lines.

Along with the railroad and signaling systems, Morse also became interested in English scientists' experiments in electromagnetism—experiments that had culminated in Michael Faraday's 1831 discovery that an electric current could be produced in metal by changing the metal's magnetic intensity. As a student at Yale, Morse had studied the sciences under Benjamin Silliman, a disciple of Benjamin Franklin who had made certain modest advances on Franklin's electrical knowledge. Morse and Silliman had remained in touch after Morse's graduation, and Morse was the first to inform Silliman, by letter from London, of Faraday's discovery of electromagnetic induction. In his letter, using his lively imagination, Morse wrote: "Wouldn't it be a thing of marvel if Mr. Faraday's current could be employed to send these words to you through magnetized wire, in some form of electric pulses, so that they might reach you more quickly than I daresay they will? Farfetched, no doubt." (It took forty-nine days for the letter to travel from Morse in London to Silliman in Connecticut.)

Without immediately realizing it, Morse had hatched the idea of transmitting signaled messages through electricity. Silliman wrote back that his concept might not be so far-fetched, since a young American scientist in Troy, New York, had apparently stumbled on the same notion.

The scientist was Joseph Henry, a teacher at a school in Troy called the Rensselaer Polytechnic. Henry had in fact been the first to discover the electromagnet; the year before, working independently of Faraday in England, he had found his own way to produce a current in a piece of metal by varying its magnetic intensity. What's more, utilizing the same technique, he had learned how to reverse the current so as to produce what amounted to the world's first crude electric motor: a device that generated power and could actually, through a belt-and-pulley system, move another object.

Joseph Henry, whose obsession was scientific experimentation with little thought of the commercial application of his work, was America's first purely abstract laboratory scientist. Faraday's later independent confirmation of his own discovery of electromagnetic induction, and the exclusive credit Faraday received for it in the scientific world, produced no professional resentment in Henry. Rather, it impelled him to further experimentation in the still-arcane field of electricity. His studies would soon lead him to the discovery of the principle of the transformer as a device to step up or step down the intensity of electrical currents as they traveled from one point to another, and to the foundation of the first tentative theory of the voltage and amperage of currents, each of which made possible the later application of electricity to everyday life.

In the meantime, having learned from Benjamin Silliman of Henry's work on sending a current through a metal wire and varying its intensity, Samuel Morse, still in London, began to ruminate more avidly about finding a way to use the method to create electrical "pulsations" that could be transformed, by some system of semaphores, into words and sentences—that is, into messages. Not surprisingly, since he still had only a layman's knowledge of the principles of electricity, his thoughts focused mostly at first on a semaphore system. Semaphores—systems of hand, light and flag signals—had been in use since ancient times for transmitting messages across a distance. Even the primitive Indians of the American continent had devised a sophisticated semaphore system: smoke signals.

As a child, Morse had learned a great deal about the Indians' smoke codes from his father. The Reverend Jedidiah Morse had done extensive missionary work among the Indians prior to his son's birth and had become so expert on Indian culture that the federal government commissioned him in 1819 to write a report recommending a method by which to settle Indian territorial claims.* Samuel Morse, then, had grown up steeped in Indian lore and had retained his interest in it into his adult years, mostly through correspondence with his father. Although he never mentioned it later, it is probable that Morse's efforts to marry traditional semaphore ideas to an intermittent electrical current were inspired in part by his acquaintance with the American Indians' smoke-signal systems.

At any rate, consulting with several English associates of Faraday in 1831, Morse learned that the pulsations he had in mind could, at least in theory, be created and transmitted through a metal wire by electromagnetic induction. This knowledge pro-

---

*Morse's father's report was submitted in 1822. It recommended resettlement of all the Indian tribes from the eastern and central portions of the country into an area of the still largely unexplored Northwest. It even raised the idea of a separate Indian state. The senior Morse's recommendations were never formally adopted. Nevertheless his report was later reconsulted when the government set out to establish the Indian reservation system after the Civil War. Jedidiah Morse became known in some circles as the architect of the reservation system.

vided him with the final impetus he needed. He theorized that if he could stretch a wire between two distant points, attach it at one end to an electromagnetic "inductor," and at the other to a terminal that would receive the electric pulsations and translate them mechanically into a semaphorelike code, he could transmit intelligible signals or messages between the two points. He surmised, too, that such a system would be highly prized by the soon-to-be-established railroad system in America; its far-flung network of tracks was sure to extend through sparsely populated regions of the country.

With these prospects in mind, Morse returned to New York in 1832. Aboard ship he met Robert Stevens, the son of the American steam pioneer John Stevens and an inventor in his own right. The younger Stevens, who had recently conceived the idea of the iron T-rail, was returning from England after a trip there to obtain a British patent on the new rail and raise money for its manufacture. When Morse mentioned his "telegraph" idea to Stevens, who was also engaged with his father in trying to charter their own railway, the railroad man endorsed it enthusiastically. Morse thereupon spent the rest of the voyage devising a code for the projected telegraph. By the time he landed in New York, he had the beginnings of one. His system was based on the theory of a series of short and long pulsations of electric current, each series a fixed representation of a number or a letter of the alphabet—dots and dashes, as they would soon become known, just as the entire system would become known as the Morse Code.*

Morse arrived in New York with a rough code, then, but still without the device to put it into use. Achieving a working telegraph would prove a much more nettlesome and time-consuming endeavor. His first step was to consult with Benjamin Silliman in Connecticut. Although Silliman had become the country's foremost popularizer of science—he had embarked on a program of tours during Yale's summer recesses in which he appeared before large crowds, somewhat in the fashion of a magician, to demonstrate scientific phenomena—he was unable to help Morse except to give him a crash course in the latest-known principles of electricity. Then he referred him to Joseph Henry at the Rensselaer Polytechnic in Troy. Morse journeyed by steamboat to Troy, met

---

*The conventional historical wisdom is that Morse invented the telegraph first, and then devised his code. Actually the code, or at least a primitive version of it, came first.

with Henry, and outlined his idea for an electrical telegraph. Henry, still the pure scientist indifferent to the idea of transforming scientific principles into practical (and profitable) gadgets, was lavishly generous in his advice to Morse. He declared that Morse's notion was practicable and all but wrote down detailed directions on how to construct such a device.

Armed with Silliman's up-to-date electrical knowledge and Henry's specific outline, Morse returned to New York and set to work. He gave up the pursuit of portrait commissions and got himself appointed instead to a meagerly paid art-teaching position at the University of the City of New York—more, he conceded later, to gain access to the university's primitive laboratory equipment than out of any desire to instruct students in painting. Within a year, with the help of a university science teacher and several students, Morse managed to put together a rudimentary electromagnetic transmitting device that sent his pulsations along a short length of wire. He was temporarily stymied, however, when he could not generate a controllable current beyond forty feet. Only further consultations with Henry (whose contributions, incidentally, he never publicly acknowledged) put Morse on the road to solving the problem. Henry proposed a series of electromagnetic "relays" that would "gather up" or "renew" the fading current as it proceeded along the wire and transmit it at full strength toward the next relay.

Once he had mastered the relay device in 1835, Morse turned his attention to developing the final requirement of his system. This was a mechanism to receive the electrical impulses and convert them into mechanical symbols which, in accordance with his code, could be deciphered into ordinary language. In 1836 he succeeded in devising a terminal that worked in conjunction with his electromagnetic sending unit. It received the short-long electrical impulses fed into the wire by the manipulation of a magnetized key and mechanically converted them, by means of a crude magnetic circuit breaker, into a series of clicking sounds.

Morse and his assistants first successfully demonstrated the contrivance in public in a New York University laboratory in 1839. The demonstration was met not with the wonderment and offers of financial backing Morse had anticipated, but with disbelief and scorn. Electricity was still more feared than understood in America; most citizens, even enlightened and educated ones, remained convinced from their experiences with lightning that electricity was a force only God had a right to employ. Those who witnessed Morse's demonstration believed that by "playing" with electricity, Morse was toying with Divinity in a way that could have only disastrous consequences.

So disheartened was Morse, and by that time so poor, that he did not even bother to apply for a patent. Yet he continued to work on the improvement of his telegraph, adding to his coterie of disciple-assistants Alfred Vail and John Goffe Rand, each a young artist and aspiring inventor.* Vail was especially supportive of his mentor, but it took another five years before Morse attained his dream. What he then needed was to carry out an actual long-distance demonstration, but he could not raise the money to finance it. Repeatedly rebuffed by private industry, including the railroads, in his quest for financing, Morse finally turned to the federal government in 1842.

It was no small irony that the South, increasingly alienated from the rest of the country over the issue of slavery, and the nation's least industrially advanced region, would play an important role in the success of a device that radically changed human life. Morse approached several southern senators whose family portraits he had painted twenty years before, when he lived in Charleston. He convinced two of them of the potential value of his telegraph to the country, particularly to the South, which knew that its economic recovery, following the Panic of 1837, depended largely on catching up to the North in railroad and other industrial development. The two senators, overcoming stiff resistance in Congress, managed to pass a bill in 1843 which mandated that the government finance, to the tune of $30,000, the laying of a metal wire between Washington and Baltimore to test the long-distance feasibility of Morse's device.

With government money guaranteeing the project, dozens of private industrialists bid for the contract to fabricate and lay the wire between the two cities, which were thirty miles apart.† Finally, on May 23, 1844, the wire was in place and the experiment

---

*In 1841, Rand would invent a flexible collapsible metal tube to hold artist's pigments; the tube was the forerunner of the modern toothpaste tube and thousands of other such containers. In 1844, Vail would invent a technique for mechanically converting Morse's telegraphic impulses into printed dots and dashes, a development that helped significantly to bring about the acceptance of the telegraph.

†The winning bidder was Ezra Cornell, later the founder of Cornell University.

was ready to proceed. Morse, surrounded by dozens of congressmen, stood at one end of the wire in the chamber of the Supreme Court at the Capitol. At the other end, in a room in Baltimore, waited Alfred Vail. In order to ensure that the experiment could not be rigged in any way, several federal officials had insisted that they be allowed, at the last moment, to supply the message Morse was to attempt to send to Vail. Vail was then to send the message back in exactly the same form; neither Morse nor Vail were to have any foreknowledge of the words to be telegraphed. Morse had agreed to the conditions. As he stood poised over his telegraph, he was handed a piece with a quotation from the Old Testament. He studied it, nodded, and began to tap out in code: "What hath God wrought?"

Once Morse was finished, a tense two minutes passed while Vail, in Baltimore, decoded the message. Then the return message began to click back, received not by Morse but by a congressional clerk who had been instructed to learn Morse's code in order to doubly ensure the authenticity of the test. When the terminal key in the hushed Supreme Court chamber ceased its clicking, the clerk, unaware of the message sent by Morse to Vail, decoded the transmission from Baltimore. He wrote the words on a piece of paper and handed it to one of the senators. "What hath God wrought?" it read. Samuel Morse was on his way to riches and worldwide fame.

But not as quickly as one might have imagined. The populace at large was still suspicious of Morse's "magic-in-a-wire," and it took several more years for the telegraph to come into general use. It was one thing to have the actual machine at hand, another to mount a long-distance wire-and-relay system that would bind the country together telegraphically. Two companies, leasing Morse's patent rights in the telegraph, were formed to accomplish this: the American Telegraph Company, which erected and controlled the lines in the East, in 1855; and the Western Union Company, which covered the West, in 1856. But it would not be until 1861, when a coast-to-coast wire was completed and the onset of the Civil War proved its benefits in providing instant long-distance communications, that Morse's invention was wholeheartedly accepted. When it was, American history—world history—was changed forever.

*   *   *

It has become a relatively recent American custom to view the nation's history in the context of a few specifically demarcated decades. It is as if each particular ten-year span encapsulated a special cultural reality that was of much more relevance to the country's development than that of other decades. We tend also to give these distinctive decades catchy phrase names: the Roaring Twenties, the Gay Nineties, the Fabulous Fifties. Had such phrasemaking been the practice in mid-nineteenth-century America, popular historians and social commentators might well have looked back at the decade of the 1840s and dubbed it the Furious Forties. For furious it was in the pace of its technological development and in the suddenness with which it altered the American character.

In addition to Morse's telegraph, other vital technological milestones of the 1840s were Charles Goodyear's accidental discovery of a method to vulcanize rubber, Charles Thurber's prototype of the mechanical typewriter, Elias Howe's sewing machine, Richard Hoe's development of the rotary printing press, dentist William Morton's discovery of ether as the first useful surgical anesthetic, and John Deere's improvement of his invention of the steel moldboard plow. Even Walter Hunt's innovation of the seemingly insignificant safety pin was of major importance, not so much because it at last spared mothers from the trauma of accidentally pricking their infants and infecting them with lethal bacteria, but because it led the way to the technology of mass-manufacturing precision instruments.

Rubber had long been known to the world, but its utility was severely limited by the fact that it invariably melted at high temperatures and disintegrated at low. Charles Goodyear, born in New York in 1800, had gone bankrupt in the hardware business in 1830. When he was released from debtors' prison in the mid-thirties without a penny to his name, he decided to try his hand at producing rubber articles. He was confronted by the same problem everyone else who worked with raw rubber faced, however: its lack of integrity except within a narrow temperature range.

Goodyear began to experiment with ways to improve the reliability of raw rubber. One day in 1839 he accidentally dropped a mixture of rubber and sulphur on a hot stove. The mixture immediately melted, creating a smelly, molten mess. Annoyed at his clumsiness, Goodyear angrily scraped the odiferous glop into a bowl with the intention of discarding it after it cooled. A while later, when he picked up the congealed substance to toss it on his rubbish heap, he noticed that it felt markedly different from the rubber he was accustomed to handling. He bent it and it flexed easily instead of cracking in two. He placed it over a flame and it did not soften. He packed it in ice and it did not flake.

By complete accident Goodyear had discovered vulcanization—a process that turned a substance of limited use into one of the world's most important and valuable raw materials. The discovery also created an entirely new industry that in turn spawned countless subindustries, each of which would contribute mightily to the ever-accelerating pace of human progress, comfort and safety. Goodyear never obtained the fortune he expected to accrue as a result of his discovery, though. After perfecting the process so that it could be carried out on a large industrial scale and not just on a workshop stove, he received a patent for it in 1844. However, the satisfaction of his past debts swallowed up most of his income from the patent. He died sixteen years later, embroiled in lawsuits and still in debt.

Quite a different destiny awaited Elias Howe. Crude sewing machines, based on the idea of the power loom, were already in use in France and England by the time the Massachusetts-born Howe went to work, at the age of sixteen, as an apprentice in a cotton machinery shop in Lowell. After three years of learning the mechanics of spinning machinery, Howe moved on to a metal-shaping job at the Cambridge shop of a maker of nails, needles and pins. The year was 1839, and one day Howe, just turned twenty, overheard a conversation between his employer and a visitor. The discussion had to do with the latest developments in labor-saving mechanization in the mills. Howe suddenly heard the visitor remark that despite the great mechanical improvements in producing fabrics for clothes, people still had to make clothes by hand. "Do you realize," the visitor asked his host, "that the making of clothes is the chief occupation of half the human race?" Whoever invented a machine to replace the time-consuming and eye-straining process of hand-sewing garments, the man went on, would do the world a great service and become a very rich man in the bargain.

Thus inspired, Elias Howe went to work in his spare time to produce such a machine. Unaware that others in Europe and

America had already embarked on the search for a genuinely workable mechanical stitcher, and that a few patent applications were even on file in Washington, he spent many months on a machine designed to copy the complex motions of his wife's arm when sewing. No matter how hard he tried, though, he could not devise an articulated mechanical movement that allowed a single thread to be stitched and "locked." Then he hit upon the idea of using two threads, operating with separate opposing but synchronized mechanical motions, aided by a shuttle device, to form and lock a stitch.

The idea was feasible, Howe discovered after five more years of tinkering and experiment. His next task was to construct an actual prototype that would put it into action. This took only a year, and in 1846 a patent was issued on Howe's invention. The machine embodied a curved, eye-pointed needle that carried an upper thread from a spindle and operated horizontally in conjunction with a shuttle for the lower thread to form a lockstitch. The whole affair, however, hand-operated by a crank, allowed only one stitch to be made at a time.

Howe could not find a machinery maker in the Northeast with tooling sophisticated enough to produce his bulky but precise contrivance in quantity, so he traveled to England to have it manufactured there. Soon the machines began to be exported back to the United States. Within a year they became nationally celebrated and in great demand, although Howe discovered when he returned from abroad in 1849 that his role in their invention was largely unknown. Most people assumed the device to have been an English creation.

If Elias Howe was the true inventor of the first useful sewing machine, another man, Isaac Singer, was its best exploiter. Also a native of Massachusetts, Singer was a journeyman mechanic in Boston when he first espied one of Howe's imported machines in 1848. He studied it and decided he could improve on its function by working out a way to make it sew continuously rather than one stitch at a time. He succeeded in 1850 by creating a foot treadle which, through a system of belts and gears, allowed the operator to sew successive stitches without having to stop to reposition the cloth. To support these innovations he built a prototype which, although he claimed it to be of his own independent creation, was actually a blatant copy of Howe's machine and also incorporated the patented improvements of several other innovators, such as the vertical needle, the continuous feed, and the transverse oscillating shuttle. Singer received a patent on this much handier machine in 1851, thereby making Howe's virtually obsolete.

Elias Howe refused to stand still for this, however. With its blizzard of mechanical inventions, major and minor, the 1840s had introduced into American life an equally intense storm of patent litigation. A fast-multiplying corps of lawyers stood ready to assist inventors with their inevitable claims against other inventors and manufacturers and in many cases lawyers practically bent prospective clients' arms to sue. In 1849, Howe had started a series of lawsuits against others who had received sewing-machine patents, based on various improvements, while he was in England. His most celebrated and long-lasting action, though, was instituted in 1852 against Singer and his "continuous machine," which was rapidly destroying the market for Howe's English-made machines.

It took until 1854, but Howe prevailed and was awarded a handsome royalty on every sewing machine manufactured in America by anyone else, including Singer. At the height of the sewing-machine mania that began in 1860 with the start of clothing mass-production and the implementation of retail marketing techniques such as those pioneered by Cyrus McCormick, Howe's royalties often amounted to $4,000 a week. Ironically, Howe would finally establish his own manufacturing company in 1865 to compete with Singer's. What made it ironic was the fact that the machine Howe put out was almost a direct copy of Singer's, but with further improvements. The Howe organization would not win the competition battle, however. Howe died two years later, and the further mechanical improvements and aggressive business tactics of the Singer Sewing Machine Company relegated Howe's company to second place, and eventually to extinction. Nonetheless, both men died rich.

"Next to the plough," wrote Louis Antoine Godey in 1856, "this sewing machine is perhaps humanity's most blessed instrument."

A curious observation, in view of Morse's telegraph; but an understandable one for the times, for it reflected the nation's continuing distrust of electricity and of the arcane aspects of other "scientific" invention. As late as the mid-1850s the American people were comfortable with mechanical progress—it was something they could see, touch and comprehend. Scientific progress—advance based on the exploitation of nature—was another matter altogether. Most could not understand the principles behind it and many still believed that it represented a biblically proscribed infringement of powers reserved exclusively to the Creator.

The momentum that progress had gathered in America during the 1830s and 1840s would soon change that narrow, fearful outlook, however. The decade of the 1850s would be the crucible of the change—that and the gruesome Civil War that followed.

Chapter 9

PROMISE AND PARADOX

What first helped to broaden the nation's outlook at the beginning of the 1850s was the Great Exhibition in London in 1851, the world's first international industrial trade fair. The exposition was conceived originally to show off to the world the fruits of England's scientific and industrial prowess, and to generate further and more widespread demand abroad for its machinery and other advanced products. Representatives from around the world were invited, but many from the other industrialized countries refused to attend unless they could exhibit their own wares. The British acceded and the affair was opened to all who cared to display their products.

Most American industrial pioneers expressed little interest in the exhibition. But not Cyrus McCormick. Invoking the aggressive marketing philosophy that had made his company such a success in Chicago, McCormick entered his reaper in the competition for the most important new mechanical invention of the previous half-century. The reaper, by then also called a harvester, not only won the blue ribbon at London, it garnered first prizes at later fairs, that year and the next, throughout Europe as well.*

The value of these awards was enormous to McCormick and his company, since they translated into thousands of new orders for the harvester from abroad. But the fame the machine accrued in Europe was just as vital to the United States as a whole. Suddenly

*McCormick's success turned his company into America's first multinational concern and led to its eventual rechristening as the International Harvester Corporation.

the accomplishments and future potential of American industry were being recognized by British and European commentators. Even Morse's telegraph was extolled as a monumental advance. "If these cunning American devisements are a portent of that nation's future capabilities," wrote the British economic philosopher John Stuart Mill in a letter to a London scientific journal late in 1851, "we in this country have good cause to be concerned for the well-being of our industrial treasure. Every sign points to the prospect of these Americans creating a Colossus of industry the size of which is beyond the ability of current imagination to grasp."

Mill's letter and other commentaries like it following the harvester's introduction to Europe were given broad public notice in the American press, which itself was growing by leaps and bounds in the 1850s in the wake of Richard Hoe's invention of the rotary printing machine. With an immodest, jingoistic vulgarity that might have made a Tocqueville cringe, American editorialists outdid themselves in boosting and boasting of the nation's industrial recognition abroad.*

"It is proof," wrote Robert Bonner in the weekly New York *Ledger* in 1852,

> that the nation, admittedly still raw and infant in many of its institutions, stands at the ready to best the entirety of Europe and all which that continent has [had] to offer. . . . We shall turn the tables, and rather than existing as poor and lowly thought of progeny of our European forebears, shall become as their fathers and protectors in the new order of things. . . . Forever more let no European man claim that the United States of America are but a collective footnote in the tide of human history; rather be it seen and learned by him that we are history itself, and his contentious mutterings about us the true footnote.

Richard Hoe's steam-powered rotary press had revolutionized newspaper production, making it possible to turn out 8,000 four-page papers an hour as compared with the 200-per-hour capacity

---

*Although Tocqueville had written favorably of physical America when he toured the country in the 1830s, his assessments of the people were not so favorable. He described them variously as "barbaric," "vulgar," and consumed by "petty passions."

of existing hand machinery. Hoe, New York born in 1812, had grown up in his family's printing-press business and in 1830 had taken over a factory owned by his father.

At that time the factory specialized in the manufacture of the single small-cylinder press that was the staple of the industry and the bane of newspaper proprietors throughout the country because of its labor-intensiveness and cumbersome pace. The nation's rapidly spiraling growth rate in the 1830s had intensified the demand for newspapers which the existing printing technology could not economically satisfy. In order to produce, say, 8,000 daily papers, a New York publisher had to have a plant filled with at least six single-cylinder presses running simultaneously, and a correspondingly large labor force to operate them. The resulting costs threatened to erase any profits the publisher might expect to make from selling the 8,000 papers. If he tried to raise the price of his paper to compensate, he would quickly lose his readers to the competition. It was for this reason, principally, that most American papers, even the major-city ones, had remained weeklies.

But the advent of the electrical telegraph changed all that in the 1840s. Newspaper proprietors were among the first to realize the implications of Morse's invention. Once it became available for general use throughout the country, it would radically speed up the transmission of news. As a result, the daily newspaper would be no longer a luxury but a necessity.

Richard Hoe recognized this even before most publishers. He had been among the few witnesses to Morse's first tentative demonstrations of the telegraph at New York University in the mid-1830s—Morse had even sought Hoe's financial backing for the device. Hoe declined to invest, but he helped to bring the telegraph's potential to the attention of the many newspaper proprietors who were his customers. And once Morse successfully carried out his first long-distance transmission in 1844, Hoe turned his own attention to developing a high-speed, high-capacity printing press that would accommodate the revolution in communications presaged by the telegraph.

Hoe solved the problem two years later with the help of several machinists in his New York factory. The solution consisted of a huge multicylinder rotary printing machine that was capable of printing at a much higher speed than ever before. It took only the addition of a steam engine, hooked up to the machine through the by-then standard array of belts and pulleys, to render all previous newspaper presses obsolete.

Hoe sold and installed his first steam-driven rotary press in the plant of the Philadelphia *Public Ledger* in 1847. Thereafter, as the telegraph entered more common use during the 1850s, newspapers throughout the country began to convert to the new machine, transforming themselves from weeklies to dailies and expanding not only their print runs but their physical size and diversity of subject matter too. In order to finance the purchase of the expensive new presses, many weekly papers merged and became dailies. As for Richard Hoe, his already prosperous printing machine business became the giant of the industry, and soon the rotary press was in demand all over the world.*

Hoe's press and Morse's telegraph thus sharply altered the nature of American communications. To newspaper offices in one part of the country the telegraph began to bring fast and reasonably accurate reports of important events in other regions. And Hoe's rotary press enabled newspapers to disseminate such news with greater economy to growing audiences on an increasingly common daily basis. When there was a steamboat explosion near New Orleans or a significant vote in Congress in Washington, citizens of Boston and Chicago learned about it within a day or two, rather than weeks later. When the price of cotton fell at Charleston or a British steamer arrived in New York, the news was available to many other sectors of the country practically overnight.

During the early 1850s then, thanks mainly to the telegraph and the rotary press, America found itself changing from a loosely linked system of regional enclaves into a tightly meshed continental entity. The consequences of this change, positive and negative, were enormous. The revolution in communications would, on one level, at last create a unified American identity and sense

*Hoe went on to develop the web press in 1871, which increased capacity to 18,000 paper an hour and was first used by the New York *Tribune*. He also invented the automatic folder in 1881. This, in combination with his web press, the curved stereotype plate, and the linotype machine invented in 1884 by Ottmar Mergenthaler, became the foundation of the modern newspaper printing process. Today, a mammoth automatic printing press based on these pioneering components—but using computerized typography instead of Mergenthaler's hot-metal linotype—can print, fold, cut, collate and assemble 70,000 copies of a 144-page newspaper in an hour.

of common national purpose, while on another it would threaten to tear the country apart.

Both the unity and the polarity fostered by the advances in communications were primarily in the economic consciousness of the country. The Panic of 1837 and the economic depression that followed had profoundly confused the nation. Until that time, the principal collective concern of the populace had been the success of the political experiment represented by the United States. The Constitution was almost exclusively a political and social charter, with the role of the federal government set forth specifically in political terms. Yet throughout America's first forty years of existence, the federal government had tightly controlled and regulated the nation's internal economic situation, mainly through its national banking system. But then Andrew Jackson, starting in 1832, had dismantled the system, ostensibly because it favored the few and discriminated against the economic opportunity of the many. In short, Jackson contended, the system was undemocratic and therefore unconstitutional.

Jackson's actions, along with his later Specie Circular restricting the speculative purchase of federal lands by private citizens, had been directly responsible for producing the 1837 Panic. During the years that immediately followed, the country's private-sector financial network was reconstructed under a system of state-chartered banks. The states, vying avidly with one another to promote commerce and enterprise, passed liberal legislation enabling banks chartered within their borders to attract private money. In turn, state-chartered banks went into a feverish competition of their own to lure deposits.

But the sudden broadening and upsurge in private-sector economic activity at first served only to confuse the issue even more in the eyes of most Americans. Until that time, the concept of democracy had been viewed largely in political terms. Now, however, it was being advanced as an economic idea. There was little in the Constitution, however, that guaranteed, or even addressed, the notion of individual economic democracy. How could economic democracy be secured in an environment of intense competition unregulated by the federal government? There would always be winners and losers in such an environment. What to do about the losers?

The question was aired and debated with increasing regularity by the press during the 1840s, but it was never resolved. In the meantime the country gradually adjusted to the new economic reality. Jackson had removed the federal government almost completely from the private-sector business and financial milieu of America, telling the American people in effect that the responsibility for economic prosperity—their own and the country's—lay soley with them. Thus was the blueprint of the modern American capitalist system handed to the country. Attempts to revive the federal banking system during the 1840s were defeated, mostly for political reasons, and for the next half-century the federal government would remain generally aloof from the shaping and growth of private enterprise. Yet the unresolved paradox of winners and losers would come back to haunt the country with increasing nettlesomeness as time went on.

Although the basic paradox of the new American system would never be fully resolved, at least the confusion generated by Jackson's fiats would. And it was the expanding and steadily more opinionated press that played the largest role in resolving the confusion. Through the public airing of the new economic issues during the 1840s, the country began to learn that although the national credo had taught that every American was first and foremost a political individual, he or she was now in fact primarily an economic one. The American political experiment was over. The "economic experiment," as one newspaper put it, was about to begin.

This sharp shift in American self-perception produced, in its turn, a growing awareness of what the new economic order promised. It opened up the possibility of future riches not just in the realm of mechanical invention but in every mode of human enterprise, in fields of endeavor that theretofore had not even been contemplated. Thanks to the press, Americans began to see that the country's emerging economic system was potentially a mammoth tree from which an almost infinite number of interrelated branches could grow, each feeding the others through its central organizational roots of competition, pragmatism and free enterprise.

Too, the late 1840s had brought the final fulfillment of the promise of Manifest Destiny. The country's 1848 war against Mexico had resulted in the acquisition of Texas, the rest of the Southwest, and California—the Northwest had been acquired

from Britain two years earlier—each with its immeasurably abundant treasure of natural resources. The United States had
"completed" itself politically and territorially. The nation had become genuinely a territorial colossus, vastly greater in size than
any other nation in the world unified under a single sovereign
government.* The time had now come to think about how best to
integrate and cultivate what amounted to a United States that was
entirely different from the one that had been created half a century before.

Given the inherent stability of the American political system,
this was no longer so much a political problem as it was an economic and logistical one. Since the federal government was, at
least temporarily, out of the business of influencing the direction
of the American economy, the task fell to the people. And since
the people were in the process of reformulating their perception of
the basic purpose of the United States in economic terms, it was
inevitable that they would perceive their greatly expanded country in the same fashion.

By 1851, the year of the London industrial exhibition, the
West had been won, at least on paper, and that was the result of
federal politics. But if it had been won on map-paper, it still remained to be won in fact. The actual winning of the American
West—its settlement and incorporation into the nation—would be
much more a matter of commerce and economics than of politics.
And the struggle to win it would complete the transformation of
the American system from one whose emphasis was almost exclusively political into one whose focus was almost exclusively
economic. The concepts of free enterprise, economic democracy,
commercial competition, and the manipulation and expansion of
private capital were not original with the United States. But the
United States was about to become their most active testing
ground.

Nothing more vividly exemplified the mid-century shift from political to economic consciousness in America than two further
mid-century events, the first of which occurred in 1848 and the
second in 1853.

---

*Other nations that are today physically larger than the United States did not exist
then as national entities. Rather, they were conglomerates of principalities or were loosely
linked nation-states.

During the mid- to late 1840s, while the federal government resorted to war and political maneuver to acquire the territories of the Far West, the eastern rail magnates were busy extending their lines toward the upper and lower Mississippi Valley. Other railroad men were just as busily organizing government support for the idea of an eventual transcontinental line that would link both coasts—an idea as revolutionary in its time as the Erie Canal had been forty years before. In effect, the railroaders became the country's first special-interest lobby. By 1847 the lobby had persuaded a group of eastern congressmen to introduce a bill under whose provisions the federal government would grant public lands in the Mississippi Valley states and the territories beyond for private railroad development. The bill was passed in 1848, its rationale being that such federal subsidization was in the public interest and therefore did not violate the Jacksonian proscriptions against government involvement in the private-sector economy.

Many of the congressmen who backed the Railroad Land Grant Act owed their election to the financial support of various railroad organizers. It was the first major instance in the nation's history of private economic interests playing a direct role in the legislative process, although such practices had already become tradition within many state and municipal governments. The 1848 Land Grant Act was a benchmark, then. Not only did it represent a silent, subtle repeal of Jackson's "democratic" policies of a decade and a half earlier, it also signaled the beginning of an era in which the federal government would play an increasingly active role in the selective fostering of private-sector economic interests and development. By its 1848 law the government, reflecting the changed outlook of the nation as a whole, symbolized its own transformation from an exclusively political organism into an increasingly economic one. It also deepened both the promise and the paradox of the concept of free-enterprise competition capitalism in America.

The 1848 act launched a new round of railroad fever as well. In the early 1850s some 21 million acres were granted to subsidize the construction of railroads in the Mississippi Valley. By 1855 there were 24,000 miles of track in the United States, more than twice that in all of Europe and Britain. In the same year, Chicago was joined to New York and Boston by a continuous line of rail. Land grants soon extended this line farther west to the Mississippi

River, and the construction of the Chicago and Rock Island and the Illinois Central railroads established Chicago as the principal rail hub between East and West. In 1856 the Rock Island completed the first bridge to span the Mississippi, and railroad development spread rapidly into Missouri and Iowa, again through the procurement of land grants.*

The second event that marked the mid-century swing from political to economic consciousnes was the Gadsden Purchase of 1853. This, too, was the inspiration of the railroad lobby. The legislation of 1848 had launched a wild scramble among the nation's railroad entrepreneurs for further land grants. As a consequence, the railroaders' influence in Congress became more pervasive than ever. It could be said, in fact, that at the start of the 1850s the eastern railroad interests firmly controlled much of the federal legislature. That control was fragmented, but only because there were so many different railroad organizers competing for the same favors. Nevertheless they had thoroughly convinced the House and Senate, as well as the Millard Fillmore White House, of the nation's need for a transcontinental railroad.

The only issue that remained to be settled had to do with the route. Since railroad construction technology was still fairly primitive, those who promoted the southernmost route—which avoided the seemingly insurmountable escarpments of the Continental Divide and the High Sierras, along with the nasty winter weather of those successive barricades—at first prevailed. A route from Chicago down through St. Louis and Kansas City, and then on an even more southerly tangent through the flat country of Texas and the recently acquired Mexican territories into southern California, was adjudged the easiest and least troublesome to construct and maintain. The sole problem was that a considerable stretch of land along part of the desired right-of-way still belonged to Mexico by virtue of the Treaty of Guadalupe Hidalgo, which had ended the Mexican War.

To solve the problem, the government dispatched South Carolina railroad president James Gadsden to Mexico early in 1853 with an offer to purchase the land. After several months of negotiation, Mexico agreed to cede the territory—a roughly rectan-

---

*In 1856 only four states existed west of the Mississippi, not counting distant Texas and California. They were Iowa, Missouri, Arkansas and Louisiana. The rest of the trans-Mississippi region was organized into federally administered territories.

gular strip of desert about four hundred miles long and seventy-five miles wide—for $10 million.*

The Gadsden Purchase, as it soon was called, was ratified by Congress in the spring of 1854. Although the vast arid tract would never figure in the eventual development of the first transcontinental railroad, the fact that the United States had purchased it for that singular purpose was taken by thousands of entrepreneurs as a clear signal that the federal government was more fully than ever committed to promoting private business and industrial development in America. As a result, manufacturers, inventors and financiers descended on Washington in droves during the mid-1850s, all of them seeking the kinds of favors and advantages the government was granting the railroads. It marked the beginning of an era of close cooperation between government and private industry, a relationship that would come to play a major role in the lightning-fast expansion and diversification of the country's industrial complex.

It also marked the birth of a tradition of corruption and malfeasance in high places of officialdom in America. Government functionaries all too soon became aware of the personal power they exercised over private interests vying for federal favors, and it was not long before public favors began to be traded for private ones. During the decade of the 1850s, then, the American system of governance underwent its final transfiguration. The American political experiment, having proved successful, was clearly over. It was now time for the economic and industrial experiment to begin in earnest. With it would come the first major manifestations of the paradox that had been spawned by the Jacksonian presidency.

---

*The territory forms what is today the Mexican border with Arizona and part of New Mexico.

CHAPTER 10

THE MONEY FACTOR

When England wrested the settlement of New Amsterdam, at the southern tip of Manhattan Island, from the Dutch in the 1660s, Wall Street was nothing more than a rough sentry path that ran alongside the settlement's northern stockade-type fence. Over the next hundred years the English gradually transformed the village into the small, crowded colonial port city of New York, extending its northern boundary a mile or so beyond the old Dutch wall. In the process, Wall Street became a narrow dirt lane that, as one contemporary observer noted, linked the two dominant symbols of the city's immediate pre-Revolutionary life: religion and commerce. At its head stood Trinity Church on the thoroughfare known as the Broad Way. At its foot were concentrated the East River wharves, storage sheds and countinghouses where the city's main business was done. It was altogether natural that as the city continued to develop following Independence, its commercial activities would spread farther along Wall Street from the waterfront. That is what happened, and in the early 1800s, when banks and the offices of private investment syndicates began to replace the countinghouses and shipping firms of colonial times as the primary vehicles of commerce, Wall Street and its satellite lanes became the center of the city's bustling trade.

The street had another symbolic significance—one, however, that even the most prescient observer of the time would have had difficulty in perceiving. This lay in the fact that it was the city's only east-west through-street. Running as it did in an almost straight line from the East River to the Broad Way, which bordered the city's western precincts, Wall Street could be viewed as a symbolic lifeline between the Old World to the east and the

New World to the west. At its foot lay the port that connected much of the North American continent to Europe. Beyond its head, across the Hudson, extended the vast continent itself, all of it ripe for settlement and development. Although no one divined the symbolism at the time, Wall Street would soon make the symbol a reality. In so doing, it would turn the name of a simple city street into another kind of symbol altogether.

That symbol did not begin to take shape until after the War of 1812, however. Until then, Philadelphia and Boston were the country's main financial centers—Philadelphia because that was where the first federal bank was established, Boston because that city remained the nation's busiest port and chief source of private investment finance and banking. It was only when the state of New York set out in 1817 to raise funds for the construction of the Erie Canal that New York City—Wall Street—began to rise to prominence as a national financial hub. Investment syndicates and banks in Boston and Philadelphia had followed a tradition of aristocratic exclusivity in their private financing operations, limiting participation in important investment schemes to select members of the local monied classes. The financing of the Erie Canal was by far the largest fund-raising endeavor ever attempted. Because the canal was to be a uniquely New York enterprise designed to improve the economic fortunes of the city and state at the likely expense of Massachusetts and Pennsylvania, it was roundly resented in those regions and failed to attract significant funds from exclusivist Boston and Philadelphia sources. Thus, almost by default, the financing of the canal became the first instance in which ordinary citizens and organizations were invited to invest their money in the hope of future profit.

The fact that the state guaranteed every individual investment in the canal project sweetened the lure, and the response was overwhelming. Because New York City was the chief locus of the state's private banking, trading and legal network, most of the financing was conducted from there. Private banks and one-man investment firms were created to broker the canal-funding, and storefront offices were established along Wall Street and its tributary lanes to handle the complex handwritten paperwork connected with it. Soon the district was saturated with a dense mix of private banking offices, money exchanges, canal-business firms, land speculators, commodities brokers, and the like.

Wall Street might have remained just another busy small-city Main Street, had it not been for the immediate success of the Erie Canal and the resultant canal fever it generated in the rest of the country. The Erie recovered its construction costs out of revenues within a few years and began to pay handsome dividends to its investors. Since Wall Street had demonstrated such expertise in canal financing, canal builders from other regions of the country called upon the New York money and brokerage firms to handle their financing.

The success of the Erie also made New York the preeminent commercial city in the nation generally, and more and more foreign investment money gravitated to Wall Street. By 1830, New York's stock exchange, dealing primarily in canal securities but also promoting shares in new industrial companies formed to exploit the transport benefits provided by the Erie, far outstripped the Boston and Philadelphia exchanges in volume of trading and number of companies represented.

First steamboats, then canals—Wall Street had cornered the market on the new transportation financing, and with it the financing of most of its ancillary industries. It was only natural, then, that when the nation turned to railroads in the 1830s, it would look again to Wall Street for their funding, as well as for the financing of much of the new industrial enterprise that would grow out of the railroad boom. Wall Street was still just a street, however. Not until Andrew Jackson put the government out of the banking business in 1832 were the conditions right for the street's transformation into a worldwide symbol of the aggressive new style of American capitalism. As early as 1838 a newspaper in Cincinnati, reporting on the difficulties of the national economy in the wake of the 1837 Panic, headlined its story: "Wall Street Foresees Revival of Confidence Soon." It was the first time the street was referred to not just as a physical place but as a metaphor for the nation's basic economic mechanism.

The 1837 Panic had produced insolvency and disarray in every financial center of the nation, New York included. But New York was the first to bounce back. In 1838 the state legislature passed the pioneering New York Free Banking Act, which removed state-charter restrictions on private banks. By so doing, it enabled dozens of new banks to open immediately, each capitalized by groups of money syndicators with access to British and European investment funds, and encouraged fierce competition among them. Although local depositors were initially hesitant about patronizing the new banks, their doubts were quickly erased by the apparent health of the city's banking system, restored by the influx of fresh foreign capital. By 1840, Wall Street was once again at the forefront of the nation's private financial and investment network. It would be several years before Massachusetts and other states introduced similar banking legislation. By the time they did, New York was far ahead in the refinement and expansion of competitive commercial banking. The New York Free Banking Act not only lured increased foreign capital into Wall Street, it also brought competing foreign commercial and investment banks, led by the experienced London firm of Baring Brothers, from which New York bankers soon learned more sophisticated and daring business methods. Simultaneously, two other forms of private banking and investment were on the rise: savings banks and life insurance.

Although the idea had been around for some time, the first American commercial firm to deal exclusively with life insurance was the Pennsylvania Company for Insurance on Lives and Granting Annuities, founded in Philadelphia in 1812. The high early-mortality rate of the times put the cost of premiums at first out of reach of all but the wealthiest citizens. After the War of 1812, however, several life insurance companies were formed in New York for the express purpose of gathering capital for investment in the Erie Canal. The companies, competing furiously for citizen money, quickly lowered their premium rates in the expectation that they could pay eventual claims out of the profits they earned on the investment of the money they amassed through the premiums. The bargain premiums succeeded beyond expectation in attracting purchases of life and other forms of personal insurance, and the new business proved to be one of the most productive sources of funding for the canal and its associated enterprises.

American savings banks, first started in Boston in 1816 as repositories for the excess funds of the Brahmins, quickly spread to New York, but in a different form. There, one such bank, deciding to compete against the commercial banks, financial syndicates and insurance companies for the public's investment money, introduced the lure of paying interest on deposits. So powerful was the enticement that, by 1819, New York savings banks were able to contribute considerable sums to Wall Street financing ventures.

During the 1820s, life insurance firms and interest-paying savings banks spread throughout the rest of the country, creating further large pools of investable capital, more and more of which gravitated to Wall Street during the first railroad-financing boom of the 1830s. Indeed, it was this concentration of money that enabled New York to weather the Panic of 1837 more easily than other financial centers like Boston and Philadelphia; banks that would otherwise have collapsed because of overextension of credit were able to tap their surplus capital to stave off disaster. When the panic was over, they were able to reorganize quickly under the provisions of the 1838 Free Banking Act, pay off their debts, and reenter the marketplace in time for the even greater railroad boom of the 1840s.

The 1837 crash and the resultant Free Banking Act did bring a marked change in the way Wall Street conducted its business, however. The panic had proved that the commercial banks were not equipped to monopolize the investment-and-financing system, as they had tried to do prior to 1837. As a consequence, the city's private money syndicates, which had theretofore worked solely through the banks, began to form their own separate entities, calling themselves investment houses. These houses were in reality a new kind of private bank—one that dealt not so much in everyday commercial currency as in securities. Modeled on the English merchant banks that had established branches in New York, the new Wall Street firms—usually partnerships of two or three syndicators—began to draw the business of marketing stocks and bonds away from the commercial banks. Thus began a spontaneous division of Wall Street's basic function: the banks specializing in the extension of short-term business credit and acting as vehicles of currency exchange; the investment firms focusing on the arrangement of long-term credit for both existing and new companies through private and public securities issues. As the new system evolved and became more formalized during the 1840s, the investment houses took over the New York stock exchange, until then more of a haphazard, every-man-for-himself, street-corner operation than an organized institutional facility, and began to impose order and system on it. Thereafter, Wall Street, already the dominant symbol of the nation's aggressive new capitalist style, quickly developed into the nation's foremost financial monolith.

Laissez-faire was a term coined in eighteenth-century France to denote the desirability of allowing that nation's capitalist economy to develop without government interference. Andrew Jackson's withdrawal of the American government from the nation's banking system in 1832, and from direct involvement in the improvement of the nation's industrial structure, were together a firm if unconscious imposition of the doctrine of *laissez-faire* on the United States. As we have seen, Jackson's rationale was that anytime the government engaged in commercial business with the private sector, it provided unfair advantage to those who were in a position to get the government's business, which in turn encouraged monopolization and stifled free competition. The competition Jackson unleashed on Wall Street and in the nation's other financial centers in the 1830s was certainly salutary at first. But as time and experience would show, free marketplace competition and the doctrine of *laissez-faire* did not act as a deterrent to monopolism.

The first test of Jackson's divorcement of the federal government from the private economic sector came at the time of the outbreak of the war against Mexico in 1846. The government soon found that without a commercial banking system of its own, it could not finance the war except by going directly to private funding sources. Suddenly the government, through the recently formed Washington firm of Corcoran and Riggs, was doing business—big business—with the private commercial and investment banks of New York, Boston and Philadelphia. Out of the $23 million in emergency federal treasury borrowings authorized by Congress at the end of 1846, almost three fourths came from Wall Street alone. The war cemented Wall Street's reputation as the country's primary financial motherlode and, as well, its preeminent relationship with the nation's capital. Thenceforth, Wall Street and Washington were joined by the glue of common cause.

The federal government had thus found a way to get around Andrew Jackson's proscription against government involvement in the private economic sector. In this case it was not a temporary emergency detour but the opposite—the kind of sophisticated circumvention that would lead to the development of the very trend toward government-abetted monopolization in the private sector that Jackson had feared. Nevertheless it was imperative that Washington cultivate its new relationship with Wall Street. One of the lasting lessons of the Mexican conflict was that the United States could not effectively prosecute a war without the help of the nation's private financial and industrial complex. Had the Jackson administration not cut off federal support of internal improvements fifteen years earlier, such vital components of modern nineteenth-century warfare as transportation, communications and arsenal-building would have been considerably more advanced throughout the country and its western territories in 1846, thus shortening the war and probably ensuring a more favorable conclusion. Thereafter, as noted in the previous chapter, the federal government embarked on a course of intensifying cooperation with the private sector.* The new approach was Jacksonism in a different guise: noninvolvement with private enterprise directly, but concrete support of those aspects of it that promoted the national political and economic interest. Thus the Railroad Land Grant Act of 1848, and the Gadsden Purchase five years later.

The 1850s, then, were a period of roiling revision and consolidation in many different spheres—in population shifts, in social and cultural ideas, in political imperatives, in economic consciousness, in industrial outlook. The decade saw by far the greatest influx of immigrants yet—a few thousand short of 3 million, more than twice that of the decade before and almost a million more than the total immigration of the previous three decades combined. The major eastern cities were well on their way to losing their postcolonial character as they expanded well beyond their original borders to form impersonal residential-industrial gridworks. The newer cities of the Mississippi and Ohio valleys and of the Great Lakes region, founded primarily to attract industry, reflected in their layouts and their drably uniform architecture that purpose and little more.

Inspired by the writings of Ralph Waldo Emerson, the Tran-

*Morse's telegraph had been largely ignored by the American military establishment, whereas early military support of the device might have hastened its deployment. Early railroad development was similarly ignored in the 1840s; the military still viewed large-scale troop movements in terms of horse, caisson and wagon train. As the war drew to a conclusion early in 1848, many in Congress were against ending it without annexing Mexico itself. As it was, the United States, in exchange for Texas, the Southwest Territories and California, was required to pay Mexico close to $20 million in reparations.

scendentalists were complicating the simple precepts of Yankee pragmatism and imposing on the country—or at least on its northern and western regions—new ideas about the connection between work, money, moral conduct and divine purpose. This enlightened consciousness was spilling over into the political arena as well as the economic one, provoking an increasingly fierce schism between North and South over the issue of slavery. At the same time it produced additional sharp revisions in Americans' perceptions of themselves and their roles, individual and collective, in the rapidly changing context of the nation's society.

Further galvanizing the new thinking was the revolution taking place in the country's traditional modes of life. The United States had lost its physical compactness and demographic uniformity. It was spreading out, becoming more diffuse and multiregional, less socially cohesive and interdependent. The ready availability of land was turning the traditional, almost religious, reverence for land into a commercialized, exploitive hunger for it.

Agriculture was still the nation's primary economic enterprise. But as new machines and implements were introduced that made agriculture not only easier but more efficient and productive, their manufacture became as vital as farming itself. And as the railroads spread their tendrils into the most fertile farming regions beyond the Mississippi in order more rapidly to transport ever greater loads of agricultural produce to the commercial markets, the manufacture of railroad equipment became just as vital. As did coal and iron mining and the increasingly complex heavy-metal fabrication that supported the fast-expanding railroad industry. As did, too, the equally complex financial manipulations and machinations of Wall Street, without which the rest could not flourish and without which the rapidly spreading telegraph and newspaper industries would not exist to inform the nation almost immediately of all the changes taking place.

The America of the 1850s might have been described at the time as experiencing a form of "future shock," to use today's phrase. Yet as rapidly as life was changing in some vital aspects, it was changing not at all in others. True, farming had been made easier; more and more citizens were working in mills and factories; city values were replacing rural ones in the shaping of the national character; interdependent commercial pursuits were replacing independent subsistence activity as the primary way of economic life; the corporation was beginning to nudge aside the single proprietorship as the backbone of many regions' economies; interregional communications and transport were radically improving; and, through newspapers and books, the American people were being bombarded with questions about what it all meant and what the future held.

At the same time, however, the quality of life and standard of living of most Americans had advanced only marginally from what it had been at the time of the Revolution. Even in the most settled areas the roads and streets were still crude, the horse still the primary means of personal transportation. Household life was still for the most part cramped and tediously routinized, the increasing availability of expensive gas illumination having been the only significant domestic improvement. Spectator diversion in the form of sports (baseball rules were codified in 1858) and theatrical entertainment were just beginning to appear in the larger cities, but the cities themselves were becoming more crowded, dirty and disease-ridden as people filled them faster than they could expand. Under the pressure of expansion, the cities grew progressively uglier and more regimented, the drab multifamily tenement becoming the residential standard for most. Although several inventors had tinkered with the concept of central heating systems, none had yet perfected the idea.* Coal was gradually replacing wood in the cities as the primary personal heat source, but handling coal was just as cumbersome as handling wood, especially when wrestling it up two or three stories to a tenement flat's stove; and, while somewhat less expensive than firewood, coal was infinitely filthier.

Nor had the recent invention of gravity-fed indoor plumbing, introduced in the late 1830s in a few select big-city hotels, yet reached the populace at large. The common outhouse was still the rule throughout the country—in city and on farm alike—and the portable wood-tub kitchen bath remained the weekly washing ritual, with the same bath water generally used by successive members of the family.

Had indoor plumbing been available, it would no doubt have

*A modest form of central heating existed, however, in the form of the iron stove invented by Benjamin Franklin in the 1740s. The Franklin stove had been a great improvement over the open fireplace; under its principles of convection, one or more rooms could be heated comfortably.

been slow to be accepted, for many Americans were extremely wary of bathing too often. Although it may seem hard to credit today, in the 1840s the belief was prevalent that washing oneself caused a wearing away of the skin, and that too-frequent bathing would eventually destroy one's protective dermal layers and lead to the sudden exposure of one's internal organs.

One of the first Americans to challenge this myth was none other than Martin Van Buren. After a stay at Manhattan's New York Hotel, where he had his first encounter with a private bathroom—toilet and tub—he decided to install such a congenial facility at Lindenwald, his Kinderhook estate home. When the news reached Albany and then New York, it was bannered in the newspapers in the most derisive fashion. And when Van Buren was quoted as saying that thenceforth he intended to bathe every night before retiring, the derisiveness turned to public concern that a former President of the United States was in danger of washing himself to death. Van Buren, then sixty years old, managed to live another twenty years despite his nightly ablutions, thereby contributing to the demise of the superstition. When he passed away in 1862, indoor plumbing was no longer an object of ridicule but an amenity most Americans coveted, even if they could not yet afford to have it.

Such groundless suspicions about bathing were probably due to the fact that despite America's progress in other fields by mid-century, medicine was still mired in myth and mystery. The only major American breakthrough had been in anesthetics, with a Boston dentist, William Morton, having demonstrated the efficacy of ether, first in dental treatment and then in general surgery, in 1846.* By the 1850s, as a result of Morton's discovery, painless surgery had become established as an experimental means of medical treatment. Nevertheless, ailments treatable by surgery remained relatively few, and most surgical procedures were still doomed to failure because of the high rate of infection they produced. Nonsurgical treatment of the myriad other diseases that afflicted the American populace, often en masse, was equally

---

*It has been claimed that a Georgia physician, Dr. Crawford Long, and not Morton, was the first to discover and employ ether as an anesthetic—in 1842. Others give the credit to Charles Jackson, a Boston chemist who introduced Morton to the unconsciousness-inducing effect of ether when inhaled. The fact remains that Morton was the first publicly to demonstrate the use of ether in surgery when, in 1846, he supervised its administration to a surgical patient in Boston from whom a neck tumor was removed.

futile. Although some inroads had been made against smallpox, such epidemic diseases as cholera, yellow fever, tuberculosis, scarlet fever and typhus, as well as the less lethal illnesses of the time, stubbornly resisted all efforts to overcome them.

Although significant advances in medicine did not begin to appear in America until the 1880s, the groundwork for them, as for advances in many other fields at the time, was laid in the 1850s and resulted from that decade's deep changes in American society's perception of itself and its future. One of the most vital changes was in the country's attitude toward science. Earlier in the century, in Britain and Europe, abstract scientific research and experimentation had undergone a massive reinvigoration in reaction to the realization that Isaac Newton's seventeenth-century system did not provide the absolute answer to all of nature's mysteries—electricity, for example. Although Europe's lively scientific spirit had begun to migrate on a small scale to the United States in the 1820s, its integration into American culture was at first resisted by the country's still-powerful religious character. Consequently, it was not until the 1840s, when the nation's narrow but pervasive religious orientation began to loosen its grip on the society, that abstract science began to be taken seriously. And it was not until the 1850s, when the major American colleges—until then primarily religious training schools—began to encourage aggressive scientific research, that organized science began to play a role in the nation's experience.

The event that finally endowed science with a measure of respectability occurred in 1858, when Harvard College established a full-scale chemistry department and scientific research facility at its campus in Cambridge. A controversial move that provoked the wrath of many among the college's overseers, it nevertheless brought an immediate influx of scientific faculty and science-minded students to Harvard and was soon copied by several other influential schools.

Of all the "pure" sciences, chemistry seemed to touch on every aspect of human life, and its understanding was essential to the development of the nascent biosciences upon which medicine depended for its progress.* Also, chemistry was the central compo-

---

*The initial sudden interest in abstract science in America derived from the realization that although the United States was catching up with Europe technologically, Europe was still far ahead in scientific endeavors, and particularly in medical research.

nent of most of the technological ideas that were being consolidated and integrated into the American industrial process during the 1850s. Innovation and progress in industry, it was seen, depended as much on broadening the nation's knowledge of chemistry and its adjunct sciences as it did on manpower and mechanical invention. The expansion of agricultural productivity through mechanical farm implements, for instance, was one thing; its further expansion through the use of fertilizers was another. The use of fertilizers would stimulate the need for more and better agricultural machinery. This in turn would increase the need for more and better fertilizers, which in turn would call for more machinery, and so on.

American industry, including Wall Street, began to recognize the vital link between industrial progress and scientific learning— a concept the British had pioneered as early as two centuries before, and the concept that had produced the original Industrial Revolution. This recognition represented the final stage in America's 1850s' process of revision and consolidation, and it brought the country finally to the threshold of its own massive industrial and technological revolution.

CHAPTER 11

CROSSING THE THRESHOLD

Although the 1850s were a time in which the United States paused to revise, consolidate and integrate old and new ideas among science, economics, politics, technology and social thought, the decade nevertheless produced a number of important additions to the nation's still-spare industrial skeleton. Steam-engine and metallurgical expertise grew more sophisticated during the period, not only improving the capacity of river and railroad transport through the construction of larger and more powerful boats and locomotives, but spreading the application of steam power to the factory industries as well. The rapid substitution of steam for waterpower in textile manufacture promoted the building of much larger factories, with corresponding increases in work force, output and markets, domestic and foreign. And when steam proved successful in textile manufacture, it quickly began to be applied to other forms of mechanized manufacture, further diversifying the American factory system and expanding the principle of mass, and massive, production within the country's economy. Based on the developments in American steam technology in the 1850s, mass steam-powered manufacture would become the standard a generation later, marking the start of the country's "smokestack age."

Moreover, the advances in steam technology freed mass manufacture from its previous geographical constrictions. No longer did the sites of factories need to be limited to the banks of the Northeast's fast-flowing streams and waterfalls. So long as there were railroad tracks or navigable waterways nearby to provide access for raw materials and for the fuel that generated the steam power, factories could be built anywhere in the country. Given this new freedom, they were. What had been mere midwestern and southern frontier villages prior to the 1850s sprouted, seemingly overnight, into important industrial cities afterward, while in the East what had been separate major manufacturing cities began to merge into huge, economically complex industrial regions. Illustrative of the change was Minneapolis. In 1850 a remote Mississippi River outpost in the Minnesota Territory, by 1858 it was a fast-growing metropolis built around lumbering and, increasingly, an intensive commercial steam-powered flour-milling industry. The transformation of Minneapolis symbolized the new trend in industry which the refinement of steam factory power encouraged—the shifting of specific manufacturing operations as close as possible to their basic raw-material sources, thus reducing one of the major costs of production. It was Minneapolis's proximity to the vast fertile wheatlands of the Upper Plains that so quickly turned it into the center of the mechanized flour industry.

The advances in steam power could not have been made, however, without correlative advances in the various technologies upon which steam depended: coal and iron mining, metallurgy and metal fabrication, machinery design and manufacture, and the network's underlying transport system. Most of the advances evolved through the gradual refinement of existing engineering know-how. But one was an almost totally new discovery, and it would not only soon become the single most important catalyst of advancement in every other industrial enterprise of the period, it would also open American industry to countless new manufacturing possibilities. The discovery was the process by which steel, until then a high-cost, low-yield material, could be mass-produced economically.

The principal cause of the great increase in foreign immigration into the United States during the 1840s and 1850s was a further succession of potato famines in Ireland, the potato having been the staple—practically the sole—foodstuff of the Irish. Irish immigration had started as a trickle in colonial times. Increasing slightly during the post-Revolution years, it became a modestly steady flow after the War of 1812, when canal-building required large contingents of cheap, unskilled labor. But beginning in the

1830s it turned into a virtual floodtide, with Irish comprising 44 percent of the total number of immigrants during that decade and 49 percent during the 1840s. The sudden concentration of impoverished Roman Catholics in what had been largely a homogeneous Protestant society provoked a wholesale oppression of the Irish that was second in scale and intensity only to the treatment of the blacks in America. In many respects the Irish were the country's new Negroes, excluded from all but the most menial, ill-paying work and ruthlessly ghettoized into its most squalid urban slums. There was one Irishman, however, perhaps because of his singular Gaelic stubbornness and luck, who managed to escape much of the oppression imposed on the "Irish race" in the United States of the 1840s. His name was William Kelly.

Kelly, born of immigrant parents near Pittsburgh, was apprenticed to a local iron forge in his youth. After a few years there, during which he learned all aspects of iron manufacture, he moved to the Louisville, Kentucky, area and started his own small kettle-making business. In 1848, working alone one day at his shop's forge, Kelly tried to hasten the cooling of a bucketful of molten iron by pumping his bellows at it. Suddenly he felt dizzy and nauseated, and barely made it to the outside door of the shop before he passed out. When he regained consciousness a while later, he returned to his forge, profoundly puzzled and wondering if he had had a heart stoppage.

A few days later Kelly once again picked up his bellows and trained it on a bucket of molten iron fresh from his furnace. Once more he passed out. But this time, after drifting back to consciousness, he made the empirical connection. Although his knowledge of chemistry was scant, he had learned a little about carbon monoxide gas at the forge where he had worked in Pennsylvania and about how it rendered people unconscious—even killed them—before they knew what was happening. He concluded that by blowing air through the molten metal in his bucket, he had inadvertently produced an invisible carbon monoxide gas that had filled his shop.

When Kelly consulted a local doctor, he learned more about the chemical process of carbon monoxide—specifically, that the gas was produced when burning carbon fumes combined with the oxygen in air. With that information lodged in his mind, he began to reflect on what had occurred. He knew that to transform a piece of iron into steel required the reduction of the iron's carbon content, a slow, tedious process of heating and separating that used up huge amounts of iron to yield minuscule amounts of steel. Had he stumbled upon something? Did the process of blowing air into his molten iron, by producing carbon monoxide, mean that the carbon in the iron was being burned away and thus reduced?

Kelly determined to find out. He set up a venting system in his shop, then built a crude mechanical bellows that he could operate for an extended period of time by remote pedal power. He directed a steady stream of forced air into another bucket of molten iron for about half an hour, employing several assistants to relieve him periodically at the bellows and using his free time to ensure that the hot fumes and gases rising from the bucket were ventilating fully through his jerry-built chimney. When the molten mass cooled and hardened, it was more like hard steel than soft iron. Kelly had discovered the rudimentary technique of converting iron into steel on a bulk basis.

His announcement of the process was at first met with disbelief by others in the American iron industry, earning him the sobriquet "Crazy Kelly." Undiscouraged, Kelly spent the next three years perfecting his process, building a large "conversion" furnace in 1851 and applying for a patent the same year. Unfortunately for him, but partly due to his own reticence and his Irish background, he would not receive lasting public credit for the process. While Kelly awaited action on his patent, an English ironmaster, Henry Bessemer, discovered the same conversion principle at a forge in Britain. Whether Bessemer's separate but later discovery was aided by intelligence from America was never determined, but he received the first American patent on his conversion process in 1856. Thereafter, because so much big-industry investment money came from England, most American bankers, anxious to cultivate British money sources, promoted the importation of the Bessemer process and ignored Kelly's method, although the two were virtually the same. As a consequence, Bessemer became celebrated as the sole inventor of the process that made possible the mass manufacture of steel, while Kelly's name faded into obscurity.*

*It has been claimed that when certain Wall Street financiers learned of Kelly's process in about 1850, they declined to market it—as the American iron manufacturers who heard about it declined to test it—because Kelly was Irish. However, go the claims, the bankers ensured that the details of the process were conveyed to the British iron industry, at which time they were copied and possibly improved upon by Henry Bessemer, a more sophisticated metallurgist than Kelly. Nevertheless, after Kelly learned that Bessemer had been issued the first American patent, he protested. Eventually the issue was resolved in his favor and he was credited by the Patent Office as the true inventor.

Notwithstanding the historical injustice, the Kelly-Bessemer process, once it began to be widely adopted in the mid-1860s, quickly changed the pace of American industrial development. Before the advent of steel, the United States had continued to lag well behind England and many parts of Europe in the breadth of its industrial and technological sophistication—this despite its landmark mechanical and electrical inventions of the previous fifty years. But with the arrival of steel, the gap would rapidly begin to close. With its unprecedentedly vast untapped stores of the specific natural resources required to make steel in quantity—coal, iron ore and limestone—the United States was poised in the 1860s to leap ahead of all its European cousins in industrial and technological achievement.

Contributing to that status were advancement and improvements in many other fields during the 1850s. The beginnings of a national system of compulsory, free education for children had been established. The electric-arc commutator, invented in 1839 by the American Thomas Davenport, was in the process of being perfected and was being applied to experiments intended to develop the first electric motor powerful enough to drive machinery. Factory-machine manufacture itself was growing more precise and consistent as uniform, detailed engineering and design standards began to replace the trial-and-error method of machine making. The craft of mass-producing precision tools and small machine parts with finer tolerances out of iron instead of wood had been achieved on a widescale basis after J. R. Brown of Rhode Island began manufacturing the vernier caliper in 1851, making possible measurements in thousandths of an inch. McCormick's harvester was joined by a mechanical thresher that separated wheat from chaff in the field, thereby further increasing the productivity of the commercial farm, and agricultural engineers were already contemplating ways to reduce the size of the steam engine and apply its power to farm machines in place of the horse. Elisha Otis in Vermont had invented the first practical elevator, fostering another revolution in personal transportation and preordaining an equivalent revolution in building construction. At the same time, architecture began to be practiced on a wider and more formal scale in response to the expansion of the nation's cities. Where before only public buildings and the mansions of the rich were carefully predesigned, now many other types of structures were submitted to the architectural pen, and organized city planning began to develop under municipal governments.

Although Ralph Waldo Emerson had complained in the 1840s about the lack of a vital cultural consciousness in the United States, the fine arts—painting and architectural design—were singular exceptions to his indictment. Each of these related fields had a long and active tradition in America that reached back to the early 1700s. By Emerson's time, each had produced numerous accomplished practitioners, although much of their work was strongly influenced by—even blatantly derivative of—Europe. The exceptional early American appreciation for visual and pictorial art is interesting to reflect upon in view of the high priority given to the visual and pictorial arts and crafts today. It is interesting also that three of the country's most important early inventors—Robert Fulton, Samuel Morse and Peter Cooper—all began their careers as artists. This suggests a powerful correlation between artistic imagination and mechanical ingenuity, the linkage residing in the gift of technical drawing or design. Each conceived complex new mechanisms and then translated his ideas into reality, principally through his powers of design. Morse, probably the most accomplished artist of the three, was especially committed to design. He founded the National Academy of Design in New York in 1826, primarily to further education in the fine arts. However, as he became more deeply involved in mechanical pursuits in the late 1830s, he moved the academy at least partially into the technological arena, encouraging the cross-fertilization of ideas between art and industrial endeavor. It would not be an exaggeration to suggest that the explosion of invention and industrial progress in America after Morse owed much to the design concepts he fostered, for accuracy and detail of design were ultimately at the heart of the country's astounding industrial and technological achievements.

As primitive as the country in many respects remained, material progress, or the seeds of it, were found everywhere in the America of the 1850s. Although oil had been seeping out of the ground in certain areas of western Pennsylvania for as long as anyone could remember, it had been ignored except as a kind of medicinal remedy until a chemist discovered its flammable properties in 1851. Almost at the same time, another chemist devised a method of treating the soft bituminous coal with which Pennsylvania, Ohio, West Virginia and Kentucky were abundantly endowed so as to convert it into high-carbon, anthracitelike "coke"—much the preferred fuel for efficient iron manufacture and, as it would turn out, absolutely necessary for steelmaking. Self-propelled steam-powered carriages were being contemplated as a replacement for the horse and buggy, the team-drawn urban omnibus and the stagecoach, and a few visionaries were already thinking of the possibility of an internal combustion engine to be fueled by the coal gas that had been introduced a few years before for street lighting purposes. The streets of the major cities of the East began to be paved with cobblestone and brick, although the development of underground sewers and other improvements in municipal sanitation were still in the future.

In 1856, Gail Borden developed a process of condensing and preserving milk that, along with the development of meat processing in Cincinnati, gave birth to the modern retail food-supply industry. Until the 1850s food was either homegrown or, in the case of cities, acquired through a system of central retail markets supplied by nearby farmers. Thereafter, thanks to American improvements in food processing, preservation and packaging (the vacuum-sealed jar), and to the rapidly expanding transportation network, specialization and diversification in food provision began. The same kind of diversification soon spread to other forms of goods, and the specialty store—foods, dry goods, hardware, and so on—began to replace the huge central market as the main vehicle of local commerce in personal staples.

Yet throughout the 1850s, even while American society was extending one foot into the brighter future promised by improved technologies, its other foot remained stubbornly mired in a darker legacy of the past. That legacy was slavery. For all practical purposes, slavery had been legislated out of existence in the northern states. In the South, however, it had become, if anything, more tightly woven into the fabric of the social, political and economic order. The federal government had waffled over the issue for decades. But by the 1850s, rising antislavery sentiment in the increasingly industrialized North began to exert powerful pressures on Washington. The eventual result was the Civil War.

Given the numerous strategic and material disparities between the two sides, it is surprising that the war lasted as long as it did—four years. The population of the North was more than three times that of the South. The North had the advantage of a richly mixed economy and a powerful resource base: an advanced, widely spread industrial complex; a prosperous, diverse agriculture; a strong financial network. It also possessed a well-developed railroad grid, stretching from the Northeast to the Mississippi Valley; a complementary system of river and canal transport; a large, experienced merchant marine and dozens of ports to expedite the importation of war materials; and a sizable navy to blockade the few ports of the South.

Indeed, the Confederacy had no advantage whatever unless one counted its fanatical dedication to the continuation of slavery. With an economy based almost exclusively on agriculture, it possessed little in the way of machine industry and suffered from a lack of advanced technological skills and equipment. Although it had abundant vital natural resources—iron, coal, and the like—it was largely without knowledge of how to extract and exploit them. Its railroad system was vastly inferior to that of the North in complexity and reach. It had no navy to speak of, and its financial resources, based largely on cotton, were slender.

In retrospect, the long, brutal conflict was not just a civil war; it was America's second social revolution. The fact that the war brought about the political and military end of slavery was only a minor aspect of its revolutionary character. Its more far-reaching significance lay in the impact it had on the entire American system. Before the war, despite the gradual rise of industrial enterprise and the increasing ferment of social and economic ideas, the country had remained primarily agricultural in its economic base, still widely agrarian in its outlook. Had there been no Civil War, the likelihood is that American industrial and technological progress would have advanced at the same leisurely pace it had set during the previous half-century.

What the war did was to prove the intrinsic value of the idea of the machine in America and spread its use, or the desirability of its use, into every corner of domestic life. But it was not just the idea of the machine the war validated; it was everything connected with it—from the minds that conceived and designed it, to the raw materials that formed it, to the labor that made and operated it, to the money that financed it, to the organizations that used it. The machine possessed its own underlying mechanism, a dynamic interlocking web of human endeavor without which it could not exist. And as American society began wholeheartedly to embrace the concept of the machine, it began also to see in it a metaphor for itself.

It was in the context of this figurative social awakening that the actual "machining of America" began in the late 1860s. The Civil War had put steadily increasing pressure on the still-modest industrial base of the North to produce the goods and materials needed to prosecute the war. The huge sums of money obtained and made available by the government enabled industry to respond to the challenge. As a result, the war inspired a second industrial revolution in America which, combined with the concurrent financial revolution, clearly charted the country's postwar social future. Industrialism—massive, widespread industrialism—was finally perceived in Washington, on Wall Street and throughout the land to be the key to the nation's destiny, its *raison d'être*. Industrial and technological progress up to then had been steady but gradual. The sudden expansion and diversification of industry during the war demonstrated what could be done when men of politics, men of money and men of mechanical ingenuity and manufacturing prowess meshed their efforts and aspirations. Visionaries began to talk about a future of unparalleled, barely imaginable comfort and convenience; some even predicted such bizarre notions as mass air transport, television, and trips to the moon. "Progress" became the national motto, and the country for the first time consciously committed itself to speeding it up.*

But how? Here again the Civil War provided the answer. In 1865, Edwin M. Stanton, the Secretary of War, wrote to a friend in Congress: "The exigencies of the war just concluded have created a new order of things from which there can be no wise retreat." Stanton's observation was made in the context of the immediate postwar debate over the government's future role in the

---

*The idea that progress could be accelerated by a mass commitment to intensified industrial and technological endeavor would turn out to be true. An American falling into a forty-year Rip Van Winkle sleep in 1820 would have awakened in 1860 to find little to astonish him in the changes that had taken place. But an American falling asleep in 1860 and waking in 1900 would find his senses overwhelmed by the changes. The first slumberer would have been surprised by the telegraph and probably by the railroads, but everything else about the environment would have been more or less as he had known it. The second would be confronted by countless changes in the landscape: electric lighting and power, enormously expanded cities beginning to sprout skyscrapers, electric streetcars, the first automobiles, the telephone, central heating, and so on.

shaping of America. Many politicians and newspapers were calling for a "retreat" of the federal government to its prewar status—in theory, at least—of dealing only with the nation's political and constitutional concerns. Stanton sided with those who saw in the lessons of the Civil War the value of government's coalition with the private sector in large-scale economic and industrial pursuits.

Stanton was in a good position to judge. A noted peacetime business and patent lawyer, in his role as War Secretary he had organized and masterminded much of the government's enlistment of northern private industry and finance in the war effort. He, better than most, could appreciate the salutary effects of the coalition—the "new order of things"—on both government and the private sector. Stanton had been appointed Secretary of War in January 1862 to replace Simon Cameron, who had been forced to resign because of his wasteful incompetence in organizing private industry in the early stages of the war. On entering office, Stanton took his lead from Gideon Welles, the Secretary of the Navy, who had already awarded large sums of government money to the private shipbuilding industry to create a modern war fleet. At the start of the war the American Navy was small and antiquated, made up mostly of wooden sailing vessels left over from the War of 1812. Welles's aggressive encouragement of the Union's shipbuilders quickly resulted in the *Monitor*, the world's first steam-powered, propeller-driven, iron warship, a vessel that revolutionized naval warfare.* In addition, Welles promoted the development by private industry of such other naval innovations as torpedoes, submarines and more powerful cannon.

Because the Civil War was much more of a land than a sea war, Stanton's challenge throughout the world was infinitely greater: to organize, train, arm, equip, feed, clothe, doctor, transport and otherwise sustain an army of more than 2 million troops and support personnel over a period of four years. Compounding his problem was the fact that vital imports of military matériel had been almost completely cut off because of the neutrality policies of Britain and the European industrial countries; and that the North's industrial base, although it had expanded and matured considerably since the Mexican War, was still modest in size, ca-

---

*Not just because of its iron structure, but because it featured the first revolving gun turret.

pacity and variety compared to those of England and the Continent.

But Stanton had increasingly vast sums of money at his disposal, most of it raised by eastern financiers. Because of that, during the war the North's industrial and technological capacity and diversity grew at a rate unprecedented in any nation. What's more, in the process of its growth and under the wartime discipline of the government, the American industrial complex acquired what it had theretofore lacked: a cohesive system of organization and management. If by the end of the war the United States hadn't yet surpassed England in its industrial breadth, productivity and technological sophistication, it was certainly on the brink of doing so. Edwin Stanton alluded to this in another letter he wrote after the war:

> The most expeditious path to the progress for which all yearn has already been charted by our experience of the war. [The path] is in that willing cooperation between government and industry which served us so well therein. All we must needs do now is to broaden and smooth it. The tools of its broadening will be the minds of our inventors. The material by which it is smoothed will be the skills of our administrators. . . . By such means will we rise to the industrial pinnacle of the world.

And in yet another letter to another congressman, he wrote:

> The recent hostilities have many lessons to offer to the nation's sober contemplation. Among them I count as foremost this: that its public political interests are identical with its private economical [sic] dealings. Let Providence deem that henceforth the government shall go forth with industry arm in arm, for if we are to suppose ourselves a nation blessed and guided by Providence, so must it be.

CHAPTER 12

SURVIVAL OF THE FITTEST

Stanton's and others' vision of government, finance and industry working in conscious and carefully orchestrated unison to expedite the march of material progress—a vision that in itself called forth an image of a giant abstract machine—was not original to America. It had already become the foundation of progress in England and the countries of northern Europe—most recently in Germany, which had set out to rival England as the world's foremost industrial and scientific Goliath. The reason the vision worked so much more effectively in America than in Europe, once it was put into practice, was due simply to the size and social nature of the United States. The small and often bickering imperial nations of northern Europe had grown excessively crowded. At the same time, they had depleted many of their indigenous natural resources in their early rush to industrialism. As a consequence, during the mid-nineteenth century they were forced to roam farther afield in search of the basic raw materials needed to keep their industries thriving. This led to an intensive upsurge in colonialism among Europe's industrialized countries, and a correspondingly bitter competition between them as they vied for control over various undeveloped but resource-rich regions of the world.

Along with the industrial and colonial conflict came increasing intellectual and social discontent in Europe. In America, higher education was just beginning to shed its restrictive religiosity. European education, on the other hand, had long been emancipated from religion. While America was still struggling over the liberating social ideas advanced by such native thinkers as Emerson, Europe had become thoroughly imbued with the spirit of scientific inquiry and its social relevance. While America was still arguing over the morality of slave labor, Europe was already embroiled in a dispute over the morality of labor in general. The Germans Karl Marx and Friedrich Engels had published their *Communist Manifesto* in 1848, the same year the English philosopher John Stuart Mill had completed his *Principles of Political Economy;* both of them, in their different ways, attacked the established capitalism of Europe. While the United States was just tentatively embarking on a coalition of government and business, the European countries had already become weighed down by the addition of a third, antagonistic element of the capitalist equation: organized labor.

Working in America's favor, then, were its size and its relative industrial and political innocence. Despite its own internecine conflicts at mid-century, the United States had no need to engage in distant colonial adventurism, since it possessed an abundance of undeveloped land and resources of its own.* And despite its growing pre-Civil War industrialism it had had little significant exposure to labor unrest. In the first place, many among the low-skilled working classes in America were recent emigrés from job-scarce Europe and were happy to find any kind of work at all, no matter how much the work exposed them to exploitation; furthermore, the sharp rise in industrial employment occasioned by the Civil War compounded labor's contentment with its status. In the second place, American society, if only in a residual way, still equated work with religious virtue, and this effectively militated against the immediate introduction of the kind of insurrectionary labor reformism that was bedeviling industrial Europe in the 1860s.

Finally, there was the nature of the American social compact. Following the Revolution, the country had set out to organize itself in a mold markedly different from that of England and the Continental industrial nations, with their small, aristocratic ruling classes and huge, tightly circumscribed labor masses. And following the War of 1812, as the United States began to develop a modest industrial base of its own, although it copied many of Eu-

---

*In 1853 an American fleet headed by Matthew C. Perry had arrived in remote, under-developed Japan—not to colonize it but to establish diplomatic and trade relations. Had the Japanese rejected the American overtures, the story might have been different, for Perry had orders to impose American will on Japan, by arms if necessary.

rope's techniques and methods, it again eschewed to a large extent the rigid, institutionalized class systems of Europe.

As a consequence, the popular perception of America as a land of personal opportunity based on work was more than just an empty slogan. For many among the white Christian majority it turned out to be a happy and remunerative reality. As thousands of individuals each year became better off than their immediate forebears had been, the idea of work in America took on a special mystique. In Europe, rather than an opportunity, work was a kind of life sentence that further embedded a man and his family in the bleak social stratum of his preordained class. In America, on the other hand, work was the primary means by which ordinary men could free themselves of their lower-class shackles and move up and outward into other classes. In Europe, work was a vehicle of enslavement; in America, to a certain extent, a vehicle of liberation. Even if one was forced to start at the bottom of the work ladder in America, one was not doomed by social custom and cultural imperative to remain there, so long as one had the proper social and cultural qualifications. In Europe, with infrequent exception, the opposite was the case.

In the America of the 1860s, then, work—even the most menial work—was still being glorified, while in Europe it was under increasingly hostile attack. Whereas in Europe capitalism had begun to stagnate and grow synonymous with evil and social oppression, in America it was forming its own more democratic identity and gaining its own progressive vitality. At the very time the labor-inspired civil wars and revolutions of mid-nineteenth century Europe were spelling the end of capitalism in its original, semifeudalistic form, the Civil War in America was in the process of launching a more democratic and pluralistic capitalism. Since capitalism had been conceived and refined by a feudal, aristocratic civilization, however, it remained to be seen whether it could survive its merger with the advanced American principles of political democracy, and whether the framework of American political democracy, as charted in the Declaration of Independence, in the Constitution and in the Bill of Rights, could survive the application of the new capitalism.

The beginning stages of the merger were auspicious—again thanks to the Civil War. The boom in manufacturing began, naturally, with weapons, then spilled over to less directly war-related industries. Throughout the four-year war a host of new systems, innovations, products and inventions emerged, all slanted toward the war effort. Because of the new weaponry that was developed—the ironclad, the submarine, sea and land mines, the breech-loading rifle, the Gatling gun (forerunner of the machine gun), the swivel cannon, the mortar—the Civil War was the first large-scale "modern" war in history. It was not just the radically new weapons that gave war production its distinctly modern cast, however; it was also the new systems of manufacturing that were developed in response to the need for greater productivity. If there had been any public doubt about the virtues of mass production before the war,* they were for the most part dispelled by the experience of the war as a steadily wider variety of domestically mass-produced goods became increasingly plentiful.

The American weapons revolution had started modestly twenty-five years before the war, in 1835, when Samuel Colt, a Connecticut inventor caught up in the country's fascination with things mechanical, had devised the fast-fire revolver. Colt's gun— a single-barrel revolver that could fire several bullets in succession before requiring reloading—was a vast improvement over the conventional single-bullet, muzzle-loaded pistol. As a result it was one of the few among America's early inventions that, instead of being greeted with skepticism, found itself almost instantaneously in demand.† In 1836, Colt established a factory in New Jersey, modeled on the Whitney system of interchangeable parts which he improved, to mass-produce his new revolver. Later, in 1854, gunsmiths Horace Smith and Daniel Wesson went into competition with Colt by devising a shorter-barreled revolver of their own. The revolver, then, was in plentiful supply at the start of the Civil War.

But short-range handguns had little utility in land warfare, which was conducted largely by medium-distance infantry fusillade and longer-distance artillery barrage. Although the new revolver might have been useful in the cavalry charges of traditional combat, such close-order tactics were quickly done away with during the initial battles of the Civil War. A company of

*There *were* doubts. Most were voiced by handcrafts representatives and preacher-editorialists who saw mass production as a grave threat to the country's spirit of individualism and personal liberty.

†In pre-Civil War America, the common handgun was the one mechanical device few citizens were without, particularly in the country's rural and frontier regions.

charging cavalry was no match for a battalion of enemy infantry laying down a carefully timed and coordinated field of long-range rifle fire from fixed positions. The only trouble was that at the start of the war there was no rifle equivalent of the fast-fire repeating pistol. Several gunsmiths had developed such weapons in the 1850s, but they were undependable and had been rejected by the armies of both sides on the grounds that they were ammunition wasters.

The standard infantry weapon at the start of the war was the rifle equivalent of the old-fashioned pistol—the slow, muzzle-loading, powder-and-ball American-made Springfield or British-made Enfield rifled-barrel musket. At best, although accurate in the hands of an efficient infantryman, it was capable of only three shots a minute. The successes of the outmanned Confederate forces in the early battles of the war evidenced Southern superiority in the use of these weapons, and it was not long before Lincoln and Secretary of War Stanton recognized that if the Union was to prevail, newer and better field weapons would have to be supplied to its troops. Stanton, overriding Union commanders' fears about ammunition wastage, implored several arms manufacturers to come up with more advanced infantry and artillery weapons. The result was, first, a breech-loaded, single-cartridge rifle that did away with the musket and was capable of up to fifteen shots a minute; then, an automatic carbine that fired seven shots in succession from a spring-loaded cartridge clip; and finally, the Gatling gun, a revolverlike multibarreled rifle that fired upward of 250 rounds in rapid succession.

Due to manufacturing irregularities, each of these weapons performed poorly when first introduced—they *were* ammunition wasters. But once they were refined and improved, they contributed significantly to turning the tide of the war in the North's favor. Most of the improvements in the weapons themselves came about as a result of improvements in their manufacture, particularly in the fine machining of their key parts. As Stanton later said in yet another letter to a congressional official in 1866: "If the war . . . had no other virtue, at the very least it had that of advancing greatly the exacting knowledge and skill of our manufacturing men." In the last year of the war there were thirty-eight factories in the North turning out thousands of rifles and carbines a day. Southern industry, such as it was, had tried to copy the new

Union weapons from models captured by Confederate forces. But at its peak it was able to produce only fifty a day.

As quickly as war manufacture expanded, innovated and diversified, so too did the tangential industries. Scores of new factories were built in New England and the central states and then filled with improved sewing machines to produce uniforms and other military garb. Based on the sewing machine, a novel boot-stitching machine was developed by Lyman Blake and Gordon McKay, and factories were rapidly erected in Massachusetts and elsewhere to mass-produce boots for the Union Army. Peter Durand's 1818 invention of the cheap metal can as a food container and preserver had been perfected, and large food-processing and packing factories were established in and about Chicago to provide canned field rations to the fighting forces. The war-accelerated expansion of the North's railroad and telegraph systems brought about an explosion of sub-industries in these fields, too, along with a corresponding expansion in coal mining and, with the introduction of the Kelly and Bessemer processes, in iron mining, ore transport and steelmaking. Agriculture also became more organized and industrialized as the war, and the 1862 Homestead Act, brought increasing numbers of farmers to the prairie states.

The emerging new industrial order had three principal features. The first was specialization. Whereas before the war a product and all its parts were generally manufactured in a single factory, now—because products were growing more complex and varied—it was *assembled* in a single plant after many of its vital parts were fabricated in other factories. Specialization brought with it the need for a much greater variety of machinery, as well as a much larger corps of trained and educated labor to design, build, service and operate it. This in turn encouraged many existing colleges to expand their scientific curricula. And it inspired the founding of several new private colleges devoted exclusively to scientific and technical studies, Massachusetts Institute of Technology among them, along with a host of government-subsidized free public vocational colleges.*

The second feature was location. The wartime demand for a widening variety of products required a faster and more efficient bringing together of the diverse elements of a particular product's

---

*By a corollary measure to the 1862 Homestead Act, the government granted 30,000 acres of federal land to each northern state for the establishment of public colleges specializing in agricultural and mechanical training.

manufacturing and distribution processes. The new mass-production manufacture of shoes was centered in New England, for instance, because it was closely akin in method to textile manufacture and the region already had a pool of machine-experienced labor. In addition, the New England shoe-manufacturing centers were near large tracts of forest that provided the free bark needed for tanning shoe leather. Similarly, as eastern deposits of iron ore and coal were depleted and more abundant deposits were discovered in the West, the iron-and-steel industry gravitated farther westward, from New York, New Jersey and Pennsylvania to Ohio, Indiana and Illinois. The meat-packing and agricultural machinery industries settled in and around Chicago and St. Louis for the same reasons—to be as close as possible to both their raw materials and their principal markets. As the Civil War progressed, the Northeast quickly lost its monopoly on machine industry. The factory system was on its way to becoming a nationwide phenomenon, spreading out with the expansion of the railroad system and stimulating even further railroad expansion as it went.

The 1850s construction of the Sault Sainte Marie Canal between Lake Superior and Lake Huron assisted as much as the railroads in turning the region encircling the Great Lakes into an industrial nation-within-a-nation during the Civil War. Conceived and engineered by a young entrepreneur from Vermont named Charles Harvey, the canal, which bypassed the nonnavigable rapids connecting the two lakes, opened up the vast, recently discovered iron and copper deposits of Minnesota to industrial exploitation. And along with the Canadian-built Welland Canal, which linked Lakes Erie and Ontario around Niagara Falls, the "Soo," as it came to be called, gave the entire Great Lakes region a direct water link to the rest of the world. No longer did a McCormick harvesting machine sold for export to England or France have to be shipped overland from Chicago to an eastern port and thence transshipped to its foreign destination. Now it could sail direct from Chicago.

The third feature of the emerging industrial order grew naturally out of the first two. It was, in a word, organization. As we have noted, until the 1830s the American commercial and industrial complex had evolved in a relatively haphazard and spontaneous fashion. Most businesses were managed on a spontaneous day-to-day entrepreneurial basis by whoever had founded or owned them. In the late 1830s the banks, the railroads and the textile industry began to impose an awareness of the importance of deliberate organization, planning and management on the country's commercial community—organization in the sense of securing hard-and-fast written contracts, of setting up reliable and smoothly functioning distribution networks, of cost estimating, of training workers, of acquiring raw materials, and so on. By the start of the Civil War, industrial management and administration were moderately well advanced, but still behind England. Although each American industry had developed its own special and unique administrative techniques, what was still lacking was the organization of those techniques into an overall matrix of management principles and practices that could be applied more or less uniformly across the widening spectrum of industry.

The war, along with the specialization and regional diversification of industry that it sparked, quickly changed that. The war turned the federal government into American industry's largest consumer. Most of the consumption came through the War and Navy departments. The first year of the war had been marked by excessive waste and corruption in dealings between the War Department and industry—vital products ordered and prepaid by the government were hastily manufactured and delivered in defective condition, or were not delivered at all. As frequently as the cause was venality and corrupt profiteering on the part of many of the country's industrialists, it was just as often simple mismanagement and administrative incompetence. For instance, an 1861 War Department order for ten thousand army uniforms from a company in Massachusetts, to be delivered to Washington two months later, resulted in the delivery of three thousand uniforms with seams that would unravel on their first contact with water. When called to account, the owner of the company excused his poor performance on the grounds that he had been supplied with defective thread; that too many of his factory's sewing machines had broken down and, because his mechanic had been drafted, he could not get them repaired; and that an influenza epidemic among his labor force had required him to close his factory for almost a month.

This was just one of many instances of War Department wastefulness cited by a congressional committee convened in 1861 to force the ouster of the Lincoln administration's first Secretary of War, Simon Cameron. When Edwin Stanton was nominated to replace Cameron, he assured his confirmation by publicly condemning the mismanagement of many of the nation's industrial companies, and by promising not to grant further War Department contracts to any company managerially incapable of performing such contracts in full. Upon his confirmation, Stanton established stringent new standards for the awarding of government contracts, among which were a rigorous review of the past performance of every company that bid for a contract, and compulsory on-site government inspections of companies' management and production procedures while they were manufacturing government-ordered products. At the same time he reorganized the War Department itself, bringing in top private-sector business managers to apply tight standards and controls over all its functions.

The War Department had its own learning to do. Never before had it had to contend with war on such a scale as the Civil War's. Problems of acquisition, supply, distribution, transport, chains of command and the coordination of all these elements were monumental and manifold. Throughout the war, Stanton and his subordinates were forced to create wholly new principles and practices of effective military management. Some were borrowed from private industry and adapted to the military situation, but most were of their own invention. As the war progressed and increasingly complex big-money manufacturing contracts were put out for bid, industry began to innovate on and improve its own management methods, often seeking and receiving guidance from the War Department, sometimes feeding back effective ideas of its own. The process of cross-fertilization reached its peak in the final year of the war and was a central component of Stanton's postwar vision of government and industry going forward "arm in arm" in the pursuit of their common interest, material progress.

By war's end, then, American industry and commerce had become at once vastly more diversified and more specialized. Equally important, with the help of the government, it had formulated uniform principles of organization, administration and management in order to function more efficiently, productively and profitably.

Also, during the war the evolutionary science theories of the English biologist Charles Darwin had captured the attention of America's intelligentsia, as had the early writings of the contemporary political-economic philosopher Herbert Spencer. In the late 1850s, Darwin had propounded a revolutionary view of life based on biological evolution and on the concepts of competition among species, "natural selection" and "the survival of the fittest." Spencer had transposed Darwin's ideas to the political and economic realm, likening the evolution of human institutions to similar "natural" factors and emphasizing the positive role free, individual competition had played in the evolutionary growth of capitalism and industrialism. Spencer's writings were in part critiques of the British and European capitalist systems, which tended to stifle free competition among all the economic classes of each country in favor of fostering the prosperity of their upper classes and aristocracy. He predicted the stagnation and eventual downfall of British capitalism in particular unless it began to encourage and stimulate democratic competition among all classes in the society.

American society was not yet ready to accept Darwin's radical, antibiblical theories about the natural evolution of human life. But many of the country's political thinkers took Spencer's ideas about economic evolution to heart. In the process, they reduced them to a simpler, more pragmatic form before applying them to American capitalism. They said, in effect, that under the American system anyone could achieve economic prosperity so long as he was willing to compete.* Competition implied "the survival of the fittest." As competition grew more close and intense, the standards of fitness necessary for survival would rise. As the standards of survival fitness rose, so too would the quality of the system's institutions: its industry, its finance, its education, its social order. But to insure the rise in the standards of survival fitness, those who wished to survive—whether individuals or companies or whole industries—would continually have to improve their self-organization and self-management. Already in the 1860s, for example, the refining of kerosene from petroleum, recently discovered in Pennsylvania, was threatening the once-prosperous whaling industry with extinction; and the new technology of artificial ice-making, invented in 1866 by Thaddeus Lowe, had sounded the death knell of the profitable winter lake-and-pond ice-harvesting industry of upper New York and New England. To

---

*Of course, in the America of the 1860s "anyone" remained again a term of art. Not everyone could participate in the competition of American capitalism, only those who qualified according to the social and cultural standards of the period. These standards remained restrictive, though they were nowhere near as restrictive as those abroad.

keep up in the competitive maelstrom that American industrial capitalism was becoming, it would in future take more than luck and inventiveness. It would take individual entrepreneurial daring and foresight on the one hand, and group organization and management on the other.

Out of this mid-1860s crucible of fresh philosophic-economic ideas and practical industrial-financial experience emerged a trend toward a new, more dynamic and ambitious American industrialism. While individual invention in the mechanical arts and sciences remained just as significant as it had been, it was joined in importance by group or collective inventiveness in finance, organization and management. And just as mechanical invention required both daring thought and deliberate method on the part of inventors, so industrial inventiveness required the same qualities among financiers, organizers and managers.

At the end of the war, America's widely expanded industrial complex, so active during the previous four years, was suddenly confronted by the prospect of a considerable slowdown in activity. The government was in the process of dismantling most of the huge military machine it had constructed during the war. With the drying up of this vast federal market, most economic prognosticators predicted a prolonged postwar industrial and commercial recession. They failed to perceive three realities, however. First, with much of the wartime production having concentrated on military goods, the nation's populace had grown starved for "civilian" products. Second, a large portion of the civilian population had been employed in war-related industry during those four years, and it had amassed significant amounts of spendable money, in the form of wages, without there having been much to spend it on. Third, immigration from abroad, having slowed to a trickle during the war, resumed in greater numbers than ever before, with many of the new settlers bringing large amounts of "stake" money with them. Consequently, rather than falling into a recession, American industry continued to thrive in the years immediately following the war.

The prosperity was selective, however. Badly managed or outdated manufacturing firms suffered, many of them going out of business, while well-managed enterprises amassed greater and greater profits and sought to expand further. The combined process of specialization and diversification, started by the war, in-

tensified, as did the need for more specialized training and
management. Companies themselves were no longer the simple
organisms of prewar times; as they grew they became more complex and difficult to maintain and operate, much like the improved
but heavier and more complicated machinery involved in their
manufacturing processes. As the major industrial companies grew
bigger, often by acquiring and absorbing their smaller, failing,
mismanaged competitors, the idea of "bigness" as a business credo
began to form and take hold. Companies that before the war had
been content to operate within and serve a single region now began to function in several regions, setting up branch factories and
tapping into new and distant markets. Some were able to finance
their expansion out of their own profits. But many others decided
to follow the example set by the railroads and telegraph companies: to transform themselves into public corporations with the
help of Wall Street.

In many cases these companies were responding to the persuasion of the Wall Street financiers, whose motive was primarily
their own prosperity. But they were also reacting to the competitive economic and geographical realities of the day. The gold and
silver rushes of the late 1840s and early 1850s had brought the
first internal migrations to the Far West. The 1862 Homestead
Act had launched a larger and more organized tide of westward
migration, and the end of the war had turned it into a virtual
flood. Now the first transcontinental railroad was under construction,* and a sharper image of the vast size of the country—
the settled country that was soon to be—began to take shape in
the American consciousness.

Bigness and complexity were the conceptual outlines of the
image. Postwar newspapers, themselves grown bigger in size and
denser in coverage, remarked endlessly on the implications of
America's bigness. Editorialists, historians, schoolteachers and es-
sayists, drawing on and somewhat bastardizing the evolutionary
theories of Darwin and Spencer, equated America's bigness with
its future greatness. Bigness became synonymous in the American
mind with the notion of the survival of the fittest. America's big-

---

*Because of the intensifying slavery dispute between North and South following the
Gadsden Purchase in 1853, the building of the first transcontinental railroad through the
Southwest, as originally planned, was stalled. The Civil War further delayed the project.
By the end of the war, Northern railroad technology was sufficiently advanced, and Wall
Street railroad financiers were sufficiently powerful politically, to dictate a direct central
route across the once-forbidding Rockies and Sierras.

ness was held to be its greatest asset in the future "evolutionary" competition with the other industrial nations of the world. And because its bigness would be the instrument of its "survival"—the winning of the contest—big corporations in the essential industries were needed to nurture and complement it.

The country became fascinated by bigness in every aspect of its life. "Think big" was the advice of Ansell Kellogg, a Wisconsin newspaper proprietor who in 1861 had exploited the nationwide expansion of the telegraph to originate newspaper syndication, which, under the rubric of "readyprint," supplied up-to-date news and opinion columns to remote small-town weeklies. Railroad locomotives and steamships suddenly grew in size, and building construction went from small to large. Thanks to the development of the cast-iron beam (an offshoot of the railroad rail and the long-barreled cannon), and to Otis's improvement of his elevator, which now could be powered by steam, huge new hotels of up to eight stories in height were erected in major cities, their notoriety based as much on their size as on their possession of such modern conveniences as indoor bathrooms and steam heating. In their wake followed department stores, which were radical departures from the past not only because of their size and convenience but because of their concentration of a wide variety of consumer goods under one roof. Along with department stores came large new office buildings, three and four stories high, and cities themselves began rapidly to spread out from their prewar cores in every possible direction, in many cases even crossing rivers with the help of linked-span iron trestle bridges of the type pioneered by railroad builders in the 1850s.* In the outlying areas, soon to become known as suburbs, and even in the rural countryside, sprawling three- and four-story mansions, equipped with indoor plumbing and steam central-heating systems, began to replace the simple compact houses of prewar times.

The once small and tidy manufacturing industries also re-

*The greatest engineering problem facing the early railroad builders was how to get their lines across the country's wide rivers, particularly the treacherous, flood-prone Mississippi and other such waterways beyond the Appalachians, without having to use ferries. They solved the problem with the trestle bridge, a series of short-beamed spans linked together and anchored to stone or wooden pilings sunk into the riverbed. The first such bridge across the Mississippi was built in 1856 by the Chicago and Rock Island Railroad. Its official opening was a cause of great celebration, prompting one Chicago newspaper to write: It "proves that there is no such thing as an impossible obstacle in this land, for when American citizens are faced with the 'impossible' they see it not as such but as merely a problem to be solved."

flected the nation's fascination with size. Existing factories were expanded to keep up with the vigorous postwar consumer demand for peacetime products. Large new plants were hurriedly built to accommodate the corresponding increases in size and variety of machinery made possible by the widespread application of steam power to manufacturing. The introduction of the Bessemer process set the stage for the production of steel in great quantity, and huge steel mills, far bigger than the country's largest ironworks, began to rise in their place.

The most potent impact of America's obsession with bigness, however, came through the organization and administration of industry itself. With their development of the public corporation, financiers and industrialists had, in effect, "invented" a unique industrial system of their own. In their view it was every bit as vital to the nation's commercial expansion, economic vigor and improving standard of living as any mechanical invention. This new corporate system was the "soul" of the entire American industrial machine, its primary animator and orchestrator, the glue that held together the country's ever more complex commercial framework. Like the inventors who sought zealously to guard and control exclusive financial rights in their mechanical creations, the organizers of the new device of the corporation strove with equal zeal to protect their rights. They had no patent office at their disposal, however—their patent office became the stock market. The commercial products a company manufactured, or the commercial services it rendered, might provide a measure of collective prosperity to its managers and employees. But its potential for generating true individual personal wealth lay not in its bricks-and-machinery industrial structure. It lay in its corporate paper essence—in its stock.

As it did so many other institutions in American life, Samuel Morse's telegraph revolutionized the entire system of banking and finance during the 1860s. The principal feature of the change was the tremendous speedup in communications between the stock exchanges and banks in different cities. Until the Civil War, the country's stock markets had remained small and regionalized, each exchange specializing in local stocks. When financier Jay Cooke pioneered the use of the telegraph to sell war bonds across the country in 1862, however, he created a nationwide excitement over the concept of long-distance investing. After the war, all the stock exchanges in the major cities quickly linked themselves to each other by telegraph.

The new financial communication network immediately encouraged wide-scale speculation in the buying and selling of stocks, as did the profound psychological changes in the nation's attitude toward money caused by the wartime issue of paper currency. With plenty of consumer money available at the end of the war, people were almost as readily inclined to invest it in the expanding stock market—particularly in the stocks of the countless new-venture corporations being created by financiers and industrialists—as to spend it in stores. Stocks began to be viewed as a commercial commodity in the public mind, not much different from shoes and farm implements, and one bought stocks to improve one's personal financial situation just as one bought a product for the home or a machine for the farm for the improvements they represented. Stock buyers no longer had to wait days or weeks to learn how their shares were performing. Now they could learn in hours, and they could buy or sell in hours, depending on the rapid fluctuations in price brought about by the new telegraphic communications system. The stock market, once limited almost exclusively to trading in government securities, was no longer approached primarily as a vehicle of safe long-term investment. For many, it now became a handy vehicle for making money—potentially large sums of money—in the short term.

Because New York's aggressive financial community had already leaped well ahead of the more conservative, hidebound Philadelphia and Boston commercial centers, Wall Street and its centralized stock exchange quickly dominated the national market in stocks and bonds. And it was to Wall Street that more and more financiers, industrialists and speculators gravitated. The most daring and forceful among them focused their dealings on railroad stocks, railroads being the oldest, largest and most developed of the country's public corporations and at that time the companies with the most promising growth and profit potential. But mere speculation in the hyperactive new market proved to carry with it much greater risks of loss than gain. Out of the ranks of the pure speculators and gamblers, therefore, arose a group of men who sought to control the market and its precipitous price fluctuations by acquiring majority stock ownership of the established railroads.

*   *   *

What had distinguished America before the Civil War was its ability, through the ingenuity of inventors, mechanical innovators and political experimenters, to adapt and improve on mechanical, scientific and political ideas that had originated abroad. What distinguished it now was its reshaping of the exclusivistic, closed-enterprise capitalism of Europe into a vigorous, pluralistic, free-enterprise capitalism. The construction of the nationwide railroad system after the war was the key to this. It was the American equivalent of the building of large navies and merchant marines by the European colonial powers a century earlier. Each in its own way was the lifeline of industrial progress in its respective region. The fleets of Europe supplied their nations with all the necessary foreign raw materials needed for their industries. In America, with its abundance and wide diversity of native raw materials, the railroads served the same purpose.

There was, however, a crucial difference between the effects of the development of European commercial maritime systems and those of the American railroads. The difference lay in the fact that foreign shipbuilding and seafaring remained relatively static, self-enclosed industries, requiring little in the way of subsidiary support or improvement once steam-powered navigation made its appearance, whereas the development of the American railroad system spawned a rapid succession of large new and separate industries. The merchant marines of European nations enabled those nations to proceed with their industrial expansion, but in a slow and stately fashion. The railroads of the United States, on the other hand, would turn the once-slow pace of American industrialism into a whirlwind of growth, depth and complexity.

CHAPTER 13

CAPITALISM COMES
OF AGE

In the late 1860s much was made by editorialists and preachers of the alarming social and economic changes they perceived as having begun to stain the moral fabric of America. Particularly targeted were the sudden postwar rush toward material consumption and the new obsession with land and stock-market speculation. Both depended to a large degree on the acquisition of personal credit, which became increasingly easy to obtain once widespread borrowing, as a result of the war, emerged as the standard system of government and business financing. Credit was an evil that threatened to destroy the traditions of virtue and prudence upon which the nation had grown, warned the moral savants. Suddenly, it seemed, everyone in the country was interested only in amassing a personal fortune through credit-financed speculation, or, worse yet, in creating the appearance of a fortune through the credit-financed purchase of land, buildings and the latest sophisticated personal products and luxuries from abroad. Such extravagance, the sermonizers declared, promoted disrespect for hard, honest work and fostered the institutionalization of competitive greed, cutthroatedness and dishonesty, all of which boded ill for the future integrity of the nation.

The alarmists were right in one respect: A frenzy of mass consumption, much of it inspired by easy access to credit, had indeed seized the country. But they were not entirely accurate in the dire inferences they drew from their observations. That was the difficulty of the new brand of pluralistic American capitalism. Its dynamics were so novel and mysterious that they confounded the standard tests of religious and moral judgment. They appeared to be the embodiment of all that was wicked in the human soul. Yet at the same time they seemed to stimulate and encourage those aspects of the soul that were considered among the most virtuous—the achievement of earthly riches and the betterment of mankind.

The paradox was no more vividly exemplified than by the expansion and improvement of the railroad system in the decade following the Civil War. On the one hand the railroads were bringing increased prosperity, mobility and comfort to the masses, both directly and indirectly, and were accelerating the development, expansion and improvement of scores of other industries—steelmaking, mining, food supply, construction, petroleum and the like. On the other hand, particularly by virtue of the methods used to organize and finance it, railroad development was about to launch an era of institutional greed, personal venality and corporate ruthlessness unprecedented in the nation's history. Together, the two sides of the coin of railroad expansion set the tone and style for the future of the nation's development. Uniquely American in its daring, robustness and pragmatism, it would eventually become the basis upon which the other industrial nations of the world would try to revamp their failing systems.

In the two decades prior to the Civil War, Cornelius Vanderbilt, a poor-born New Yorker who started his career as a local fishmonger, had made a handsome fortune in that city's commercial harbor and river transport, and had become well known on Wall Street. As a prosperous maritime merchant—whence he derived his nickname, "Commodore"—he had bitterly denigrated the prewar railroad phenomenon and predicted nothing but disaster for those who invested in it. "Why expend massive sums to hack out and lay down a railway [to Albany] when God has already given us a free right-of-way by His bestowal upon us of the mighty Hudson?" was one question Vanderbilt was quoted as having posed to a syndicator who approached him to invest in the original New York-to-Albany line in the 1850s.

The outbreak of the Civil War abruptly changed Vanderbilt's mind. Impressed by the country's increasing dependence on railroads for the rapid movement of troops and supplies, he became persuaded that railroads would soon make interior canal and river commerce obsolete. Accordingly, although he was already in his late sixties, he began privately to buy into the New York–Albany railroad. By 1865 he controlled the majority of stock in the line. He thereupon sold his shipping companies and set out to gain control of the string of independent railroads that stretched westward from Albany toward Chicago. His ultimate goal was to establish a single unified road, with branches, that would capture most if not all of the freight and passenger traffic between the two cities—a privately owned, much longer and faster rail version of the Erie Canal.

Vanderbilt "thought big," but up to that time the nation's financial establishment, despite its creation of the public corporation, had not yet developed a systematic method of organizing and financing such a gargantuan project. The only enterprise of such size to have been established was the continent-spanning telegraph industry, which was largely controlled by two corporations, the Western Union Telegraph Company and the American Telegraph Company, soon to be merged into a single organization. But the telegraph business, a "light" industry, demanded little in the way of continuing capital investment as compared to railroads, a "heavy" industry that required numerous other industries to sustain it. Notwithstanding the government land subsidies granted to the railroads, their actual building, maintenance, improvement and expansion were extremely expensive affairs. Telegraph machines, and the poles and wires that linked them into an orderly system, were relatively cheap, as were their installation and the small number of workers required to operate the system. Railroads, on the other hand, depended on costly trackage, locomotives, rolling stock and a large, diverse labor force. This was the principal reason so many railroads had suffered financially before the Civil War. Although they had appeared to flourish, their revenues in the early years were insufficient to offset construction and operating costs.

The building of the first major railroads in the America of the 1830s and 1840s had been as pioneering a human venture as the first ocean voyages of the European navigators four centuries earlier. Like the early navigators, the railroad builders simply did not know what they were getting into. As they progressed, they were repeatedly confronted by unforeseen construction problems caused by terrain, weather, the frangibility of equipment and the unreliability of labor. Many railroads died aborning, their actual costs far exceeding their construction estimates and quickly draining their start-up financing. Others, financially overextended before they could begin actual operations and unable to raise further money through their original charters, laid themselves open to takeovers and forced mergers. Out of this process in the 1850s emerged a new kind of railroad financing.

The 1850s railroad entrepreneurs, particularly those who were planning to build the first lines west of the Mississippi, were determined to avoid the financing mistakes of the past. These mistakes, they concluded, had resulted from the fact that the original railroad organizers had depended on conventional funding—the selling of a fixed number of securities in the chartering corporation based on the charterer's estimate of how much it would cost to build the railroad, with no provision for acquiring additional capital to cover what are nowadays known as cost overruns. The conventional business financing of the 1850s was simple and straightforward. It could be compared today to a man giving all his spare funds to another man to open a candy store in exchange for a fixed-percentage share in the revenue. If the store succeeds, the "financier" stands to recover his investment and to profit as well. But what if the "financee" expends all of the proffered funds in acquiring the store site and refurbishing it? He will have nothing left over with which to stock the store; thus the store cannot open and there will be no revenues. The man who agreed to finance the venture, having no more funds to put into it, is left with nothing except perhaps a lease on the property for which he may also be liable. The best he can do is to find someone else to take the lease off his hands.

This in effect is what happened to many investors in early railroad stocks. And it is what the more sophisticated organizers of the 1850s railroads sought to avoid. They did so by inventing the paper device of the "construction company." The construction company was formed as a separate subsidiary of the main chartering corporation of a particular railroad, although it remained firmly under the control of the parent company's principal directors. Despite its name, its purpose was not so much to construct the railroad as it was to manipulate securities, and thereby to guarantee the parent company's supply of a continuing flow of money beyond the amount of its original stock capitalization.

In its simplest terms, the construction company functioned in the following fashion: It entered into a contract with the railroad's parent corporation to undertake the road's construction in exchange not for money payments, but for payments in the parent's stock. This was the key to the device. The parent company, having been capitalized under its original chartering issue of stocks and bonds, could not expect to be able to go back to the public for more capital, through further securities issues, until its railroad appeared sure of completion and future operation. Instead, it used part of the capital it had raised to pay the construction company for its services in building the first section of the railroad. Then, hiring a printer to create new batches of paper stock, it gave these to the construction company in payment for each additional section built. The construction company sold these stocks on the open market or used them as collateral for bank loans, thereby acquiring the necessary cash to proceed with the building of the road's next section. The process of creating successive new blocks of stock shares continued until the railroad was completed and operational.

The scheme had more going for it than just guaranteeing the completion of the actual railroad, however. By enabling construction to advance at a steady pace, without the financial collapses and work stoppages the investing public had become accustomed to during the building of the earlier railroads, the construction company served to build public confidence in the line, sending up the value of the parent company's shares well before its system was completed. The increase in value of the original public-issue shares inflated the value of the additional shares that the parent company printed and handed over to its construction company, enabling the latter to realize progressively greater amounts in stock sales and loans, much of which went not into the actual building of the railroad but into the construction company's treasury, and not infrequently into the pockets of its directors (who were also the directors of the parent company). Once the railroad was operational, it resorbed its construction company and "rolled over" the company's bank debt through periodic payments from operating revenues.

By such circular and self-aggrandizing methods were most of

America's new western trunk-line railroads built in the 1850s and 1860s, as well as the many branch and interconnecting lines of the principal eastern roads. That the railroad companies and their organizers were amassing great profits even before their lines went into operation seemed to bother no one. Nor did the fact that the organizers were able to grow still richer by buying back the inflated original-issue shares in their companies, since the sellers of those shares were happy to unload them at a tidy profit. The only eyebrows eventually raised were those of the federal government when, in 1872, a New York newspaper exposed the Crédit Mobilier scandal.

Crédit Mobilier was the name of the construction company that had been created to build the Union Pacific Railroad, which, along with the Central Pacific, had been awarded extensive government subsidies to complete the first transcontinental line.* Several prominent federal officials, including future President James Garfield, were implicated in the scandal, but only two were found guilty of impropriety in the subsequent congressional investigation. The two, Congressmen Oakes Ames of Massachusetts and James Brooks of New York, were censured by Congress, Ames for having sold and Brooks for having accepted valuable Crédit Mobilier stock at considerable discount for the purpose of influencing the government to give the Union Pacific a large share of the first transcontinental route.

The longer-term consequence of the Crédit Mobilier exposé, however, was to encourage a more watchful government eye on the construction and operation of the nation's railroads. Beginning in 1874 the public began to clamor for some sort of federal regulation over the private railroad industry, on the grounds that it had been built largely over public lands and had become a "public utility." The industry mounted a concerted lobbying effort against regulation, arguing that railroad construction, improvement and operation demanded pioneering methods. It argued, too, that the fact that such a huge rail network was being built throughout the country by private enterprise was enough to prove the industry's fulfillment of its duty to enhance the public good.

*The final link in the first transcontinental railroad was completed at Promontory Point, Utah, on May 10, 1869, when a track laid westward from Nebraska by the Union Pacific met a track laid eastward from California by the Central Pacific. Subsequently, three further transcontinental routes would be built, all, like the first, fanning out from Chicago.

Without the free and unfettered development of the railway system, insisted the apologists, the American public would be much less materially advanced than it was; the railroads not only enabled the public to enjoy a more abundant life, they had created an entirely new economy of ancillary industries, which meant greatly expanded employment and progressively greater public prosperity.

The government was persuaded, at least for a while—the first step toward federal regulation would not come until 1887, when the railroads began to take on the form of a government within a government. In the meantime the new style of railroad financing, having been perfected, became standard and was applied in the late 1860s to the refinancing and expansion of the older eastern railroads. Here a new wrinkle was introduced, one that derived directly from the western corporations' practice of printing additional lots of stock for use in payment of their construction costs. It was in essence the same practice, but it was used by organizers and financiers in the East for a different purpose: to gain individual control of established separate and independent eastern railroads and then to combine them into single large systems that would dominate a given region and, by virtue of their size, discourage competition. This was Cornelius Vanderbilt's aim when he got out of the shipping business at the end of the Civil War and turned his money and energy to the railroads. The manipulative technique he used soon came to be known, aptly, as the "watered stock."

Put simply, stock watering was the secret printing of additional batches of shares in a small, independent railroad by those who controlled the company. The additional shares, now carrying the value of the shares already on the market, would not be issued to the public. Instead they would be used as direct payment to buy an additional small railroad, or as security on bank loans for the same purpose. Once the additional railroad was bought and merged into the original company, or reorganized as a subdivision of a parent company, its shares would be similarly diluted, or "watered," in order to purchase yet another railway. And so on, until a string of once-independent short-haul lines was formed into a single large conglomerate that dominated its region.

Cornelius Vanderbilt did not invent the watered stock, but he raised its use to high art. The technique in its specific eastern details had been created by Daniel Drew and Jay Gould, two Wall Street speculators who went into competition with Vanderbilt at the end of the war, determined to monopolize the potentially lucrative railroad markets between New York and Chicago. When Vanderbilt had decided to enter the railroad business, he first cast his eye on a string of railways that cut diagonally and directly across upper New Jersey and lower New York to the Great Lakes region. Drew and Gould beat him to this direct route to the West by acquiring the majority ownership of a small New Jersey railroad and then, with the help of Jim Fisk, another Wall Street speculator, watering their company's stock to purchase several more short-haul lines along the route. The resulting combination was reorganized by Drew and Gould into the system eventually called the Erie Railroad Company.

It was because he had been deprived of the most direct route that Vanderbilt quickly bought into the indirect Hudson River line, which traveled by way of Albany and was almost two hundred miles longer. Gaining full control of the New York–Albany railroad in 1866, he promptly began to water its stock and rapidly acquired majority ownership of the New York Central between Albany and Buffalo—itself a recent then consolidation of several separate and independent lines built in the 1850s. Vanderbilt then consolidated the Central with the Hudson River line, again vastly increasing the stock of the two in order to increase public confidence in the system and to outduel Drew, nominally the treasurer of the Erie, in the battle to gain exclusive control of the main Great Lakes route from western New York to Chicago.

Vanderbilt's first tactic in this endeavor was to use his own watered stock to try, in 1868, to wrest the controlling interest in the Erie from Drew. He began by obtaining a court order prohibiting Drew and Gould from printing and issuing to themselves further Erie shares—the conventional method of combating takeovers in what had by then become the eastern railroad wars. With his injunction in hand, Vanderbilt then used his own watered New York Central stock as security for loans to buy large blocks of "frozen" Erie shares in Wall Street. As word of Vanderbilt's buying spree got around, the price of the stock spiraled upward. That did not deter "The Commodore," but after spending millions to acquire what he expected would be the majority stock in the Erie, Vanderbilt found that he was no better off than when he had started: Drew and his associates had outfoxed him by squirming through a loophole in the court order. The order had enjoined them only from printing and issuing new shares in their company. Therefore they didn't print new shares. Instead they issued to themselves, without paying a cent for them beyond their paper costs, $10 million in convertible bonds. They then converted the bonds into hundreds of thousands of shares of stock, thus blocking Vanderbilt from acquiring the majority of the Erie's "outstanding" shares. Moreover, Gould later persuaded the New York legislature to enact a law forbidding the consolidation of the Erie and the New York Central.

Vanderbilt lost the battle, but not the war. The Erie would plunge into bankruptcy in 1875 as a result of further Drew-Gould financial machinations, thereby preventing it from developing the main Great Lakes route to Chicago. Vanderbilt acquired the route almost by default, buying into the string of railroads and branch lines that stretched across northern Ohio, southern Michigan, northern Indiana and beyond, and eventually consolidating the entire network into the huge New York Central Railroad system.

In such fashion were other railroads throughout the East and Midwest consolidated into large monopolistic combines, as well as new ones in the West constructed from scratch. The decade from 1875 to 1885 was the period above all in American industrial history of great railroad building, and of the concomitant reformation of Wall Street as the unique force in corporate and industrial megafinance. But "above all" meant only that these two dominant influences blazed the trail over which the next stretch of the road to colossus would be built. In their wake came scores of associated industries, old and new, to carry out the actual road building.

First were the manufacturers of railroad construction equipment itself. Until the 1860s the building of railroads had been almost exclusively a pick-shovel-and-wheelbarrow affair. Teams of manual laborers dug and leveled the roadbeds, often progressing only a few yards a day through the rockier, hillier stretches of the line's route and not infrequently being forced to deviate from the road's surveyed right-of-way in order to bypass unexpected geological difficulties. Even the building in the late 1860s of the final link of the first transcontinental railroad, between Nebraska and California, had been largely a pick-and-shovel operation, with each of the two railroads involved in its construction employing armies of cheap immigrant labor to accomplish the job with the help of horse-drawn scrapers and plows. But at the very same time, inventors and engineers in the East and Midwest were busy contriving mechanical devices designed to cut down on human labor and speed up progress in railroad construction. Much of their inspiration came from the Society of Civil Engineers, an organization founded in 1852 to establish as an integral profession what had until then been a loose agglomeration of machinery designers and builders. America's first association of "practical" workers, the society, through its printed bulletins, took up as one of its chief causes the mid-nineteenth-century idea that later, in the 1930s, came to be called "automation"—the replacement of human labor by machinery.*

Automation was not a new idea in the United States. Indeed, it was as old as the country's first textile mills and Eli Whitney's cotton gin, and had more recently spread to the manufacture of farm machinery. But automation had not yet been applied successfully to the heavy, dirty industries. True, the steam locomotive was a heavy, dirty piece of industrial machinery, but technically speaking it did not constitute automation since it had replaced not human labor but horsepower. (It might even be said that the locomotive had brought about an increase in the need of human labor—in view of the fact that railroads created a wide variety of new mechanical and manual jobs.) Now, however, civil and mechanical engineers sought to devise heavy machines, operated by a few men, that would replace picks and shovels wielded by many. In their efforts, they combined the bulk power of the steam locomotive with the articulated hydraulic action of smaller machines. The result was the "steam shovel," the precursor of all modern, heavy excavating and earth-moving equipment.

The steam shovel and its offspring, the steam scraper or grader

---

*The American Society of Civil Engineers was formed on the model of the American Medical Association, founded five years earlier to give doctors and surgeons a common, specialized medium through which to communicate with one another and impart information about the latest epidemics and methods of dealing with them. The A.M.A., the country's first full-scale "professional" society, had its own organizational precedents in various scientific societies that had been started in Philadelphia and Boston in the post-Revolution years. The Society of Civil Engineers was the first such "practical" organization, science and medicine still being in the realm of the theoretical and experimental. It would itself serve as the model for the founding of scores of other professional associations in the post-Civil War decades.

and the steam tamper or roller, expedited the boom in railroad building in the 1870s and 1880s. Three more transcontinental routes were laid, as well as scores of additional branch and connecting lines within the existing system and a dozen new or reconstructed lines in the South, by then emerging from the paralysis of its Civil War defeat. An expansion and intensification of the Wall Street financial wars, such as the one waged between Drew and Vanderbilt in the late 1860s, accompanied the boom, but now there were many more combatants. By 1873, stock watering and speculation had grown so rampant that the stock market, supported almost solely by the trade in overinflated, credit-backed railroad securities, collapsed. It swept with it into bankruptcy some of the country's most powerful private banks and investment houses, and into impoverishment tens of thousands of individual investors.

Only a handful of nerveless and sagacious speculators benefited. They coolly watched as the market collapsed over the course of several days. Then they stepped in and began buying up favored stocks in huge quantities and at rock-bottom prices. Gradually the slide was stemmed and the market began to inch up again. The net effect was that many ordinary investors and speculators got poorer, while the numerically fewer rich got richer—not just in the sense of improving their paper wealth, but also by virtue of the fact that they were able, at nominal cost to themselves, to obtain majority-ownership positions in the stricken corporations whose stock they bought. Once again the railroads had played a pivotal if unintentional role in the shaping of the American colossus. The 1873 Panic, brought on by the railroads, permitted the further consolidation and concentration of the country's industrial wealth into the hands of a relatively few individuals and syndicates. This fact, and the psychology behind it, were soon to have enormous consequences for the nation, both positive and negative.

Too, by 1873, American material expectation had been raised so high that the country as a whole was able to escape a deep long-term economic depression such as the one that had followed the 1837 Panic. Postwar consumerism, along with the drive for individual wealth and mechanical progress, had produced a flood of new inventions and improvements on existing technology.* Al-

---

*Between 1855 and 1864, the United States Patent Office had granted 38,761 patents. Between 1865 and 1874 it granted nearly 200,000.

though not all were practical, many were, and since they represented potentially profitable new products or processes, they kept finance and industry busy exploiting them. Financial promoters and organizers themselves diversified their interests, having learned that the concentration of their resources in single industries was too risky. Thus, rather than stall the advance of postwar technological and industrial development, the financial crisis of 1873, by the further diversification it prompted, actually helped to accelerate it.

CHAPTER **14**

THE MARRIAGE OF SCIENCE AND BUSINESS

Grosvenor Porter Lowrey was the fourth-generation descendant of an immigrant Dutch farmer who had settled near the tiny hamlet of Claverack, New York, in the early 1700s. Lowrey was born in 1831 on a farm in nearby North Egremont, Massachusetts, to which his father had moved from Claverack after serving in the War of 1812. Musically gifted, Lowrey became skilled at the violin as a youngster, and by the time he was twelve he was tutoring several of his contemporaries in the Berkshire hills. Among his students was a boy named Franklin Pope, who would later play a consequential role in Lowrey's life and career.

When he was fourteen, Lowrey had exhausted all the education that was offered in North Egremont and went to work as a printer's devil at a newspaper in Great Barrington, five miles from his home. After four years on the printing side of the newspaper business, he began to do occasional reporting and editing, which provoked in him a fascination for facts and inspired an ambition to become a lawyer. Collecting his savings from his violin lessons and newspaper work, he traveled to Easton, Pennsylvania, and enrolled at Lafayette College to study law. During his first year there he resumed his violin teaching and was soon giving lessons to the daughter of Andrew Reeder, Easton's most prominent attorney. Reeder took a liking to the ambitious student and gave him a job as a clerk in his law office. And when Reeder was appointed governor of the new territory of Kansas in 1854, the same year Lowrey graduated from Lafayette with a Bachelor of Laws, he invited the twenty-three-year-old to join him as his personal assistant.

Kansas was a cauldron of violence and lawlessness at the time, all of it revolving about the question of whether the territory was to be admitted to the Union as a slave or free state. After two fruitless years trying to establish law and order as Reeder's principal deputy, Lowrey, known for his antislavery sentiments, was forced to flee the territory when the proslavery legislature threatened to imprison him. After a short stint as a newspaper reporter in Albany, Lowrey made his way to New York City in 1857. There he opened a law office and became friendly, through a mutual love of music, with Egisto Fabbri, an Italian immigrant who was in the process of making his mark in Wall Street finance. Through Fabbri, Lowrey met a number of other rising Wall Streeters and began to acquire some of their legal business. His law practice and social standing were further enhanced when, in 1862, he married Laura Tryon, the daughter of a wealthy city businessman.

In 1862, Lowrey went into partnership with three other New York attorneys to form the firm of Porter, Lowrey, Soren and Stone, specializing in commercial, business and patent law. During the latter part of the same year, on his own initiative and impelled by his abolitionist principles, he wrote a treatise setting forth a detailed legal defense of Lincoln's Emancipation Proclamation. He followed this a short while later with another brief attacking the legitimacy of England's declaration of neutrality in the American Civil War.* The two documents made a favorable impression in Washington, and Lowrey shortly found himself in demand as a lawyer for the government. His initial retainer was the

---

*The brief addressed the notorious "*Alabama Affair*," in which England was accused of aiding the South by secretly building and providing to the Confederacy a pair of specially designed steam-powered attack ships, or "corsairs," which the South used to prey on defenseless Union freighters plying the shipping lanes of the Atlantic. The two corsairs, called *Alabama* and *Florida*, destroyed 257 Union ships and forced northern shipowners to transfer another 700 vessels to foreign registries, thus decimating the American merchant marine. Lowrey's pamphlet accused England of engaging in piracy against the United States, and it was later used as the basis for recovery of $15.5 million in legal claims against the British government.

Treasury Department, for which he prosecuted cases of customs-, sales- and income-tax evasion under the recently enacted wartime tax laws. In this function he became expert in all forms of financial and business law, and by the end of the war he was one of New York's best-known and best-connected attorneys, particularly appreciated by the Wall Street community for his ready access to the machinery of government. As a consequence, his and his firm's services were sought out extensively during the postwar industrial boom, and he became an increasingly important figure in the wave of consolidations, expansions and corporate power struggles that dominated the period.

One of the consolidations Lowrey was instrumental in engineering was that which resulted in the formation, in 1866, of the giant Western Union Telegraph Company. As a result of his work, he became Western Union's principal lawyer, publicly defending it against allegations of monopolization and acting as its chief attorney in an increasingly complex web of business litigation. It was his association with Western Union that was to reunite Lowrey with his boyhood violin student Franklin Pope. That reunion would lead him to his ultimate and most celebrated destiny as the godfather, as it were, of electric light and power.

Like Grosvenor Lowrey, Franklin Pope had left the bucolic Berkshire hills of western Massachusetts in the late 1850s to seek a career in a field more congenial to his interests than farming. Pope had chosen telegraphy, and after several years of apprenticeship, and then service in the Civil War, he found a job with the Gold Indicator Company in New York's Wall Street district. The company had grown out of a device invented by Samuel Laws—a telegraphic instrument that operated a mechanical indicator that registered changes in the price of gold on a large board attached to the wall of the gold-trading room of the New York Stock Exchange. Through a network of telegraph wires, the machine also conveyed the same information to the offices of local stockbrokers, who paid high fees for the service. By 1869, Laws, who owned and personally managed the Gold Indicator Company, had made Franklin Pope supervisor of the shop near the stock exchange from which his master telegraphs operated. Into that shop one day, looking for a job, came a scruffy twenty-two-year-old wanderer with experience in the trade of telegraphy. His name was Thomas Alva Edison.

Edison, the son of poor immigrants from Canada, had been born in Milan, Ohio, a small canal town near Lake Erie, in 1847. As a child growing up in Port Huron, Michigan, where his family moved when he was seven, he evinced a profound aversion to formal schooling but a precocious flair for scientific experimentation at home. At the time, Samuel Morse's telegraph was just beginning to come into use in the remoter regions of the country, and it became, along with the entire mystery of electricity, an object of fascination to the young Edison. When he was eleven he built a homemade telegraph set between his house and a neighbor's and needed only to discover a method by which to generate an electrical current to test it. His solution to the problem was to gather together the two family cats, attach picture wires to their legs, and rub their backs hard in an attempt to create friction. The cats declined to cooperate, however, spitting and clawing at the boy before running off to hide.

Edison was undeterred. Realizing that he would have to earn some money to be able to buy the magnets and coils required to produce an electrical current, he went to work at the age of twelve on the new rail line between Port Huron and Detroit—the Grand Trunk Railroad—hawking sandwiches, fruits and candy to passengers. One day, soon after he started, he was delayed in reaching the Port Huron station to board his regular morning train. When he arrived he saw the train leaving without him. Sprinting after it, he came abreast of the baggage car and shouted to one of the men on board to haul him in. The trainman grabbed his extended hand and began to hoist Edison into the car. The boy got through the door safely enough but then, as the trainman loosened his grip, the weight of Edison's sackful of fruits and sandwiches began to pull him out again. As he lost his balance and started to fall through the baggage car's wide door, the trainman, in reaction, grasped his ears to yank him back in. As a result, Edison said fifty years after the incident, "I felt something snap inside my head." What he felt was the rupture of both his eardrums. Soon he began to grow deaf. "I haven't heard a bird sing since I was twelve years old."

Edison's deafness discouraged any ideas he might have had of further school attendance—"I couldn't even hear the teachers," he later remembered. Instead he set out in his early teens to educate himself, stopping almost every day during his train layovers in

Detroit at the free library, where he pored through as many books as he could, especially books on scientific subjects. When not at the library, he was in the Detroit railyard of the Grand Trunk, where he pretended to drive the great steam engines parked there. This nourished in him a hankering to become a locomotive engineer.

Indeed, Edison might well have grown up to be nothing more than a railroad man had it not been for an event that occurred in 1862, when he was fifteen. On a warm summer morning in that year he was standing on the platform at the station in Mount Clemens, Michigan, while his train took on water and fuel. Nearby, in the railroad yard, a freight train was in the process of being assembled. While Edison watched the cars being shunted about by a pair of switching engines, his eye caught the figure of a child toddling across the tracks of the yard. Then he saw a boxcar heading down the very track onto which the child was wandering. Edison leaped from the platform, tore across the tracks, and snatched the child from the path of the approaching boxcar. His heroics were witnessed by John MacKenzie, the Mount Clemens station agent and telegraph operator, who happened also to be the father of the child. The grateful MacKenzie asked the fifteen-year-old "candy butcher" what he would accept as a reward. Edison proposed that MacKenzie give him lessons in operating a telegraph. The Mount Clemens man agreed.

Thereafter Edison stopped at the Mount Clemens station three or four times a week to be tutored by MacKenzie in the operation of the telegraph. Telegraphy was still a relatively new trade in 1862, and speed and accuracy in the transmission of Morse code were highly valued by the railroads and telegraph companies. Also essential was a solid knowledge of all the special codes within the Morse code system that telegraph operators employed to communicate in shorthand with one another. Edison had developed a rudimentary skill at telegraphic transmission during his earlier experiments at home, and he quickly impressed MacKenzie with his aptitude. The expert's speed in taking messages was forty-five words per minute; it took extensive practice, but once mastered it meant a job almost anywhere. Edison mastered it in five months, and early in 1863, MacKenzie sent him on his way with a letter of recommendation.

Two years later, after working as an apprentice in Port

Huron, Edison applied for and won a job as a full-fledged tele-grapher with the Grand Trunk. Assigned as a night operator to a lonely station across the border in Canada, he soon left for a bet-ter-paying position with the Lake Shore and Michigan Southern Railway at a station near Michigan's border with Ohio. The fol-lowing year found him in Indianapolis as an operator for Western Union. At the end of the Civil War he was sent to Cincinnati, and after a few months there to Memphis, and then to Louisville. By 1866, as a nineteen-year-old, Edison was an experienced jour-neyman telegrapher but was growing bored with the monotony of the work.

Then he had an idea. The main reason speed was so essential in telegraphic transmission was that only one message could be sent at a time over the wire; while signals were being transmitted from one end, messages coming back from the other had to wait. The great growth of the telegraph system produced by the war had brought with it a vast increase in traffic over the main lines. Due to the one-way limitations of the system, traffic was begin-ning to pile up, causing communications to slow down. Edison thought that if he could devise a system that permitted signals to travel in both directions over the same wire simultaneously, he would have made a significant contribution to telegraphy—an improvement that might provide him with handsome financial rewards in the bargain and also free him from the monotony of his job.

Thoroughly familiar with the known principles of electricity and telegraphy by then, Edison began to experiment with the be-ginnings of such a system in Louisville, where he set up a desk-top laboratory-workshop in his telegraph office. Soon he was totally engrossed in the project, spending practically all of his earnings on additional equipment. A few months later, though, he was fired for neglecting his regular duties. Once a Western Union telegrapher was dismissed for such cause, he was blacklisted and could not get another job with the company. Edison remained in Louisville for several more months and continued to work slavishly on his experiments for a two-way telegraph machine, which he called a "duplex." After his money ran out, he packed up his laboratory equipment in a pair of steamer trunks and made his way by boat to New Orleans. His intention was to sail from there to South America in search of telegraphic work. But then he changed his mind and journeyed to Boston. Once there, he heard from a friend that he might find investors willing to back him in developing his duplex telegraph.

Edison found no backers, but in 1868 he did find a job as a receiver-decoder in the telegraph room of the *Boston Herald*. He also found, in a secondhand-book shop, a two-volume work entitled *Experimental Researches in Electricity* by the English scientist Michael Faraday—the same Faraday whose discoveries in electromagnetism had first inspired Samuel Morse in his invention of the telegraph in the 1830s. After reading the Faraday works, the most important parts of which were Faraday's descriptions of how electrical power could be produced mechanically through a magnetic dynamo, Edison redoubled his efforts to perfect a two-way telegraph. At the same time, he broadened his experiments to include ideas for other electrical inventions. One of these was for a machine that would automatically record the votes of state and federal legislators.

Edison had first gotten the idea for such a device when he was in Louisville with Western Union. While relaying telegraphed reports of the oral votes of congressmen directly from the Capitol in Washington, he had grown annoyed at the slowness of the process, which tied up the wire from Washington for lengthy periods. A visit to the Massachusetts State House in Boston, where he personally witnessed the tediousness of the serial, oral voting process, rekindled the idea for Edison. Within a few days he designed a device, based on the electrical principles of the telegraph, that would record legislative voting automatically and simultaneously through a system of wires and switches attached to the desks of the Massachusetts legislators. Before the month was out he had put together a working model, whittling most of its components out of wood.

Edison's success in designing and building his first functioning electrical machine quickly turned his interest in invention into an obsession. After a friend printed a brief article about his experiments in the *Journal of the Telegraph*, he quit his job at the *Herald* and set out to be a full-time inventor, managing to raise $600 in cash from two investors as backing for further work on his vote recorder and duplex telegraph. It was not only his sudden passion for invention but a sense of commercial urgency that impelled him to quit his job and spend all his time on his experiments, for he had learned that another Boston inventor, J. B. Stearns, was also at work on a two-way telegraph.

Altogether, Edison's efforts in Boston proved to be a failure, at least initially. Although he was able to show that his electric vote recorder worked, and even obtained a patent, he failed to find a market for it. No legislature cared to install it because, despite its efficiency, it allowed little time for filibuster and the last-minute arm-twisting maneuvers most politicians deemed essential to the voting process. Also, although the country was fast growing fascinated by the possibilities of electricity, most people were still highly fearful of it, and legislators were no less wary than others of touching their fingers to poorly insulated electrified buttons. Edison's machine did not possess enough electric current to impart a serious shock; yet a shock was a shock to the uninitiated.*

Nor did Edison have any better luck with his duplex telegraph. After perfecting a prototype machine late in 1868, he went to Western Union in Boston for permission to test it over one of their long-distance wires. He was rudely turned away. Then he appealed to the local office of Western Union's competitor, the Atlantic and Pacific Telegraph Company. They were more accommodating, granting Edison permission to try his device on their wire between Rochester, New York, and New York City. Borrowing another $800, Edison entrained to Rochester with all his equipment packed in his luggage, while a duplicate set was shipped to the company's main telegraph office in New York with written instructions on how to hook up and operate it.

On February 11, 1869, his twenty-second birthday, the confident Edison began his transmissions from Rochester to New York, his first message being a signal to the New York operator to commence simultaneous transmission back to Rochester. Nothing happened—Edison received no response. It was later learned that the operator in New York, having failed to understand Edison's written instructions, was helpless to carry out his vital role in the test. But for now, Edison's hopes and the months of solitary work he had put into his invention were wiped out, as was all his borrowed money. He returned to Boston burdened by a debt of $1,500 (an amount equivalent today to nearly $20,000) and with

---

*When automated legislative voting machines were finally adopted more than half a century later, they were based on Edison's invention, as was the automatic voting machine that replaced the handwritten ballot and ballot box in general elections.

no more sources of money available to him. Soon his creditors started to dun him. Feeling disgraced and dispirited, Edison decided that he had no choice but to skip town. Penniless, he shivered his way across Massachusetts in a boxcar, intending to make his way back to his parents' home in Michigan. But when the train reached Albany after a long night's ride, he changed his mind. Lugging his two heavy bags of equipment, he made his way to the local railroad telegrapher's office. There he found an operator he had known during his brief days with the Lake Shore and Michigan Southern Railway. The former colleague loaned Edison $5 so that the frustrated young inventor could travel to New York City and find out what had gone wrong with his duplex experiment.

Edison arrived in the city with little more than a dollar in his pocket. His visit to the main Atlantic and Pacific Telegraph office yielded no information; in fact he was turned away before he could make any inquiries. The office superintendent, who had been highly skeptical of Edison's Rochester test when he had been ordered to participate in it, could not believe that the disheveled, almost completely deaf youth at his door could possibly have anything to contribute to the advancement of telegraphy. After wandering the city for several days in an unsuccessful search for a telegrapher's job, Edison heard about a possible opening at the Laws Gold Indicator Company near Wall Street. When he presented himself at the company's shop, Franklin Pope, the supervisor, had to tell him there was no job available.

Pope, however, had heard about Edison and his experiments through the article in the *Journal of the Telegraph*. Taking pity on the younger man, he offered him a cot in the shop's basement until he could find work. Soon after, during a day when gold trading at the stock exchange reached fever pitch, the company's master indicating machine suddenly and inexplicably ceased to function. The gold-trading room at the stock exchange was thrown into an instant panic, as were the offices of the many stockbrokers who subscribed to the service. Samuel Laws, the inventor of the system, rushed from his office shouting at Pope to find out what had happened and to fix it before his business was wiped out. Try as they did, neither Pope nor Laws could discover the cause of the stoppage. Angry gold traders began to congregate outside the shop with threats of lawsuits and other dire actions. The frantic Laws was sure he faced ruin.

Just then Edison, having heard the commotion, materialized from the shop's cellar. By that time a dozen traders had barged in and were bitterly berating Laws and Pope. Edison eavesdropped for a minute, then walked over to the inert master machine and began to inspect it. Almost immediately he noticed that a spring between two of its gear wheels had snapped and dropped off. He fished around beneath the machine and found the two pieces of the broken spring. He brought them to Pope and said, "I believe this is your problem."

Laws, not even knowing who Edison was, commanded him to fix it. Edison rushed to a nearby metalworking shop and quickly fabricated a new spring. Then he returned to the Gold Indicator premises and fitted the spring to Laws's master machine. The machine began to run again, and after all its dials were reset, with corresponding adjustments made at the receiving stations at the stock exchange and in the brokers' offices, the system was once more operational. The interruption in service had lasted less than two hours; the Gold Indicator Company was saved.

The grateful Laws immediately hired Edison as Pope's assistant, and when Pope resigned soon after to go into business for himself, Edison succeeded him as supervisor. His employment was short-lived, however, since the Laws firm was bought out by Western Union in the fall of 1869 and reorganized as the Gold and Stock Telegraph Company. Nevertheless, improvements Edison made to the Laws machine during his brief job stint came to the attention of Western Union officials, and most particularly to Grosvenor Lowrey, the attorney who had handled all the legal aspects of the acquisition of the Gold Indicator Company.

Lowrey and Pope had resumed their childhood friendship, and through Pope the young Edison was introduced to Lowrey. Lowrey was impressed by Edison's ideas for improving the standard telegraphic stock printer, ideas based on what Edison had learned from his work on the Laws indicating machine. The Western Union lawyer suggested that Edison and Pope go into business together. Finding them financial backing, he helped them form the firm of Pope, Edison and Company, Electrical Engineers. In exchange for his services in putting the small company together, Lowrey asked that they give Western Union first refusal on any improved telegraphic equipment they developed.

In effect, Lowrey inspired the first corporate invention factory. Until then, invention had been the work of individual visionaries, usually unfinanced and with little public support or appreciation, tinkering away in lonely, remote solitude. With the advent of Pope, Edison and Company, the nature of invention in America was about to change. With the financial backing supplied by Lowrey, and buoyed by their commitment from Western Union, Pope and Edison were able to set up shop in quarters across the river from Manhattan in Jersey City and to hire several assistants. Their modest laboratory would become the forerunner of the country's later industrial research-and-development movement, whereby large manufacturing corporations established their own in-house facilities and staffs to pursue the invention of new machines, processes and products.

Edison quickly proved himself to be the creative brains behind Pope, Edison and Company. Almost immediately he made good on his promise to improve the stock printer, and he devised a series of other telegraphic improvements of value to Western Union. Soon, though, he tangled with his partners, who became jealous of the reputation he was earning. As a result, late in 1870 he left Pope, Edison and Company to form a new company in nearby Newark with another partner, William Unger, to manufacture Edison's patented stock printer and work on other inventions, particularly his two-way telegraph system. J. B. Stearns of Boston had already secured a patent for the duplex machine, however, so Edison started work on a quadruplex device, one that could send two messages in each direction at the same time over a single wire.

Edison got Grosvenor Lowrey to persuade Western Union to permit him to use the company's facilities for his experimental work on the quadruplex, and when he perfected the machine, he offered it to Western Union. The company was slow to respond, however, since by then it was engaged in a ferocious Wall Street takeover battle with Jay Gould, who had already gained control of the Atlantic and Pacific Telegraph Company and was out to monopolize the entire industry. Badly in debt again, Edison sold the rights in the quadruplex to Gould for $30,000. It was then that Western Union responded—by claiming that Edison had breached his agreement to give Western Union first refusal. The company went to court to force the cancelation of Edison's sale to Gould.

The litigation that followed, much of it prosecuted by Lowrey for Western Union, brought Edison, now in his mid-twenties, to the brink of bankruptcy. Curiously, though, it caused no personal rift between the two men; in fact, Lowrey, along with Western Union president William Orton, engineered a new agreement to bring Edison back into the fold. By the agreement's terms the company committed itself to paying off Edison's debts, financing a new laboratory for him in rural New Jersey and establishing Lowrey as his sole legal representative. In exchange, Edison agreed to do further telegraphic and electrical research for the company. The new laboratory was built in 1875 at Menlo Park, near Rahway, New Jersey, and close to the recently completed main line of the Pennsylvania Railroad. There, pressured by Western Union, Edison's first job was to try to beat independent inventors Elisha Gray and Alexander Graham Bell to the invention of the telephone.

The notion that the sound of the human voice might be transmitted electrically over a telegraphlike wire was first conceived by a German inventor named Johann Reis in 1861. Since then Elisha Gray in Chicago and Alexander Graham Bell, a Scottish expatriate living in Boston, had been experimenting independently in the effort to transform the idea into reality. Bell's interest in it derived initially from his vocation as a teacher of the deaf and his desire to create a device that would enable the deaf to hear. In 1873, while also working on a multiple telegraph for the purpose of improving the education of the deaf, he began to experiment seriously with a voice mechanism. When he realized the commercial implications of his work, he abandoned his telegraph and concentrated solely and feverishly on the telephone. Late in 1874, Bell went to Western Union for financial backing. With little faith in the practicability and utility of such a device as Bell described, even as competition to the telegraph, Western Union declined his proposal. Bell then acquired private backing and continued his work in secret.

A year later, Western Union changed its mind about the telephone after it discovered that Elisha Gray had perfected an instrument that enabled musical sounds to be transmitted telegraphically. Western Union purchased the rights to Gray's patent in order to study the device. Then the company commissioned

Edison to transform it into a full-scale telephone. As Grosvenor Lowrey later told a newspaperman: "When Mr. Bell first came to the Western Union with his ideas for the telephone, we had our head in the sand. When we finally awoke, we went back to Mr. Bell and offered to help him financially to complete his invention in consideration of the license to use it. By then he was close to perfecting it, and his price was too high. So we turned to Mr. Edison, who had been the one to advise us of the telephone's feasibility." Indeed, it was the apparent imminence of Bell's invention that had impelled Western Union to reconcile with Edison during the quadruplex litigation and to set him up at Menlo Park. Edison's job was to steal a march on Alexander Graham Bell and secure the telephone exclusively for Western Union at a cost considerably less than the price Bell was by then demanding: $100,000.

On January 14, 1876, Edison filed with the United States Patent Office a document called a *caveat*, a formal notice designed to protect inventors from later claims of infringement by others. Edison's *caveat* announced that he was working on an invention to be known as the telephone. And work he did, aided by dozens of laboratory assistants, most of whom were supplied by Western Union.

But it was too late. Bell, whose penchant for secrecy had left everyone else in the dark about his progress, filed for a patent on a completed working telephone exactly a month after the date of Edison's *caveat*. Edison rushed a nonworking model of his instrument to the Patent Office, as did Elisha Gray, a nonfunctioning model of the device with which *he* had been experimenting. Nonworking models could not compete against functioning ones, however, and on March 7, 1876, Bell's instrument was awarded the exclusive patent. Three days later, in Boston, Bell tested his invention successfully for the first time. Having rigged a wire between his laboratory and a distant upstairs room of his house, he stationed his assisant, Thomas Watson, in the laboratory while he took a position in front of the large telephone "box" in the bedroom. "Mr. Watson, come here, I want you," Bell said into the box. Watson appeared a few moments later at the bedroom door, declaring that he had heard every word clearly.

Bell's invention, like many of the period, was at first looked upon as a curiosity by the newspapers—one of "those devisements appearing of late which the monied classes seem to find appealing for their humorous diversion at social gatherings," as one tabloid put it; in other words, a new party gadget. As usual, history proved the savants of the newspaper business dead wrong. Bell's invention was to be another giant step in the quickening march of progress, another American device that would profoundly change the world. And it marked the start of a decade that would be furious with further invention, innovation and discovery in every field.

CHAPTER 15

A PRICKED FINGER

Alexander Bell's original telephone was based on the principle of generating a weak electrical current by the vibration of a metal diaphragm—a thin circular plate—against an electromagnet. Not even Bell understood completely how and why the phenomenon worked to convey the human voice and other sounds through a wire; in fact the whole process had been discovered by accident. Nevertheless the instrument caused a sensation at the Philadelphia Centennial Exposition during the summer of 1876. The exposition, mounted to celebrate America's industrial achievements during its first hundred years, was a showplace of huge steam-operated machinery and other improved mechanical systems. Yet Bell's relatively tiny, mysterious "talking box" was what most captured the public's imagination. People waited in lines for hours to bark a few words into the box and hear a few more come back from a site far across the grounds of the exposition. Even Thomas Edison traveled to Philadelphia and stood in line to try it.

Edison did not give up his telephone work at Menlo Park just because Bell had obtained the first patent, though. More knowledgeable about electricity than Bell, Edison immediately perceived a way to improve Bell's device appreciably. Not only was it awkward to use, since the transmitter and receiving mechanisms were in separate boxes and the user had to switch from box to box when he wanted to listen or speak, but the quality of the sound was poor, making it seem to the listener that the speaker's voice was emanating from some distant galaxy. Edison was further encouraged to pursue improvements by Western Union, which was intent on starting its own telephonic communications business before Bell could launch his.

Edison decided that the poor quality of Bell's sound was due to the weak conductive properties of his diaphragm, which was made of soft iron. Edison experimented with a number of other materials, each time improving the sound in the telephones he built to accommodate them but still not achieving the quality he thought was possible. Then, one night when he was working late in his Menlo Park laboratory, his kerosene lamp went out. While refueling the lamp, he noticed that the chimney had become smudged and coated with soot—carbon black.* Whenever that had happened before, Edison simply removed the carbon and disposed of it in a wastebasket. But now an idea occurred to him. He scraped the carbon from the chimney and then spread it onto the diaphragm he was experimenting with in one of his telephones. The volume of sound immediately grew much stronger.

The carbon transmitter Edison stumbled upon is still in use in the telephone of today. But that was not his only improvement. He also devised the combined transmitting and receiving elements—the unified voice and earpiece—that made the telephone simpler to use and improved the basic internal circuitry of the system.

Edison received $100,000 for his patented improvements from Western Union, which had begun to compete with the company Bell had formed (Bell Telephone Company) to corner the market on telephone service. Bell in turn modified and adapted some of Edison's improvements, which soon led to a legal war between the two companies over matters of patent infringements, licensing rights and territorial claims. The conflict was resolved, finally, when Western Union agreed to withdraw from the telephone business in exchange for a 20 percent royalty on Bell Telephone's future earnings and a promise from Bell that it would stay out of the telegraph business. Western Union thus earned many millions of dollars by virtue of Edison's work on the telephone. By paying the royalty, Bell Telephone was able to make use of all Edison's improvements, including the carbon transmitter and the unified mouthpiece-earpiece arrangement, so that Bell profited enormously too.

---

*Kerosene illumination had become the first commercial consequence of the discovery of petroleum deposits beneath the hills of northwestern Pennsylvania in 1859. During the time of Edison's telephone experiments, the petroleum industry was already in the process of being organized and monopolized by John D. Rockefeller of Cleveland, about whom more later.

Edison was still only twenty-nine when he patented his telephone improvements, but since the improvements were made in the service of Western Union he had yet to become widely known to the American public. His next invention changed all that; indeed, in 1877 it turned Edison into a household name. During the time he had been conducting his telephone experiments, as he was later to explain, something occurred that sent him on an entirely different tack. "I was singing into the mouth-piece of a telephone when the vibrations of my voice sent the fine steel point into my finger." That generated an idea. If he could record the actions of the electrified point on an appropriate surface, then run the point over the same surface afterward, "I saw no reason why the thing would not talk." Edison tried it first on a strip of telegraph paper. "I shouted the words: 'Halloo! Halloo!' into the mouth-piece, ran the paper over the steel point, and heard a faint 'Halloo! Halloo!' in return."*

The results excited Edison. Until that point in his career he had never actually invented anything totally original; everything he had accomplished had been but an improvement on someone else's creation. Now he saw the path to his desired destiny: the creation of a "talking machine," an electrical device that would record the human voice and other sounds—symphony orchestras, for instance—and play them back.

After further experiments with various designs, models and recording surfaces for the machine he envisaged, Edison was ready to put his idea to the test. He had settled on a crank-driven, grooved metal cylinder wrapped tightly with tinfoil as his "recording" device. To put his voice into the grooves of the cylinder, he devised a carbon diaphragm that vibrated beneath a metal needle, just as with the telephone, and a telephonelike mouthpiece, or microphone. Even his Menlo Park laboratory assistants who helped him put the concoction together were dubious. As one, John Kruesi, later said, "We thought Mr. Edison had taken leave of his senses. We were sure he was in for a great disappointment with this thing."

But no. After discovering how to glue the ends of the tinfoil so

---

*Among his other contributions to the telephone, Edison was responsible for the way we answer the phone today. Originally, people wound the telephone by cranking it, which rang a bell at the receiving end of the wire. The caller would then shout, "Are you there?" This took too much time for Edison. One day, during one of the countless tests he conducted at Menlo Park, he cranked a phone and called, "Halloo?"

as to hold it taut against the cylinder, Edison started cranking. As he did, he began to recite: "Mary had a little lamb,/ Its fleece was white as snow. . . ." When he finished the rhyme, he cranked the roller back to its starting point, put a second diaphragm into position, and commenced to crank again. Faint and distant, but distinctly in Edison's voice, the laboratory assistants who had gathered round heard: "Mary had a little lamb,/ Its fleece was white as snow. . . ."

John Kruesi later described the moment: sixteen men struck dumb with awe. "I almost keeled over in a faint." Edison invited the disbelieving Kruesi to say something into the machine. He did, in German. Edison replayed it, and Kruesi heard the strange sound of a voice—his voice—speaking the same German words.

A few days later, Edison tucked his machine under his arm, caught a train for New York and barged into the office of Alfred Beach, the editor of the journal *Scientific American*. "Well, Mr. Edison, what's this?" Beach inquired when the inventor set the device on his desk. He had to shout into Edison's ear to ensure being heard.

"Turn the crank and you'll see," Edison replied with a cat's grin.

Beach, suspicious, got the crank going. "Good morning, Mr. Beach," the machine said in Edison's voice. "What do you think of my phonograph?"

The astonished Beach quickly spread the word of Edison's invention, and the next day the New York newspapers were filled with stories about the fabulous "talking machine." In the weeks thereafter, thousands of people descended on Menlo Park to hear it, and the Pennsylvania Railroad had to run dozens of special excursion trains to handle the crowds. Edison was a national hero at the age of thirty. A few weeks later he was invited to the White House to demonstrate his phonograph for President Rutherford B. Hayes. Even the President of the United States expressed his delighted astonishment—in those days an endorsement that carried with it the force, almost, of divine blessing.

The phonograph—the result of the accidental pricking of a finger—was in the nature of an electrotelegraphic device. Therefore, under Edison's agreement with Western Union, the rights belonged to the telegraph company. Although Edison continued to improve it after he received his patent in February 1878, he soon lost interest in it, for suddenly he was confronted by a much greater challenge. The challenge was posed to him by Grosvenor Lowrey.

The idea of electric lighting went back as far as Newton's time in seventeenth-century England, when the first crude laboratory experiments were conducted with the mysterious invisible "fluid" from which a spark could be produced. It was not until the early nineteenth century, however, when such British scientists as Humphrey Davy, Michael Faraday and, later, Clerk Maxwell discovered the principles of electromagnetism, that the idea began to acquire realistic potential. As a result of their discoveries, the arc lamp had first been developed in Europe. The arc lamp operated on a simple principle: Electric current was sent along carbonized rods, which were placed with their tips almost touching. At the tips the current jumped, or arced, the gap, creating a spark that caused the tips of the rods to glow.

The main problem with arc lighting in its early stages was that because it was powered by a kind of static electromagnetic induction—the same weak current that operated the telegraph—its light was feeble and inconsistent. The invention in 1871, by the French engineer Zénobe Gramme, of the mechanical electromagnetic dynamo, driven by a steam engine, improved the arc lamp considerably by feeding it a powerful current in a direct, continuous flow. But then a contrary problem arose: The light was too bright and harsh, and was useful only in illuminating large areas. Too, it burned with such intensity that it tended to melt the rods.

The invention of the dynamo and the problems associated with the various forms of arc lamp had launched inventors and engineers throughout the industrialized world on a search for a better method of electrical illumination by the early 1870s. Edison was no less interested than others in the problem. He had even announced to William Orton and Grosvenor Lowrey his solution: the "division" of the electric current that he imagined dynamos were able to generate. But his mind and energies had been so diverted by his telephone, phonograph and other experiments that he had not had time to pursue the matter.

William Orton, the president of Western Union, died in April 1878, leaving Lowrey as Edison's only close official connection to the telegraph company. Edison's 1877 contract tied the inventor to the company through Orton, but it stipulated that Lowrey was to be Edison's attorney on all matters pertaining to his invention, not just matters in which Western Union had an interest. Consequently, Lowrey wrote to Edison in May 1878 to remind him of the efforts that were being expended in other research quarters to invent a more practical alternative to arc lighting. Lowrey told Edison that as far as he, Lowrey, was concerned, Western Union would make no claim to such an invention if Edison managed to produce it—in other words, that Edison would be free to profit solely from it. When Edison responded by saying that his present facilities at Menlo Park were too scant to support the proper research required, and that the equipment he needed would be too costly, Lowrey was undiscouraged. Western Union wouldn't pay to enlarge Edison's laboratory for the purpose of a prospective invention to which it would have no claim, but Lowrey, along with some of his friends in Wall Street, would.

Lowrey's prodding of Edison was surely motivated by his own desire to profit from the thirty-one-year-old inventor's genius, but it was not limited to that. During the 1870s, Lowrey had developed an intense and expansive interest in science and its application to industry, much of it the result of having followed Edison's work on the telegraph, the telephone and the phonograph.*
Moreover, he had come to like Edison enormously and wanted to help free him from the tethers of his Western Union obligation, which he believed had begun to constrain and inhibit Edison's inventive drives.

At first Edison resisted Lowrey's encouragement, claiming that the research venture the lawyer proposed was too risky for the large private capital outlays it required. But Lowrey persisted, writing Edison: "I think we can get money enough not only to set you up forever, but to enable you at once, if you so desire, to build and finally endow a working laboratory such as the world needs and has never seen." Edison finally agreed, but when he suggested a financially modest beginning to his research into the new electrical lighting project, Lowrey again insisted that no ex-

---

*Lowrey was among the leading industrial lawyers of his time in the 1870s and 1880s. In addition to pushing Edison, he promoted the work of dozens of other inventors and was closely involved in the technological development of the aluminum industry in America. He genuinely loved the art and science of invention; one of his law partners later described him as a "frustrated scientist, a man who, if he had had his life to live over, would have pursued a scientific rather than a legal career."

pense be spared. He would provide Edison with the money to build a large new laboratory at Menlo Park, made of brick and equipped with the latest in machinery, tools and other equipment. Furthermore, Edison "must have an engine and boiler capable of producing power for all emergencies." What Lowrey was proposing was not so much a traditional experimental laboratory as a new research-and-invention factory.

In order to raise the necessary money for the venture, Lowrey put together a syndicate of New York friends and business associates that included principals in the merchant banking firm of J. Pierpont Morgan, members of the board of directors of Western Union, and partners of his own law firm. As one of the partners later said:

> The problem of lighting by electricity was far from being solved. Mr. Lowrey's contribution came first from the fervent belief that it *could* be solved and that Edison himself could solve it, a belief that perhaps was more staunchly held by Mr. Lowrey than by Edison himself at the start of the enterprise. His second and probably more important contribution came from his ability to understand the scientific principles involved, and to explain them to his friends, thereby persuading them to invest large sums of money to underwrite Edison.

The syndicate was formed in the summer of 1878 with an initial investment of $50,000. In October, Lowrey raised an additional $300,000 by putting together and incorporating the Edison Electric Light Company. In the meantime Edison launched his research, putting aside all his other interests except for the supervision of the construction of his new factory-lab at Menlo Park. Edison proceeded from the theory of the arc lamp—a continuous spark leaping across the narrow open space between two magnoelectrified carbon rods. Rather than a sputtering, blinding spark, he realized that he would have to produce a steady, modulated glow between the two rods. To accomplish this, he would need not a gap between the rods but a connector that would glow brightly without burning up—a *filament* of some kind.

One of the early discoveries of science was that the oxygen in the atmosphere causes things to burn more intensely and quickly.

Thus, the electric light Edison sought to create would require a vacuum. His first task, then, was to perfect a container for his experimental rods and filaments from which all the air could be pumped. Naturally, for an electric light inside the container to be able to spread illumination, it would have to be made of clear glass. Edison hired Ludwig Boehm, a glass-blower, and with his help rapidly perfected a vacuum container, or bulb. Thereafter, Boehm was assigned his own shop at Menlo Park in which he was kept busy making bulbs for Edison's experiments, while another assistant manned an air pump that Edison had devised to "vacuumize" the bulbs.

The problem of finding the right material for a cheap and dependable filament proved more nettlesome. It took Edison nearly a year, experimenting with every known substance, many of them rare and expensive metals, to find the right one—a simple strand of cotton thread twisted into a helical shape, then coated and stiffened with carbon. On the night of October 21, 1879, Edison and his assistants sealed a carbonized thread into one of Boehm's pear-shaped bulbs and pumped out the air. Edison turned on the current. Rather than flicker, as previous bulbs with other filaments had done, this one "glowed like the setting sun in the dusk of early autumn," as one of Edison's assistants later described it. Each man present stared at the bulb breathlessly, waiting for the filament to burn out. But it continued to glow with an even light.

And continued to glow. Edison and assistants sat down to wait. They waited through the night and into the next day. They waited through the following night and early into the night after that before the filament died and the light went out. It had burned steadily for forty-five hours. Edison had succeeded in being the first to devise a practical electric light; he had invented the incandescent light bulb.

History has shown that any significant new invention, discovery or innovation is only part of the story of the progress to which it has contributed. Another vital chapter emerges from the manner and extent of its development, adoption and deployment—in short, its exploitation. And still another stems from the subsidiary technologies, industries and services it gives birth to. The full story relates not just to the original invention itself, but to the evolution of the entire system that springs from it. Often the development of the system is more fraught with uncertainty and trial-and-error than the conceptual and experimental process that produced the invention. Thus the history of America's material progress is also the history of how inventions were put to use, of their "systemic" effect on the nation as a whole. An invention, though revolutionary, can be useless unless a way is found to utilize it most beneficially.

We have seen how the cotton gin, the steam engine, the power loom, the reaper, the telegraph and other such pre–Civil War inventions created a host of new technological and industrial systems required to support and capitalize on them. These new systems in turn launched a variety of interlinked subsystems, all of which stitched themselves into the social and economic fabric of American society. But these systems and subsystems had evolved and intermeshed almost spontaneously; there was little conscious, concerted, systematic human guidance applied to the process. The Civil War and the spread of the railroad network imposed a certain degree of deliberate organizational direction on the development of the overall American economic-industrial complex, but it was not until the 1870s that the need was clearly seen for the application of a strong collective hand in the future shaping of that complex. More than anything else, Edison's light bulb—and, to a lesser extent, Bell's telephone—gave utmost urgency to the need. For between them they would spawn an infinitely more complicated variety of new economic and industrial systems than all of America's previous inventions together had done.

The initial problem of the telephone lay in the question of how it was to be put to use. There was no doubting its potential benefits: The fact that a device now existed by which people could communicate over long distances by voice was a remarkable advance, its implications equally remarkable. But first a way had to be found to make it not only practicable but affordable. The country's telegraph system operated over a network of intra- and intercity wires. No one had a telegraph in his home, and only a few businesses, such as newspapers and railroads, maintained telegraphic systems in their offices. Most people who wanted to use the system had to go to central telegraph offices, print out their messages as cryptically as possible, and hand them to an operator for transmission. Although telegraphic service had itself broadened and improved considerably since the end of the Civil War, there was often a long wait before a message could be sent, an even longer one before a response came back.*

At first Alexander Graham Bell and his associates in the newly formed Bell Telephone Company intended to pattern their phone system after the nation's telegraph network—that is, central urban telephone offices linked by wire to similar offices or stations within the same cities and in other cities. And so it *was* established, remaining the principal method of telephone communication during the first ten years after Bell's invention of the instrument. Bell himself established the first intercity telephone line between Boston and Salem, Massachusetts, in 1877, while his chief rival, Elisha Gray, strung a similar wire between Chicago and Milwaukee.

By 1880 nearly 150 small local and regional telephone companies had been formed throughout the country, most of them serving limited areas and all of them licensed by the Bell company and using its equipment. Later in the decade, as an increasing number of urban homes and businesses began to enjoy the benefits of electric lighting, demand rose for a decentralized telephone system that would enable phones to be installed for more convenient use in commercial offices and personal residences. Although the demand promised an enormous increase in revenues and profits, the telephone industry was technologically obstructed from responding to it. What stood in the way was the problem of "switching."

All telephone calls had to be switched or relayed by a central "operator." When there was only a modest number of users of a particular line at one time, as was the case with the centralized interconnected telephone-office systems, the process was easy— one operator could switch four or five calls simultaneously. But with a large number of decentralized users, many separate switching, exchanging and relaying operations would be required at various locations to complete just one call. The number of operators needed for switching would far outnumber the people making calls at any given time. As one telephone financier told a New York newspaper in 1887, "The possibility of a private home tele-

---

*After several failed attempts, an undersea cable had been laid and put into operation in 1866, linking the United States telegraphically to England and Europe. Also, Edison's quadruplex telegraph, and others like it, had been adopted by the telegraph companies, thus speeding up the service.

phone system throughout the country is out of the question. . . . Almost the entire working population of the United States would be needed to switch cable. Not even Tom Edison has been able to solve the problem."

Edison was not working on it. Nor was anyone else, the assumption being that the telephone system was destined to develop merely as a more convenient adjunct of the nation's telegraph network. At best, only the wealthiest individuals and businesses would be able to afford their own telephones. But then, as had so often happened in the past to produce an improvement in a basic invention, an essentially unrelated event occurred in the town of Mansfield, Ohio, that would lead to a radical change in the utility and potential of the telephone. The event was the marriage of an undertaker.

Mansfield had two undertakers when it first acquired telephone service in the 1890s. One was a man named Strowger, the other named Metz. After a time, Metz married a widow who had been operating the town's only telephone exchange out of her home. Naturally, the new Mrs. Metz moved the exchange from her residence into Mr. Metz's, which also served as his funeral parlor. Thereafter, whenever the townspeople wanted to make a phone call, they had to go to the Metz Funeral Home. There, while they waited for their calls to be put through by Mrs. Metz, Mr. Metz was able to solicit their future burial business. As a result, Strowger found his funeral business falling off. Strowger, however, had once been a telegrapher and knew something about electricity. After months of determined toil, he thought up and created a crude system for the automatic switching of telephone calls. He went to the local phone company officials, demonstrated it, and persuaded them to hook their lines to it at his funeral home, where customers would not have to wait to have their calls switched.

Strowger's device, the world's first automatic telephone switching exchange, turned him into a wealthy man and enabled him to stop worrying about competition from crosstown morticians. But what was of infinitely more importance was the fact that it touched off the true telephone revolution. After it was perfected by the Bell company, Strowger's idea eventually made the telephone available to every private home and office at moderate cost, generated the development of one of the world's most co-lossal and complex industrial and technological systems, and—directly and indirectly—transformed the entire way of life of much of mankind. Viewed at first as a kind of toy, the telephone proved to be a very serious and far-reaching instrument indeed—far-reaching in more ways than one.

Edison's incandescent light bulb was confronted by the same problem as the telephone at the outset: How could it be practically and commercially utilized, made a part of every home and office? For it to work, it needed a source of electrical current much greater than that of the telephone. Where was the power to come from? Would everyone who wanted to install an electric lighting system in his home or office or factory be required to purchase an individual power plant by which to generate the current for it—a steam boiler, engine, dynamo? Or could the current be supplied from a central source?

Edison resolved these questions, at least in part, well before he produced his first successful incandescent bulb at Menlo Park. The introduction of the principle of the electromagnetic dynamo in 1871 provided the basic answer. The dynamo had been developed primarily in connection with research in Europe devoted to improving arc lighting. By 1876 and the Philadelphia Centennial Exposition, the improvements in arc lighting, along with the large steam-driven dynamos used to power it, had traveled to America; in fact, the exposition grounds themselves were illuminated at night by arc lamps. Another exposition, this one in Paris early in 1878, had displayed even greater advances in the system.

It was the Paris Exposition, which Lowrey visited while abroad on Western Union business, that had prompted him to urge Edison to drop all his other work and concentrate on incandescent lighting. Although arc lighting had proved at least marginally useful in the electrical illumination of large outdoor areas, Lowrey had heard engineers and scientists at Paris agree that it would never be perfected for indoor use, and that the only alternative was incandescence. All that remained to be done was for someone to invent it. Among the other ideas Lowrey brought back to Edison from Paris was the concept of using huge, centrally located dynamos, or electrical generators, to supply a given geographical area with the constant current needed to light thousands of incandescent bulbs. Edison agreed with the idea, and thus the question of how to turn the incandescent bulb, once Edison had perfected it, into a usable wide-scale lighting system was settled.

But the conceptual technical factor was only one of two essential components of the question. The other was its physical aspect. Having decided that it was technically feasible to radiate current from a central source through a network of transmission cables to hundreds if not thousands of distant terminals, Edison and Lowrey had not yet determined if it was physically, geographically, or even legally, possible. Such a system would require the use of public and private property, the crossing of property lines, the infringement of property rights—every violation imaginable of the traditional American standards of property ownership. Never before had a system been created that gave one man or one organization the right to trespass at will upon the real estate of others. The telegraph companies and railroads either owned or leased their rights-of-way, and where they didn't own or lease, they possessed long-term contractual easements. There were no precedents for the laying out of an electrical power grid, though. If Edison were to be required to negotiate contracts for every foot of land his transmission wires had to cross to reach their destinations, there would be no end to the legal morass it would create. And even if it were legally practicable, there was probably not enough capital in the entire United States to finance such a venture.

Another way of making electric light available on a large and profitable scale would have to be found, both for the benefit of the Edison interests and for the benefit of the populace at large, which—after Edison's success with the incandescent bulb was broadcast late in 1879 and its advantages explained—raised a loud clamor for it.

CHAPTER **16**

THE ELECTRIC DECADE

For most of us, the major political occurrences of America's past define the nation's history. That is the way history is taught; it is the way our history is learned. From the Declaration of Independence to Watergate, political events have always dominated our perception of ourselves as a nation. Yet what is often more instructive and enlightening is the discovery of the subtexts of our political history, the underlying social and economic currents that conjoin to produce an important political event.

It is one thing, for instance, to view a political action such as the Declaration of Independence in isolation. Such a view tends to an interpretation based solely on its literal textual content, which can lead to naïve, even dangerous, conclusions. It is another thing to view the Declaration in its contextual and subtextual lights, as an action motivated not just by high-minded political philosophy but by the social and economic pressures on its time, place and participants. From that perspective we learn that the lofty idealism of the Declaration was shaped and tempered to a considerable extent by more mundane aspirations: by the need and desire of its authors, and those they represented, to improve their material, economic and social status. Once that is understood, we can comprehend the political actions of 1776 more realistically, and thereby the country's subsequent social and economic history.

But then there is the other side of the historical coin: the *political* subtext of important events in the country's past that were, in themselves, basically nonpolitical. The introduction of

Thomas Edison's revolutionary electrical system was hardly a political event at the time. Yet without the interplay of politics, the system might not have been introduced at all.

On a cold late afternoon in December of 1880, the members of New York City's Board of Aldermen—the political body that administered the city's affairs—ferried across the Hudson River to the Jersey City terminal of the Pennsylvania Railroad to board a special chartered train bound for Menlo Park. Their journey had been arranged by Grosvenor Lowrey, who, along with Edison, had devised a plan by which Edison's incandescent lighting could be put to practical and profitable use. The plan was to build a central power-generating station from which a gridwork of underground wire conduits would radiate for a distance of a quarter-mile in every direction, with the buildings along the route of each conduit wired into it. New York was the natural site for the implantation of such a system; densely populated and constructed, it stood to benefit the most. There remained only the question of how the system could be installed without creating a maze of legal problems for the Edison Electric Light Company.

Edison had already solved most of the technical and engineering problems of the proposed system. After perfecting the filament bulb, he spent most of 1880 devising the many additional electrical components needed to make an integrated, geographically widespread lighting network function. He and his assistants designed and built an improved electromagnetic dynamo at Menlo Park which was to be the model for his later commercial power-plant generators. Called the "Long-Legged Mary Ann" because of its tall twin vertical posts, its unique design made it markedly more efficient than any dynamo theretofore produced for arc lighting and electroplating. But the dynamo was just the beginning. Edison also invented junction boxes, meters, relays, fuses, blocks, even bulbs, lamps and lamp switches—everything required to enable the process to function. By the late fall of 1880 he had installed a test system at Menlo Park, lighting up the interior of all its buildings and lacing its outdoor paths with pole-supported lamps.

It was to view this display at first hand that the New York City politicians set out for Menlo Park that December. Lowrey and Edison hoped that once the aldermen experienced it, they would readily accede to the plan Lowrey had devised to avoid the legal and real-estate complications of installing the world's first commercial incandescent lighting system. His plan was, simply, to ask the City of New York for a franchise to allow the Edison company to run its conductor cables beneath the streets of the city at no cost. To achieve such an underground network, radiating from the centrally located power station Edison was already in the process of designing, would mean tearing up many of the city's streets. But, Lowrey was prepared to argue, the ultimate benefits for the city would far outweigh the temporary inconvenience. As the first incandescently lighted municipality in the world, the city's economy would benefit immeasurably from the hordes of tourists who would stream in to see the system function. Not only that, but it would profit as well from the inestimable number of new businesses that would establish themselves in New York in order to take advantage of electric lighting.

A private railroad car awaited the aldermen in Jersey City, along with Lowrey and several other board members of the Edison company. Lowrey offered the Tammany politicians cigars and whiskey as the train set forth. During the hour's ride the Edison board members, staunch Wall Street Republicans all, went out of their way to be agreeable to their usually unsavory Democratic guests. By the time the train reached Menlo Park, darkness had descended. The ward heelers, brought into Edison's dim, kerosene-lit office, were introduced to the inventor. He invited them on a tour of his main laboratory, which also had been purposefully left dark. The politicians began to complain as they stumbled over equipment and cables: Where was this famous indoor lighting? Edison, guiding them by the faint glow of an oil lamp, signaled to one of his assistants. The assistant threw a switch. Suddenly the laboratory was bathed in a bright, even light. As the assistant, Francis Jehl, later recalled, "They were stunned at first, never having seen such electric light, and then immensely pleased. . . . Mr. Edison took them to a window. They looked through and saw the area all around lighted up. They were astounded once again."

There followed a formal catered dinner for the officials from New York. Lowrey, sitting at the head of the table with Edison, rose and presented his plan, making the point that the first section of the city to be electrified would be the downtown area around Wall Street and City Hall, where the assembled politicians conducted their business.* Soon after their Menlo Park visit, the Board of Aldermen passed an ordinance giving the Edison company the right to install the pioneering system in the city. As a local newspaper wryly remarked, "For the first time in at least forty years the politicians of this city have given away something for nothing. Could it possibly be a trend?" New York's largely Irish ruling political machine, shaped and dominated for years by the recently deceased William "Boss" Tweed, was notorious for its venality and corruption.

Work on the system began early in 1881. Edison chose a building on New York's Pearl Street, near the East River wharves, to house his generators. Since he planned to start with six giant dynamos, each weighing twenty-seven tons, the building had to be specially reinforced to support them. Nearby he established a workshop in which to construct the generators and all the other components of the system. Ditches were dug in the cobblestone streets of the square-mile district surrounding the Pearl Street "powerhouse" (that new word having been added to the lexicon by Edison) and 80,000 feet of underground conduit laid—main transmission and feeder cables enclosed in iron piping; junctions, relays and crossover points in iron boxes. Since it was the first such integrated system ever installed, Edison had to design and test each component himself.

Finally, at the beginning of September 1882, everything was in place. At three in the afternoon of September 4—a steamy late-summer afternoon turned dark by an approaching thunderstorm—Edison stood in the kerosene-illuminated office of Drexel, Morgan and Company, the Wall Street banking firm that had assisted Grosvenor Lowrey in the financing of Edison's system and the various subsidiary companies formed to support it. The inventor yanked a ceremonial switch connected by wire to the Pearl Street powerhouse. The six huge dynamos started up, and a few moments later the electric lamps that had been strategically placed about the Drexel, Morgan rooms began to glow with a collective light that rendered the kerosene lanterns instantly obsolete. Bulbs

*New York's City Hall, which had been built in the early 1800s near what was then the northern boundary of the city proper, was just a few blocks from Wall Street. By 1880 the city had spread well northward along Manhattan Island; its mixed residential-commercial settlement stretched as far north as today's Fifty-seventh Street, and the region above that, though more sparsely settled, was rapidly beginning to take on its present-day urban form.

in scores of other offices and shops that had been tied into the system blinked on as well. According to the next day's New York *Evening Post:* "A pedestrian standing in lower Wall Street heard a muffled cheer emanate from the innards of the surrounding buildings." Another paper reported that a few minutes later several bolts of lightning from the approaching storm were seen to strike the New Jersey shore of the North River: ". . . a strange punctuation to the beginning of the age of man-made electricity," the writer noted.

Edison's light bulb and Bell's telephone not only inaugurated a new era of material progress, comfort and convenience, they also stretched and reformulated the boundaries of capitalism. Out of these two seminal inventions grew a whole new order of finance, industrialism and technology that was to change the very essence of life in the world. No area of life was untouched by the arrival and spread of electric power and telephonic communication. During the decades following Pearl Street's modest beginnings, electricity found its way into factories, offices, shops and homes throughout the nation. While the new form of power was adopted in communities everywhere, in no place was its impact more profound than in cities, first in those of the United States, then in the rest of the world. Edison's insight in locating his pioneer system in the heart of America's most densely populated urban area was borne out in subsequent years as the working and living patterns of cities changed, transportation was transformed, and the very look and shape of urban environments were altered under the influence of electricity. Electric motors allowed factories and workshops to be organized more efficiently and to become at once more varied and productive in their output. Applied to elevators, electricity allowed building construction to reach unthinkable heights. The electric streetcar and subway, the electromotive principles of which Edison also established, gave urban travelers welcome relief from street congestion and filth, and at the same time encouraged the rapid lateral expansion of cities. Electrical appliances for a multitude of different tasks lightened work in home, office and factory alike.

But that was just the beginning. Edison's further research into electricity provided the foundation of modern electronics, particularly radio and television, as did the further refinement of the telephone.* Just as vital was the explosion of independent scientific-industrial research and invention which the telephone and electric light triggered in the mid-1880s. Until then, the pursuit of progress had been a barely organized affair, with inventions and innovations coming at a relative snail's pace and mostly by accident. Edison, not only by the breadth and variety of his scientific interests but also by his industrial entrepreneurship, completed the transformation of the invention process and conducted the final ceremony in the wedding of science, technology and business. Thereafter, science would emerge fully from the university laboratory to become an integral component of the industrial process. Whereas, in the time of Bacon and Newton, industry was viewed as the stepchild and beneficiary of science, in the America of the 1880s the relation was reversed. Huge corporations quickly grew out of Bell's and Edison's inventions, other giant rival organizations followed in their wake, and thousands of smaller auxiliary companies arose to support or challenge them. Success on the increasingly fierce battlefield of business competition depended no longer solely on the financial sleight-of-hand and entrepreneurial skills of the Wall Street monopolists, but also on industry's scientific daring and capability. Among the first to recognize this was Edison himself. Ironically, his insistence on it led to his abrupt withdrawal from the basic industries that were born out of his inventions.

Edison had developed his electric lighting system with the full intention of controlling it in all its aspects, including its management and expansion nationwide, even worldwide. His purpose was to be not just the country's leading inventor but its most influential industrialist as well. A man of high moral principle, he had grown disgusted with the skullduggery of many of the Wall Street tycoons to whom he had been exposed—men who, in his thirty-five-year-old view, were interested less in contributing to the betterment of mankind than in fattening their own pockets.

*While experimenting to improve his incandescent light, Edison observed that electricity in the form of electrons flowed across the space between the bulb's hot filament and a cold, or unelectrified, plate at the bulb's base. He called his discovery the Edison Effect and in 1883 obtained a patent for it, but did not pursue it. However, the Edison Effect later became the basis for the development of the electron, or vacuum, tube. Because the vacuum tube functioned as an amplifier, it made possible the development of the radio and other forms of nonelectric or wireless transmission after the existence of radio waves in the atmosphere was discovered by the German scientist Heinrich Hertz in 1887.

"The one thing that is more important than any other," Edison said a few weeks before his first lighting system went into operation in New York, "is that a goodly portion of the profits which we realize from our business be directed to the expansion of our laboratories, so that we can continue to discover better products and processes for the improvement of life. Simply because we have accomplished this one improvement, we must not limit ourselves to being satisfied with it."

Edison's goal was to use the Edison Electric Light Company, which had established corporate offices on New York's lower Fifth Avenue, as the soil and seed for a virtual garden of new inventions, electrical and otherwise. To accomplish this, he realized, he would have to control the direction of the company with a firm hand. His first aim was to establish a family of subsidiary Edison companies devoted to manufacturing the components of his lighting system and installing them in cities across the country. Immediately he encountered difficulties. The Edison company had been managed since its inception in 1878 by Grosvenor Lowrey and a staff of administrators handpicked by him, while Edison labored during those years at Menlo Park. And then there was the company's board of directors, manned by Lowrey and many of his Wall Street friends who had put up the initial money to back Edison. Most of them had different ideas about how the Edison lighting system should be handled commercially. Since all the patents in the system were the property of the company, it was their desire to license the system to various other groups around the country and around the world. They were Wall Streeters, after all, and as such were content to see the Edison company serve solely as a bank for the fortune in fees and royalties they expected it to earn.

When they announced their intention to Edison in 1882, he disagreed vigorously. "[I] had run squarely up against a great difficulty," he later wrote in a personal account of the events.

> My agreement with the capitalists who had furnished the money for the experimental work did not provide for the furnishing of money to manufacture the lamps, dynamos and other essential parts for carrying the invention into effect. When I asked them to furnish capital for manufacturing shops, they were sorry (Wall

Street sorry), but "could not see their way clear" as this was an untried business, etc.

As the company held my patents, I was "up against it" for the time being, but not for long. I had unbounded faith in the future of the business and fortunately my personal credit was good. So I pawned my future and, with a little assistance from two or three of my associates, organized and established the necessary shops to manufacture the essential devices that would enable us to go ahead with the business.*

But Edison did more than that. By employing a Wall Street tactic he otherwise had little use for—the proxy fight—he managed in 1884 to gain control of the Edison Electric Light Company, in the process provoking a temporary falling-out with Grosvenor Lowrey, who had been forced for business reasons to side with Edison's adversaries on the board.

Edison's victory was a hollow one, however. While his determination to manufacture all the equipment for his electrical systems made some of his associates rich, it did not do quite the same for him. Immediately after gaining control of the parent company, he was forced to start prosecuting scores of patent infringement suits against other companies around the country that had gone into the electrical lighting business with innovations of their own. A few years later, fatigued by the litigation and unable to establish an expanded research laboratory for further invention, he sold his interests in the Edison electrical companies to a consortium of Wall Streeters headed by Henry Villard, a German immigrant and railroad financier who had recently completed the building of the Northern Pacific Railroad. Because the sale included Edison's Menlo Park laboratory, he used the proceeds to build a new and much larger research facility for himself at West Orange, New Jersey, where he also settled with his family. As Edison wrote in a letter to Villard in February 1890, he was retiring "from the lighting business, which will enable me to enter fresh and more congenial fields of work."

Edison's preoccupation with the business and legal affairs of the Edison Electric Light Company between 1883 and 1887 had

*Thomas Alva Edison, *The Beginning of the Incandescent Lamp and Lighting System: An Autobiographical Account* (Dearborn, Michigan: The Edison Institute, 1976), pp. 29–30.

diverted his attention from other developments being made at the time. The arc-lighting industry, pioneered in the United States by Charles F. Brush of Cleveland in 1878, struggled to prevent its submersion by Edison's new incandescent lighting system. Arc lighting could not compete, but in its efforts to do so it produced several electrical innovators who engineered significant improvements in the generation of electrical power. Among the most notable was Elihu Thomson, a Philadelphia inventor and high-school science teacher who discovered the principle of alternating current while experimenting to improve the Brush generator.*

Until then, all dynamos, Edison's included, were thought to operate on direct current (DC)—that is, they were believed to create a constant voltage and therefore generate a steady flow of electricity. Thomson learned that they in fact produced an alternating current (AC), one that traveled to and fro rather than constantly in a single direction. The one serious limitation of Edison's DC lighting system was the fact that the electricity created by his dynamos could not be sent over very long distances; each urban district he electrified required its own separate powerhouse. As Thomson was later to prove, alternating current had a quality that enabled it to travel over much longer distances and with much more efficiency than direct current.

Thomson worked with a partner, Edwin Houston, to develop an AC dynamo for arc lighting. In 1880 they joined the American Electric Company of New Britain, Connecticut, to manufacture the dynamo and the other electrical components, such as transformers, necessary to conduct alternating current. In 1883 the company was reorganized and renamed the Thomson-Houston Electric Company, after which it moved to Lynn, Massachusetts, in an effort to introduce AC arc lighting into the surrounding region's textile factories.

In the meantime, Charles Brush had formed his own electric arc-lighting company in Cleveland. After Edison first demonstrated his electrically powered railway car at Menlo Park in 1880, Brush created a second company—the Bentley-Knight Electric Railway Company—to exploit the potential of the electric street

*Brush, a University of Michigan graduate, had built an improved dynamo for arc lighting in 1876. By 1878 he had developed an indoor arc-lighting system which, when installed in the Wanamaker department store in Philadelphia, gained the system some favorable comment. Nevertheless, arc lighting remained visually disagreeable, as well as harder to sell once Edison's filament system was introduced.

trolley using his own DC dynamos, motors and other equipment. Concurrently, a former United States Naval Academy midshipman named Frank Sprague developed a DC dynamo and traction motor of his own. Thereafter he formed the Sprague Electric Railway and Motor Company in New York to promote the development of the electric street trolley and a revolutionary new idea—the underground railway, or subway.*

Foremost among the electrical innovators of the 1880s, though, and the man who was to become Edison's chief rival in the business of marketing urban lighting and power systems, was George Westinghouse. Born a year earlier than Edison in upper New York State, Westinghouse was already a well-known inventor when Edison began experiments on his filament bulb in 1878. His first major invention, in 1869, had been the compressed-air brake, which, together with his development of an electrotelegraphic automatic signal system a few years later, was contributing significantly to faster and safer rail transport. By 1882, Westinghouse was responsible for a number of other important industrial inventions and had formed several companies to manufacture and market them. One was the Union Switch and Signal Company, which specialized in the manufacture of his railroad signal equipment. In conjunction with that business, he began to search for a better, more efficient source of power for his signal system. His quest brought him, among other places, to Wall Street, where he learned of the difficulties Edison was having with the board of directors of the Edison Electric Light Company over the issue of manufacturing versus licensing. Because Westinghouse had proved himself as adept a businessman as he was an inventor, several financiers urged him to use his expertise in electricity and manufacturing to go into competition with the Edison company.

Westinghouse, as competitive as any personality on Wall Street, agreed. With New York financial backing he formed the Westinghouse Electric and Manufacturing Company in Pitts-

---

*By the early 1880s most major cities in the United States had established systems of horse-drawn streetcars for intercity transit. A few larger ones such as New York had also constructed or were in the process of constructing elevated steam railways—elevated in order to keep some of the noise and soot produced by their operation off the streets. The idea of developing electrified streetcars and electrified underground railways was a compelling one, since it promised not only to speed up travel but to eliminate much of the street filth produced by steam locomotives and horses. The pervasive odor of many city streets was that of horse manure; although squads of street sweepers were employed to battle the problem, they seldom overcame it.

burgh—his longtime base of operations—and in 1884 purchased patents to an unsuccessful incandescent light developed by William Stanley of Massachusetts, and to a DC dynamo developed by J. W. Swan in England. The two acquisitions allowed Westinghouse to announce the manufacture of a lighting system of his own, which Edison immediately challenged in the courts. Although Edison had obtained exclusive rights in many of the component devices of his lighting system, the entire system, including the power source and the means by which the power was conducted to its individual lamp outlets, would not receive a patent until 1887. This meant that anyone could manufacture and sell similar systems so long as they did not use Edison's specifically patented components.

It was not Edison's legal challenge that discouraged Westinghouse, however. It was the fact that the DC generating dynamo both the Edison and Westinghouse systems relied on was insufficient—again, a matter of too many power stations being needed for the electrification of a given area. The way the original Edison system operated, at least eighteen separate powerhouses would be required to serve all of New York City. The same ratio held true for the Westinghouse system. The electrification of Pittsburgh, for instance, would entail the building of five separate stations, each with six or more huge dynamos and their attendant steam engines. Although money was certainly to be made from the manufacture of all the necessary power-generating equipment, profits would be eroded by the manpower required to install, maintain and operate each limited system. The erosion of profits could be stemmed by charging customers higher prices for their electrical service, but such a policy might well discourage demand.

But then, still in 1884, Westinghouse learned about the alternating-current theories of Elihu Thomson, who at the time was trying to develop his own complete AC lighting system for the Thomson-Houston Electric Company in Massachusetts. Although Edison disagreed vehemently—partly because his preoccupation with his legal problems had left him no time to investigate the matter, and partly because he was bent on protecting the integrity of his own direct-current inventions—it was becoming clearer to many members of the electrical engineering fraternity that alternating current was the key to cheaper power. All that remained was for one or more people to invent the necessary components. With Edison having denounced alternating current and having disclaimed any interest in trying to exploit it, Elihu Thomson appeared to be the only one in a strong position to produce the first AC system. If he did so, Westinghouse realized, it would mean the ascendancy of the Thomson-Houston company over both the Westinghouse and Edison companies. Westinghouse sought a truce with Edison in the hope of persuading the inventor that the two should join forces to beat Thomson to the punch. Edison rebuffed him, just as he had rebuffed an earlier visitor to Menlo Park.

The earlier visitor was Nikola Tesla, a young European physicist who had recently immigrated to the United States after discovering, while conducting research in Budapest, the principle of the rotating magnetic field.* theory of the rotating field, as it would turn out, held the secret to the creation of electrical machines capable of generating and using alternating current. Tesla had heard of Edison's skepticism about alternating current and had gone to visit him, first to persuade him of its potential and then to offer his services toward developing an Edison-sponsored AC system. In turning him down, Edison nevertheless testily mentioned that Westinghouse was looking for someone to work on alternating current. So confident was Edison of the impracticability of AC power that he had no qualms about putting Tesla on to his principal rival. It was a mistake in judgment Edison would be unable to bring himself to acknowledge until ten years later.

Tesla sought out Westinghouse. He received an enthusiastic reception and an immediate job as Westinghouse's chief AC researcher. By 1886 he produced the electrical designs needed for the Westinghouse Company to build its first successful AC generating station at Buffalo, New York. In the same year William Stanley, who had sold some of his DC patents to Westinghouse in 1884 and had learned the theory of alternating current from Tesla, developed a commercially practical AC transformer. He used it, along with Tesla's AC generator, to install the world's first AC

---

*By 1885, physics and mathematics, particularly in Europe, were beginning to isolate and define the natural laws and principles according to which electricity worked. As a result, electrical invention would become less the province of unschooled technicians like Edison and more that of formally trained scientists.

lighting system in Great Barrington, Massachusetts—ironically, a stone's throw from Grosvenor Lowrey's birthplace. Suddenly it appeared that the Thomson-Houston company, which still had not perfected Elihu Thomson's AC system, no longer held the advantage. What seemed even more certain was that the Edison Electric Light Company, which with all its manufacturing subsidiaries was committed exclusively to DC power, stood in danger of being totally outdistanced in the race to dominate the commercial lighting field.

The race between Westinghouse and Thomson-Houston drew tighter in 1887, when Elihu Thomson finally perfected his own AC incandescent lighting system. His company began to manufacture and sell it to cities and towns around the country in competition with the Westinghouse-Tesla-Stanley AC system and Edison's DC system. Edison's reputation as the original "wizard" of electricity, and his repeated warnings about what he alleged to be the unreliability and dangerous instability of alternating current, enabled the Edison company to remain marginally competitive with Westinghouse and Thomson-Houston during the mid-1880s. But by 1888 it had become clear that AC was the system of the future, not only for lighting but for all forms of electrical machinery. Both Westinghouse and Thomson-Houston had started to diversify into the manufacture of AC electric motors, welding equipment, railway propulsion and mining drills.

All of this intensifying business competition, coupled with his enervating patent litigation and his chagrin at having been proved wrong about alternating current, motivated Edison to sell his majority interest in his company to the Villard group. By then, most of the Edison manufacturing operations had been consolidated and moved from the New York City-New Jersey area to upstate Schenectady. For Villard and his associates, the first order of the day upon gaining control of the Edison General Electric Company, as they renamed it, was simultaneously to bring the company into the AC age and to diversify its manufacturing operations so as to be able to regain the competitive edge over Westinghouse and Thomson-Houston.

They took their first step in this direction in 1891 by acquiring the Sprague Electric Railway and Motor Company, which had developed the first electric streetcar line in New York City and had contracts to build similar lines in several other cities, as well as to develop elevated and subterranean electric railways. Then, in 1892, they completed their plan by using their considerable Wall Street financial resources to acquire none other than the Thomson-Houston Electric Company itself. This merger not only gave them a flourishing AC electric technology, it also provided them with the means for further diversification. Thomson-Houston, during the mid- and late 1880s, had acquired a number of separate pioneering electrical equipment companies of its own, including the Brush Electric and Bentley-Knight Electric Railway companies of Cleveland, and the Van DePoele Electric Railway Company of Chicago.

The merger was celebrated by renaming the combined companies the General Electric Company. The Edison company contributed to the new conglomerate such major assets as its Schenectady manufacturing complex, the fundamental incandescent lamp patents,* the Edison system of distributing electrical energy, and its growing Sprague-Edison electrical traction business. Thomson-Houston contributed its Lynn, Massachusetts, plant, its patents on arc-welding, electric traction and electric locomotives, and its various AC power and lighting systems.

In the same year, the General Electric Company set out to improve and expand its AC power capabilities by hiring Charles Steinmetz to function as the counterpart of Westinghouse's Tesla. Steinmetz, also an immigrant scientist and electrical engineer, had his own theories on alternating current which would soon allow General Electric to surpass the Westinghouse applications of it. The company further reinforced its technological expertise in this field by acquiring the Stanley Electric Manufacturing Company of Pittsfield, Massachusetts, which had been formed by William Stanley in 1890 after he left the Westinghouse Company. By 1893, General Electric enjoyed more than $20 million in gross sales and employed more than 10,000 people. Westinghouse was almost as big. In a mere ten years, both companies had grown from small invention-and-engineering shops into giant technological and industrial monoliths based largely on the fundamental discoveries of a single man, Thomas Edison.

---

*Thomas Edison's 1880 patent-infringement litigation reached a climax in 1889 when the consolidated suits finally went to trial. Represented by Grosvenor Lowrey, with whom the inventor had reconciled, Edison prevailed, thus providing General Electric with the exclusive rights to the basic filament lighting system. It was this victory in 1891 that helped to foster the merger of the Edison company with Thomson-Houston.

*   *   *

The two companies were symbolic in many ways. First, they reflected the enormous speedup in growth, prosperity and material
progress that had occurred in practically every area of American
life in the decade of the 1880s. Second, they represented the rapid
transition from individual to corporate invention, entrepreneurship and management which was to accelerate progress even
more rapidly in the decades thereafter. Third, they symbolized
the final transformation of America from an agricultural to a technological and industrial society. Fourth, by balancing the principle of mass progress with that of individual and corporate profit,
they became pathfinders and exemplars for the future evolution of
industrial, technological, big-business America.

But beyond all these, the rapid growth of General Electric and
Westinghouse symbolized the lightning journey the American
spirit itself had taken. During the 1870s and 1880s the country
had gone through a frenzy of expansion, invention, construction,
mechanization and discovery, all of it accompanied by the immigration from abroad of nearly 8.5 million people, many of them
unable to speak English, and by the ceaseless shifting of large
parts of the expanding internal population westward and northward. Quite simply, the nation no longer bore any resemblance—
physically, demographically, technologically or psychologically—
to the United States of antebellum times. Although its basic political and religious underpinnings had been retained, the structure
that had spontaneously risen atop that foundation was of a
breadth, diversity and complexity unparalleled in the experience
of man.

Moreover, the orderly organization, consolidation and management of the General Electric and Westinghouse companies in the
early 1890s served in an abstract fashion as an unconscious guide-
line to the reorganization, consolidation and management of
American society. In response to the many radical changes and
expansions it had undergone in the previous twenty years, the
populace of the United States began figuratively to "incorporate"
itself. In fact, that may have been the most significant of all the
consequences of the process started by Edison's invention of the
light bulb. America sensed that electricity and the telephone were
not just the miraculous final links in the chain of material progress
of the previous half-century, but were also the anchor links in a

future chain that stretched far beyond the horizons of imagination. Since progress was now ineluctably identified in the public mind with the country's corporate canvas, American society felt an increasing need to remodel itself in the corporate mold. For if corporateness was what stimulated material and economic progress, so too would it, on a different and more abstract scale, foster social, political and moral progress. The country needed to keep up spiritually with the changes that were occurring materially. Incorporation was perceived as imposing a very definite and favorable control and order on the material realm. Thus, it was intuitively believed, incorporation in the figurative sense would impose the same kind of spiritual control and moral order in the face of all of society's new material stimuli.

The intuition was continually fueled and reinforced in the 1890s by editorialists, lecturers and other advocates of the idea of America as a corporate and business utopia. Even traditionally nonbusiness institutions such as schools, churches and civic groups reorganized themselves in the image of the business corporation. It was at this time, too, that the phrase *corporate America*— meaning not the community of the country's formal corporations but the notion of American society as a single abstract corporate entity (akin to the "body politic")—gained cachet. Most Americans began to think of themselves as integral members of a giant national corporation, each with a specific function to fulfill in the interest of ensuring the profitability and progress of the organic whole, spiritually as well as materially.

This rising corporate consciousness would have many salutary effects on the way the country developed after 1890, to be sure. But it would also have negative consequences. On the one hand it would encourage personal initiative, individuality and daring. On the other it would promote homogeneity, conformity and timidity. The two trends would begin to act like contrary electrical currents, alternately charging and draining the dynamism of American behavior and endeavor.

CHAPTER 17

BRIDGE TO COLOSSUS

In the early 1940s, when I was a youngster just starting out in school, there were elderly men and women still alive who had been born in the 1860s and possessed rich memories of what life in America had been like in the last three decades of the nineteenth century. I recall one such man distinctly. Approximately eighty years old, the grandfather of my second-grade teacher, he appeared in our classroom one day to tell us about his life when he was our age, and to impress us children of the twentieth century with the vastness of the material change that had occurred between the time of his youth and ours.

As a second-grader I probably paid only desultory attention to the oldtimer's lecture, which, as I remember it, was conducted in a question-and-answer fashion with the teacher. Yet a singular image etched itself in my mind then and has remained vivid ever since. The man told us of having worked in his youth on the final stages of the building of the "Great East River Bridge" in New York, which I later learned had taken fourteen years to construct and had been completed in 1883.* The fact that he repeatedly referred to the span as the Great East River Bridge, although at the time he spoke to us it had long been known as the Brooklyn Bridge, was not what imprinted itself so indelibly on my memory; rather, it was his shuffling to the blackboard, drawing a sketch of the bridge, then turning to us and saying, "That's where it all began." What he meant, he went on to explain, was that—more than the railroads, more than the telephone, more than the light bulb, more than electric power, more than anything else—the

*The bridge was started in 1869, the same year the Suez Canal was completed in Egypt, the same year the first transcontinental railroad was completed in the United States.

222

construction of the Brooklyn Bridge was the single most important event behind the change from the America of old (the America into which he had been born) to the then-modern America into
which we seven- and eight-year-olds had been born.

At the teacher's insistence, the old man proudly elaborated.
He wasn't denying the importance of the telephone, the light
bulb, and all the other things that had been discovered or invented
in America in the period during which the bridge was being built.
Nor was he discounting the vital milestones that came later: the
automobile, the radio and the airplane, for instance. What he was
pointing out was that just as the successful completion of the
Brooklyn Bridge served concretely to bind together two cities previously separated by a wide and turbulent river, so too did it serve
figuratively, more than any other contemporary event, to unite
the American people and ignite their belief that nothing was technologically beyond the country's ability to achieve.

Why? Because the bridge had started out in 1869 as a conceptual and structural impossibility. When municipal leaders had
first discussed the desirability of a bridge between New York and
Brooklyn (then a separate city) before the Civil War, they were
limited to thinking solely in terms of a low, railroad-type trestle
span with a short drawbridge in the center to permit boats to pass
through. That notion was quickly put aside, however, when it
was realized that because of the density of traffic on the river, the
drawspan would need to be open almost continuously. What was
required was a high, arching bridge that would allow the river
traffic, even the most tall-masted of schooners, to pass beneath.
But given the one-third-mile distance between the two shores,
such a bridge appeared out of the question—a construction problem beyond anyone's solving.

But then a man named John Augustus Roebling appeared before the New York Board of Aldermen with a plan. Roebling had
emigrated from Germany in 1831. Though trained in Berlin as an
engineer and road builder, he had pursued farming when he first
settled near Pittsburgh. After his farm failed in 1837 he had gotten work on the construction of the Allegheny Portage Railway, a
unique cable rail line that was being built to haul canal and railroad freight over the steepest inclines between Philadelphia and
Pittsburgh, near Altoona. In the course of working on the Portage
Railway, Roebling invented a mechanical process for combining

thin metal wire into thick cable. Thereafter, he applied his cable process to the concept of building suspension bridges—bridges whose spans were attached to and suspended from cables anchored in towering piers. He built his first successful bridge over the narrow Monongahela River at Pittsburgh in 1846, followed it with a suspended double-tier span for rail and road traffic at Niagara Falls between 1851 and 1855, and followed that with a second bridge over the Ohio at Cincinnati.

Roebling's landmarks had already earned him considerable acclaim by the time he presented his preliminary plan for a bridge between New York and Brooklyn in 1857. But although he had proved the safety and efficacy of suspension bridges, the New York project posed an infinitely greater scale of difficulty than any bridge yet constructed. The principal problem was its distance. With his previous bridges, he had been able to build the supporting piers on hard ground. In order to span the width of the East River, however, he would have to construct his support structures on the river bottom itself.

No one but Roebling believed it could be done and for ten years his plans, repeatedly refined, were rejected. But then, in 1867, a group of Wall Street financiers became convinced that such a project, despite the fact that it had never been executed before, was feasible. They thereupon bribed the Tammany bosses into granting them a franchise, organized the New York Bridge Company, and over the next two years raised $5 million in financing through the sale of securities in the company. This meant that everything about the bridge was unprecedented; not only was it to be the largest private construction project ever undertaken in the United States, but its financing constituted the greatest amount of money ever raised at one time for a private venture.*

Since the bridge was to be operated as a toll span, the organizers of the company were able to promise investors generous long-term profits, once the construction costs were recovered. Still, the financial risks were as monumental as the prospective bridge itself promised to be. Despite his optimism, not even Roebling could be absolutely certain the bridge was buildable.

---

*Railroad financing tended to be carried out on a serial basis, with money raised in increments, over the period of several years of a railroad's construction, through new stock issues. Although the Brooklyn Bridge would require more than thrice again its original $5 million before it was completed, its initial financing was nevertheless a record for a single nongovernment enterprise.

Even more enigmatic was the question of whether, if built, the span wouldn't collapse into the East River. The sketches Roebling had drawn of the proposed structure, which according to him would be strong enough to carry the heaviest cargoes imaginable, made it appear very doubtful indeed. His drawings pictured an impossibly long roadway arching high over the river, held up by cables that seemed as fragile as sewing thread compared to the bulk of the bridge's lofty stone caissons.

Roebling barely lived to see the start of construction. While conducting surveys with his son, Washington Roebling, from a dock on the Brooklyn side of the East River in late June of 1869, his foot was crushed when a ferry from Manhattan slammed into some pilings. He was taken to a nearby doctor's office where his toes were amputated, without benefit of an anesthetic. A few weeks later, on July 22, 1869, he died of tetanus infection. It was left to Roebling's son to carry on.

Washington Roebling, then thirty-two, had studied engineering at the Rensselaer Polytechnic Institute and had later been one of the Union heroes at the Battle of Gettysburg. After the war he had gone into his father's bridge-building and cable-winding business. If John Roebling had been the inspiration for the concept and design of the Brooklyn Bridge, Washington Roebling was to become the driving force behind its actual construction.

His first task, when the work began later in 1869, was to realize his father's uncompleted plan for the erection of the huge twin river-based caissons from which the main span and its approaches were to be hung. Combining his engineering knowledge with an equal amount of blind faith, he borrowed a British method by which two gigantic, inverted wooden boxes were floated on the surface of the river, several hundred feet from each shore, and anchored to its bottom. He then began to build the stone caissons on top of each box. As the weight of the caissons increased, they slowly forced the boxes downward until they reached the river's silt bottom. Compressed air was then blown continuously into the boxes to keep the water out, while gangs of laborers descended into them to dig away at the riverbed with picks and shovels. With the tons of stone overhead increasing steadily by the month, each box was driven deeper and deeper into the silt until it reached bedrock. Once each box rested firmly on the bedrock, its interior was filled with cement, bonding it to the bedrock. Then the Gothic-arched stone towers, designed to soar almost a hundred yards above the river's surface, were completed.

For its time it was an awesome job in the conception, even more so in the execution. Newspapers printed vivid accounts of the underwater work and expressed amazement that anyone could endure the conditions below. The only illumination in the slowly sinking construction boxes was from oil lamps and later, calcium lanterns called limelights. The compressed air was uncomfortably dank and heavy, with temperatures often reaching ninety degrees. Journalists who went down into the boxes to observe soon found themselves drenched in perspiration, and more than one compared the atmosphere to that of an equatorial jungle. Voices had a thin, eerie sound because of the compressed air, and walls, tools and laborers were constantly draped in muck and slime. "Compared to it," wrote a reporter for *The New York Times*, "the filthiest coal mines of Pennsylvania are as fine resorts."

As each caisson sank deeper, the pressure of the air within had to be increased. In December 1870, almost a year and a half after construction first began, a fire broke out in the Brooklyn-side caisson that threatened to bring an end to the entire project. The compressed air sent flames shooting deep into the overhead timbers of the construction box, timbers that supported the countless tons of stonework of the superstructure above. The fire created a sensation in the press. "I don't believe any man now living will cross that bridge," wrote New York diarist George Templeton Strong the next day.

Washington Roebling led the fight to save the caisson, struggling throughout the night in the interior of the sunken box until he and his men finally conquered the blaze. After collapsing from exhaustion, he was rushed to the surface for fresh air, whereupon he was stricken suddenly with excruciating pains and paralysis. It was the first known attack in America of caisson disease, which later came to be called "the bends," and was caused, it was discovered in 1876, by emerging too quickly from high atmospheric compression. Roebling survived, but another agonizing attack two years later drove him into almost hermitlike seclusion in his Brooklyn home for the remaining ten years of the bridge's construction.

The second attack occurred during work on the Manhattan-side caisson in 1872 and was occasioned by a problem that Roebling had not anticipated. By then the Brooklyn caisson had settled on hard rock that was forty-four feet below the river's surface. Roebling had assumed that the bedrock ran on a level across the width of the river. When the Manhattan caisson reached a depth of forty-four feet, however, it found no rock. Nor did it at fifty-four feet, nor at sixty-four feet. The deeper the construction box sank, the more the air within had to be compressed, increasing attacks of the bends suffered by other laborers, three of whom had already died.

Finally, the caisson resting on sand at a depth of seventy-eight feet with still no sign of bedrock, Roebling made a decision upon which his reputation and career would hang. He ordered a halt to further digging—the caisson would stand permanently where it was, on sand. True, it was hard-packed sand, but sand nevertheless. Yet if the caisson went any deeper in search of bedrock, Roebling determined, it would be impossible for anyone to work. He examined the sand through the open bottom of the construction box and made an educated guess that it would support the caisson without ever eroding or shifting. It was immediately after he made that decision, while emerging from the solitude of the sunken box, that he suffered his second attack of the bends.

The only treatment for the affliction was morphine. Some observers at the time hinted that Roebling went into seclusion because he became addicted to the drug. Others credited his withdrawal to a deepening anxiety over his decision to allow the Manhattan tower to rest on sand—he could not face being at the site in the event the caisson shifted. Whatever the case, Roebling was hardly ever again seen in public during the bridge's construction. Instead, he dispatched his wife to construction headquarters each day from their home in Brooklyn with instructions for his engineers and foremen. Emily Roebling became such a familiar sight at the bridge during the next seven years that *The New York Times* insisted that she, not Roebling, was its chief engineer.

The financial crisis of 1873 marked the end of the four-year period within which Roebling's father had predicted the completion of the bridge. But by the fall of that year the construction of the towers had yet to be finished, the initial $5 million in financing had been exhausted, and the New York Bridge Company, unable to raise further funds due to the economic sag that followed the crisis, stood on the verge of bankruptcy. After a further round of bribery and other political chicanery in 1874, the directors of the bridge company got the cities of New York and Brooklyn to relieve them of their financial burden. Thereafter, the bridge became the co-responsibility of the two cities, and over the next nine years they fed an additional $11 million into its construction.

When the two granite towers were finally completed in the fall of 1876, they were the tallest free-standing man-made structures in the United States. In the world they were exceeded in size and majesty only by the great pyramids of Egypt, and it was not long before writers were comparing them favorably to the pyramids as marvels of both engineering and aesthetics. An English voyager passing through New York harbor in the winter of 1876 likened their stark beauty to that of the legendary cathedrals of Europe, their "haunting mystery"—as they soared without apparent reason from the depths of the East River—to that of his native Stonehenge. Those who lived in New York and Brooklyn were no less awed by the towers' stately majesty. From wherever one looked in either low-roofed city, they loomed like twin colossuses, their height and bulk dwarfing every other structure—even the highest-steepled churches—and jarring long-accustomed perceptions of scale and perspective.

Next came the "spinning" and anchoring of the cables from which the roadway would be suspended. The spinning was carried out at the site and took a year and a half to complete. Thousands of miles of thin, metal wire were formed into four thick, rigid cables that dipped in identical graceful curves between the two towers, then snaked through the tops of the towers before descending again to the two shoreside caissons in which they were anchored. If anything, the cable-spinning process was even more of a wonder than the construction of the towers had been. The spectacle of dozens of workers scrambling high up among the cables, nothing between them and the river below but hundreds of feet of open space, was one that passengers on New York-Brooklyn ferries would long remember.

Once the main cables were completed in the fall of 1878, the construction crews embarked on the building of the roadway span itself. This consisted of bolting together giant prefabricated steel trusses and then attaching them to wire "ropes," or suspender cables, that were hung vertically like harpstrings from the main cables every few feet. Although the arching span would be held up principally by its attachment to the main cables at the bridge's centerpoint, the thousands of suspender cables were designed to assist by spreading the suspensory stresses along the entire length of the main cables. Added to them were crosshatching stays, also thin cables, that radiated from the towers to impart further lateral stability to the span.

The span was built in two sections, beginning from each shore and progressing toward the middle. The work consumed nearly four more years. When it was finished in 1882, all that remained was the laying of the plank roadway, the building of an elevated pedestrian promenade, and such finishing touches as the installation of a lighting system and railings. By then everyone in New York and Brooklyn was able to view the bridge in its final form. No less an engineering wizard than Thomas Edison, preparing at the time to inaugurate his first electrical power station a few blocks south of the Manhattan approach to the bridge, sang the praises of Washington Roebling's feat. "I am hard put," he remarked, "to judge my achievements in electricity to be any more stunning a 'miracle,' as some people are given to characterizing [them], than the building of that great bridge to Brooklyn. If we are to talk about the miraculous, then by all means I defer to Mr. Roebling and his subordinates."

When the roadway was completed in the spring of 1883, Emily Roebling was chosen to test it by driving the first carriage across. A few weeks later the bridge was officially opened amid the greatest ceremonial fanfare the city—indeed the country—had ever seen. Hundreds of thousands of spectators thronged both approaches, and the river below became jammed with boats of every description. The President of the United States, Chester A. Arthur, led the first parade across from the Manhattan side.* Those who followed marveled at the experience. As they started up the ascending curve of the roadway, all they could see was sky through the tower ahead—it was like walking into a void. When they reached the center of the span they were 135 feet above the river, considerably higher than most had ever been in their lives. Those brave enough to stand at the roadway's edge and gaze down at the river, and at the rooftops and harbor beyond, experi-

---

*Arthur wore a pair of brand new "Easy Walking" shoes given to him by an enterprising New York merchant, who thereafter advertised them as the first shoes in history to carry a President of the United States "dry shod" across the East River.

enced the eerie feeling of vertigo. For months thereafter countless tourists poured into New York and Brooklyn to trudge back and forth across the bridge, particularly after P. T. Barnum "proved" its safety by pounding a herd of circus elephants over it.

Today the once-awesome towers of the Brooklyn Bridge are all but lost in the maze of skyscrapers, shipping terminals and other bridges that surround it. At the time of its construction, though, the bridge was a harbinger of the America to come—the America of huge vertical cities, of massive manufacturing complexes, of mammoth industrial, technological and economic enterprises. The soaring monument presaged another pioneering aspect of America as well—the America that would learn to girdle the globe with an endless bridge of radio communications and air transport, that would even, eventually, reach across the chasm of space to touch other planets.

Of course no one in 1883 could divine what the building of the Brooklyn Bridge had helped to unleash in the American spirit. But unleash something it did, just as did Edison's concurrent light bulb and electricity system. It was doubtless nothing more than an accident of fate that the installation of the first commercial incandescent lighting system and the completion of the Brooklyn Bridge occurred within six months of each other. One was a triumph of invention and what might have been called light, or "delicate," design and engineering. The other was a victory of massive design and heavy engineering. Both were testaments to human will, tenacity and ingenuity. Together the two created a powerful new incentive for the country's already lively imagination and resourcefulness. The engineer had joined the inventor and financier as a symbol of America's burgeoning "know-how" virtuosity. After a stroll across the Brooklyn Bridge in 1883, a French visitor wrote, "You see great ships passing beneath it, and this indisputable evidence of its height confuses the mind. But walk over it . . . and you will feel that the engineer is the greatest artist of our epoch, and you will own that these people have a right to plume themselves in their audacity."*

*Quoted in "The Great Bridge and the American Imagination" by David McCullough, *The New York Times Magazine*, March 27, 1983.

CHAPTER 18

OILING THE MACHINE

An American, Thomas Edison, had fulfilled in the broadest sense the dictum set forth two and a half centuries earlier by Francis Bacon: "That the true and lawful end of the sciences is that human life be enriched." Certainly between Bacon's time and Edison's, there were many important breakthroughs that had enriched human life. But even in the most technologically advanced societies, all had been limited in their reach and effects. Although major breakthroughs on both sides of the Atlantic had gradually raised the standard of living and quality of life of certain segments of those societies, and had increased their overall economic prosperity, their blessings did not extend to everyone within them. In Great Britain, in Western Europe, in America too, large portions of the population, mainly for economic reasons, had remained excluded from many of the life-enhancing benefits of material progress. It was not until Edison's invention of the light bulb, and of his system for transmitting electrical power that the opportunity for a much wider scale of life-enrichment presented itself. As the generation and transmission of cheap electricity spread during the 1880s and 1890s, almost anyone within a transmission area, regardless of his economic resources, could share in its advantages.* Commercial electricity, then, was the first truly democratizing in-

---

*The early generation and transmission of electricity followed the Edison formula of steam-powered dynamos operating from central power stations. Because great quantities of coal were required to fuel the steam engines that drove the dynamos, electricity, though not expensive, was not cheap either. Also, it was limited to large urban areas. Soon, how-

vention of history. Fittingly enough, it was invented and perfected in the one country in the world that, more than any other, prided itself on its democratic aspirations.

But the democratizing aspect of electricity was only one part of its Baconian significance. What made it equally important for America was its final validation of Bacon's doctrine that the ultimate goal of science should be the improvement of human life. The doctrine was one that was scarcely known up to Edison's time; in fact the majority of Americans had never heard of Francis Bacon, or of Isaac Newton, for that matter. Except in certain narrow academic and intellectual circles, science was still an activity likely to inspire more in the way of suspicion, or contempt, than admiration. In Europe and Britain, both scientific research and the teaching of science were well established in universities, and significant practical and socially beneficial advances, particularly in medical chemistry and physiology, but also in the theoretical sciences, had been achieved.*

Edison, more than anyone, changed all that for America. Indeed, just as his inventions were more "democratic" in their benefits than those of anyone before him, so too did his work, more than anyone else's, serve to revolutionize, democratize and popularize the pursuit of science in the United States. Although untrained in science and basically a mechanical engineer, Edison, because of his mastery of the arcane mysteries of electricity, was perceived in the public mind as a scientist of the most rarefied kind. Yet his personal style, abetted no doubt by his deafness, was homely and congenial; he never displayed the eccentric, aloof or icily superior demeanor most Americans associated with scientists. The country's newspapers played up his comfortable "common man" image, thus reinforcing the view that science possessed a redeeming humanistic dimension and was not exclusively the domain of the remote, idiosyncratic "brain."

---

ever, it was made cheaper and much more widely available by the building of huge power stations, first at the sites of great waterfalls, then at mammoth river dams constructed especially for the purpose of providing waterpower for turbines that drove the much larger generating dynamos, and by advances in the technology of alternating current.

*Joseph Lister, a British surgeon, pioneered antiseptic surgery in the 1860s—except for anesthesia, the greatest single advance in medicine up to then. Louis Pasteur, a French biologist-chemist, was the first to identify germs as the cause and transmitters of certain diseases. Most of the great strides in medicine remained the province of Europeans until the mid-twentieth century.

Added to that was the fact that Edison's inventions created an entirely new industry, the rapid growth of which was unparalleled in history. The industry entailed more than just creating the means of generating and transmitting electrical power on a progressively wider and more potent scale; it also involved manufacturing an increasing variety of devices and products designed to exploit electricity. The dynamos, meters, fuses and light bulbs made by Edison's original manufacturing companies, and then taken over by General Electric and other companies in the early 1880s, were merely the beginning of an industrial complex that would expand seemingly without limit. To meet the demand for electricity and electrical products, and to sustain its dizzying growth, specially trained engineers, mechanics and service people were required in abundance. And as countless electricity-based manufacturing enterprises proliferated—from streetcar manufacturers to makers of electric fans—and competition intensified, the need also arose for practical scientific researchers and abstract theoretical scientists.

As a consequence, science was no longer viewed by most in America as an alien pursuit. Edison had proved that scientific skills were the key to further material progress, that scientific and technical education was needed not only to service, expand and improve such recently invented systems as the telephone and electricity but to create new life-enhancing devices and systems as well. Even the financiers, lawyers and industrial entrepreneurs of Wall Street began to promote the virtues of scientific endeavor. Although few possessed more than a superficial understanding of the sciences, they were quick to recognize that the nation's future industrial prosperity, and therefore their personal prosperity, were dependent on scientific enterprise. "The day has ended in which the gifted business organizer and manager is paramount to the success of an industrial enterprise," said Andrew Carnegie, the Pittsburgh steel tycoon, to a local newspaper in 1885. "Scientists and engineers are to be the new wealth of industry, the coadjutors of the managers, for without them no manufacturing business will succeed."

As a result of the need for trained scientists and engineers, science curricula expanded rapidly in the nation's colleges and universities during the 1880s, and scores of new colleges and technical schools were founded. Rudimentary science instruction—

mathematics, physics and chemistry—was introduced on the public high-school level too. Professional engineering and scientific societies proliferated, as did journals and other publications specializing in scientific and technological subjects. Students were publicly urged to study for scientific and engineering careers on the twin rationale that these occupations were the keys to the country's future progress and that they provided new routes to personal employment prosperity—a way for a young man otherwise fated to be a "blue-collar" laborer to become a "white-collar" professional who would be every bit as important in the future scheme of things as the lawyer, financier or business manager.

The major industrial companies themselves promoted and supported the shift in educational emphasis. The General Electric and Westinghouse organizations began to contribute money to select universities in the 1890s so that electrical-research laboratories and advanced courses in electrical engineering could be established. At the same time, the steel industry, led by Andrew Carnegie, provided funds for the establishment of courses in metallurgical and geological research, and of engineering courses designed to improve the technology of mining and steelmaking. Large machine manufacturers such as the McCormick Harvester and Singer Sewing Machine companies subsidized courses in mechanical engineering. The success of the Brooklyn Bridge triggered an immediate enthusiasm for the creation of college courses in civil engineering. As one educator put it in 1894, the inspiration for the new educational wave was "the astonishing rapidity of invention and discovery during the thirty years past. To support and propagate the gains [that] have been made, we urgently require armies of men especially tutored in each field. Without them our progress, heretofore so miraculous, will wither on the vine."

Edison's discoveries, along with those of Westinghouse and his colleagues, had yet another vital impact on the industrial and technological colossus that was taking shape in the America of the last two decades of the nineteenth century. Commercial electricity not only created its own mammoth industry, it also enabled scores of other industries to function and expand more quickly and efficiently. Moreover, it spawned scores of newer industries which, although not based on electrical inventions, required electricity in order to flourish. It is commonly assumed, for instance, that the modern automobile industry owes its beginnings to the development in the 1880s of the internal combustion engine, which in turn was made possible by the earlier discovery of oil, and of the process of refining it into gasoline. The assumption is only partially correct. Without the application of the principles of the electric dynamo and the spark, there would have been no internal combustion engine and thus no automobile industry, and no vast complex of sub-industries that support, and are supported by, the automobile industry.

Petroleum was known in colonial America as early as the late 1600s. Indians in the wilderness of what is today northwestern Pennsylvania found it seeping from the ground and floating on ponds, and when they smeared it on wounds and aching joints, or swallowed it, they discovered that it had healing properties. They introduced this crude curative to colonial settlers, and by the mid-1700s there was a brisk trade in the substance between whites and Indians. The Indians had learned to soak up surface oil with blankets and then wring them out into clay containers, which they sold to the settlers. Soon a few colonists began to bottle and resell the foul-smelling goo for medicinal purposes, and "American oil," as it came to be called, began to enjoy a medical vogue throughout the colonies.

The opening up of the trans-Appalachian wilderness after the Revolution brought not only coal and iron mining to the far reaches of Pennsylvania and beyond, but salt mining too. Salt was harvested by drilling deep wells into underground saltwater deposits and then evaporating the water to recover its salt content. By the late 1830s many of the salt wells in western Pennsylvania were being contaminated by oil that was sucked up with the water. So pervasive did the problem become that when Samuel Kier, the son of a local salt producer, took over his father's business in 1845, he decided to give up salt making and concentrate on marketing the "medicinal" oil that was being pumped up in greater and greater quantities through his wells. By 1854, Kier had become the country's leading "tonic" manufacturer and, by virtue of his flamboyant advertising techniques and network of traveling salesmen, the father of American hucksterism. Kier sent his salesmen by horse-drawn wagon into every populated corner of the nation. With their entertaining, albeit highly exaggerated, spiels about the medicinal virtues of his bottled oil, they inspired the coinage of such phrases as *medicine show* and *snake oil*.

Kier's elixir might have remained just that, snake oil, had it not been for the need at the time to find a better and more economical source of illumination—the same need, ironically, that led Edison and others, two decades later, to perfect electric lighting. By the 1850s, whale oil, because of the logistical problems involved in acquiring it, was growing increasingly expensive. Candles, though cheap, gave a feeble light and were annoyingly short-lived. Coal gas, while suitable for city street-lighting systems, was also expensive and beyond the means of the ordinary householder. Camphene, a distillate of turpentine (an oil extracted from pine trees) which had been developed in 1830 by a New Yorker named Isaiah Jennings, had proved unpleasantly odoriferous as well as dangerously explosive.

It was not until the discovery of kerosene—an oil first extracted from coal—in Boston in 1852 that an important new source of lighting became widely available. Kerosene-fueled lampwicks burned without an unpleasant odor, gave a generously magnified glow beneath a clear glass "shade" and posed little danger of explosion. Nevertheless the process of extracting and refining coal oil remained expensive, and although more than a million kerosene lamps were sold by 1857, most Americans still relied on candlelight for whatever interior illumination they required.

The greater significance of the discovery of kerosene lay in what it portended for the underground petroleum deposits of northwestern Pennsylvania. Theretofore usable only for bottled medicine, so much oil-laden water had been pumped up through that region's salt wells that by 1854 the supply far exceeded the commercial medicinal demand that had been created by Samuel Kier.

In the summer of that year, however, a young entrepreneur named George Bissell, a graduate of Dartmouth College, paid a visit to the New Hampshire campus of his alma mater. During his stay, one of Bissell's former professors showed him a bottle of oil from a spring in the tiny town of Titusville, Pennsylvania, and also a brochure boasting of the curative powers of Samuel Kier's "natural rock oil." Bissell, a city-trained businessman, perceived a greater commercial potential in the Pennsylvania oil than Kier, with his rustic marketing methods, had realized. Shortly thereafter Bissell traveled to Titusville to scout out sources of oil. He was amazed to find them in plentiful supply in the form of seepages and springs in the hills around the village. He returned to New York and, with an investor-partner, chartered a company designed to compete with Kier's home-remedy organization.

Calling themselves the Pennsylvania Rock Oil Company, Bissell and his partner purchased one hundred acres of land rich in surface oil near Titusville and acquired oil rights to an additional twelve thousand acres. Their first year of operation proved unprofitable, however; despite their more sophisticated business methods, they were unable to break Kier's near-monopoly on the oil-as-medicine market. As a consequence, Bissell began to consider other possible uses for his oil. A query to his old Dartmouth teacher put him in touch with Benjamin Silliman, Jr., a chemistry professor at Yale and the son of the scientist who had been so instrumental in Samuel Morse's invention of the telegraph.

The younger Silliman accepted Bissell's commission to analyze samples of the Titusville surface oil. His report, when he delivered it a short time later, completely transformed the modest medicinal promise of rock oil. Silliman described the oil as having "exceedingly fine" machine-lubricating qualities when it was separated from the watery medium in which it was borne. But even more important, natural oil was "chemically identical with illuminating gas in liquid form." It was identical, in other words, with coal gas and coal oil, or kerosene. The one vital difference was that gas and kerosene had to be extracted and liquefied, through complicated and costly refining processes, from coal. Rock oil, on the other hand, was "coal already in liquid form." According to Silliman, the fluid distilled from natural oil burned with as much light as coal gas and coal oil, and it did so "more economically, and the uniformity of the light was greater than in camphene, burning for twelve hours without a sensible diminution, and without smoke."*

Silliman's Pennsylvania rock-oil distillate was nothing less than

---

*Although camphene was seldom used for illumination because of its volatility and odor, the light it produced was much admired for its brightness and nonflickering steadiness.

a new, cheap kerosene—new and cheap because it skipped the most expensive and time-consuming process of producing the "old" kerosene. For that reason alone the Bissell oil lands at Titusville suddenly vaulted to a much higher level of value. There remained, however, the problem of how to obtain enough oil from the land's springs and seepages to make the distilling of the new kerosene commercially worthwhile. Although the oil that bubbled to the surface of Titusville and its environs was sufficiently abundant to support the tonic business, there was not enough of it to produce kerosene in bulk.

It was Samuel Kier's salt wells that suggested the solution. One of the features of Kier's initial medicinal advertising had been the claim that his "miraculous" rock oil had come, via his salt wells, "from four hundred feet beneath the earth's surface." Indeed the numeral *400* became an integral part of the Kier logo; it was printed prominently on his labels and advertising brochures and was meant to signify the purity of his product and its superiority over those of his competitors, who obtained their oil from surface pools.

In 1857 an unemployed former railroad clerk named Edwin Drake, then living in New Haven, overheard a conversation between Benjamin Silliman, Jr., and James Townsend, a local banker who had joined Silliman as a principal in George Bissell's faltering Pennsylvania Rock Oil Company. The conversation centered on the problem the company was having in finding a way to obtain oil from its Titusville lands in quantities sufficient to make its burning and lubricating properties commercially profitable. Drake, once a regular user of Samuel Kier's rock-oil tonic, interjected himself into the discussion. Recalling Kier's "400-feet-beneath-the-surface" advertising claims, he wondered aloud if boring or drilling for oil, much as one bored for salt, might not be the answer to the problem.

Drilling for oil itself was a concept that had never before been advanced. For that reason, Drake's suggestion engaged the interest of Silliman and Townsend. Yet they challenged it. Kier's salt wells brought up mostly water, they said; the oil the wells sucked from the depths was merely a by-product, and it appeared in no greater quantity than was obtainable from Titusville's surface springs and pools. What made Drake believe there was any advantage in boring further wells? Wouldn't it simply be a more costly method of getting what was already available on the surface?

Drake, who had not gone beyond grade school and possessed not a whit of geological or technical training, had a ready reply, although a theoretical one. It came in the form of several questions of his own. If oil had long been seeping out of the earth of Titusville, wasn't it possible that large pools or reservoirs of the substance existed deep underground—just as reservoirs of pure water existed? And that underground pressures forced it to percolate upward, during which process it mixed with and was thinned by underground water before bubbling out of the ground.

Silliman and Townsend remained doubtful, yet they were still interested enough in Drake's theory to accept his offer to travel to Titusville to look over the Pennsylvania Rock Oil lands. When Drake arrived in December of 1857, he gained a clearer understanding of the reasons for his sponsors' skepticism. That most of the surface oil of Titusville flowed from springs in the steep hills around the village supported their contention that if in fact there were pools of oil, they were situated within the hills; thus, any boring to be done should be carried out laterally into the sides of the hills. But then Drake inspected the creek that ran through the valley in which Titusville lay. The stream was called Oil Creek by locals because of the petroleum that oozed from its rocky bed at various spots and fouled its waters. Writing later, Drake said that he could not understand why oil was seeping from the creekbed—the lowest part of the terrain—"if it came from the Hills, as it is so much lighter than Water that it would be impossible for it to go down of its own accord." From this he concluded that oil indeed percolated upward from underground vats. "I made up my mind that it could be obtained in large quantities by Boreing [*sic*] as for Salt Water. I also determined that I should be the one to do it."*

The practically penniless Drake was unable to persuade the Pennsylvania Rock Oil Company to finance his attempt to drill for oil—Silliman and Townsend still clung to the belief that the only experiment worth trying was a horizontal probe into one of Titusville's hillsides. The company did agree to lease some of its land to Drake, however, if the neophyte prospector succeeded in

---

*As quoted in *The Americans: The Democratic Experience*, by Daniel J. Boorstin (New York: Random House, 1973).

obtaining drilling money elsewhere. It took him well over a year, but by the spring of 1859, Drake finally had put together enough of a stake of borrowed funds to make a payment on his lease and begin construction of a crude drilling rig. He hired an experienced local salt-well driller, William A. Smith, to actually build the rig at a site near an oil spring selected by Drake. In June 1859, Smith started to drill. After two months of almost daily drilling, the bore pipe had reached a depth of only sixty-five feet, half of it carving through bedrock that yielded only a few inches a day. Because of Samuel Kier's advertising slogans, Drake was sure that the well would have to be sunk considerably deeper than four hundred feet to learn whether his theory about the existence of a pure-oil pool was correct. He began to worry about the slow progress, afraid that he would exhaust his funds before getting anywhere close to that depth.

On Saturday, August 27, Smith reached 69½ feet. Then, late that hot afternoon, he locked up the drilling shed for the rest of the weekend—although concerned about the tedious pace, Drake was a religious man and forbade Smith to work on Sundays. Nevertheless, the next day Smith returned to the shack with one of his sons to replace a cracked pipe-joint in the drill. As he hoisted the pipe out of the hole, he was startled to notice oil on his gloves. He looked into the well box and saw a pool of oil beginning to form, gurgling gently up from the pipe hole. He took off one of his gloves and dipped his fingers into the rising pool. Then he sent his son to fetch Drake.

Drake arrived at the shack a few minutes later. Smith beckoned him to the well box and pointed inside. "Oil?" said the disbelieving Drake. "Push your fingers in it," Smith said. Drake dipped his fingers into the black substance and rubbed them together. "Feel it?" Smith said. "That's the pure stuff. No water in it. You've found your fortune, Mr. Drake."

Thus was discovered the world's first modern oil well. But like every other invention or discovery of consequence, the climax of Edwin Drake's hunch-inspired search marked just the beginning of a much more complex process, in this case the development of systems by which to refine, transport, distribute and market the various useful products capable of being extracted from crude oil.

Drake's discovery triggered a stampede of oil prospectors to the region around Titusville that was almost as feverish as the California Gold Rush ten years earlier. But the problems attached to crude oil production were far different from those of gold. First, although oil rose naturally through the scores of wells that were subsequently drilled in the region, it would not flow with any force but had to be pumped, first by hand, later by machine. So a whole new technology of drilling and pumping was born of Drake's discovery.

Then there was the matter of refining the oil into kerosene and lubricants, initially the two major commercial by-products of the Pennsylvania oil field and of similar fields discovered soon after in Ohio, Kentucky and West Virginia. It was this need in the 1860s that produced the first great awakening of interest in chemistry and physics in the United States and inspired the establishment of specialized courses in these sciences in the nation's universities and colleges. As time went on and practical knowledge about the technology of oil refining grew, it was discovered that oil could be put to other valuable uses beyond lighting and lubrication. It could be refined into combustive agents for heating and propulsion; into paving and protective coating materials; into heating and cooking gases; and into substances from which, in combination with other materials, a wide variety of plastics could be made. Moreover, as early American oil technology matured, stimulating the development of such practical subsciences as petrochemistry and geology, it discovered and learned to corral the combustive properties of natural gas, applying them to commercial use.

But the greatest immediate problem posed by the early 1860s oil boom lay in the question of how to transport the crude oil in bulk from the isolated regions in which it was found to the distant urban and industrial markets in which its refined by-products— kerosene and lubricants—were in demand. As much as anything else connected with the early science and technology of oil, the solution of this problem played a singular role in the shaping of the modern American colossus.

The two cities closest to the northwestern Pennsylvania oil lode were Pittsburgh, about a hundred miles south, and Cleveland, Ohio, a hundred miles west on the shore of Lake Erie. By 1860 both had become iron-manufacturing and transshipping centers, and it was from them that most of the oil prospectors and speculators rushed to the Titusville region. Refineries for making kerosene were established in both cities, and by 1861 a steady traffic in crude oil was flowing from Titusville and Oil City to Cleveland and Pittsburgh.

Oil City, a village a few miles south of Titusville, was situated at the place where Titusville's Oil Creek spilled into the Allegheny River, which followed a meandering course south to Pittsburgh. Oil from the first wells of Titusville was hauled in barrels to the river-landing at Oil City and the barrels were put on barges to Pittsburgh; oil destined for Cleveland was carted overland by wagon to that city, also in barrels. By 1862, however, so much oil was being drawn from the ground at Titusville that the overland cartage could not keep up with it. As a result, and also because the region's primitive storage facilities were inadequate, much of the crude oil had to be wasted, dumped into Oil Creek and the Allegheny River.

In the meantime the Civil War had increased demand for kerosene and machine lubricants. In order to speed up the transport of crude oil and thereby increase production, and also to gain an edge on Pittsburgh as a refining center, a group of businessmen in Cleveland formed a company to build an oil-hauling railway between their city and the Titusville region. With the completion of the railway in 1863,* more oil began to travel to Cleveland than to Pittsburgh and refineries proliferated in the Cleveland area. One of the early refinery founders was a twenty-four-year-old native of upper New York who had moved to Cleveland as a boy and made a small fortune during the first two years of the war as a food broker. His name was John D. Rockefeller.

In 1863, Rockefeller was approached for financial backing by Samuel Andrews, a Cleveland oil prospector who had invented a cheap refining process. Rockefeller, his nose for the value of commodities already finely developed, agreed to go into partnership with Andrews. Two years later their refinery had earned more than a million dollars. Although Rockefeller knew little about the technology of oil, he decided thereafter to devote all his time to the new enterprise. He bought out Andrews for $72,500, enlisted his younger brother, William Rockefeller, in the business, and in

*This railway was a branch of the Atlantic and Great Western Railway, which later tied into the Erie and New York Central Railroads and eventually allowed refined oil from western Pennsylvania and eastern Ohio to be transported quickly to the East and West.

1870 reorganized and enlarged the refinery under the name of the Standard Oil Company of Ohio.

Taking his lead from the emerging railroad tycoons of Wall Street, Rockefeller then set out to monopolize the country's fast-growing oil industry. What helped him succeed, ironically, was his repugnance toward the railroaders' monopolistic business methods. As the oil industry enlarged in the late 1860s, it became increasingly dependent on the railroads for the transport of its products—from the remote oil fields to the nearby refineries, and from the refineries to the distant markets. The major railroads, vying fiercely with one another for this lucrative traffic, began to manipulate shipping rates and priorities, favoring certain refiners over others. At the same time, refiners began to indulge in the habit of random price-cutting in order to gain market advantages over their rivals. This pattern of fluctuating prices and unstable shipping rates, along with a sudden glut of oil due to overproduction, threw the oil business into financial chaos in 1869. It was then that Rockefeller resolved to control the industry. His motive was not his own personal enrichment, he would later claim, but "to put an end to the destructive competition."

Rockefeller began to buy failed and failing refineries, merging them into his Standard Oil Company in a fashion similar to that in which the rail barons were consolidating various short-line railways into huge, centrally controlled railroad systems. By 1872, Standard Oil was refining 10,000 barrels of kerosene a day, a production rate greater than that of all the country's remaining independent refining companies combined. In accordance with Rockefeller's dictum against oil's dependence on other industries, however, that was not all the company was engaged in. He set up subsidiaries under the Standard Oil umbrella to develop its own oil fields; to manufacture its own barrels; to build its own railroad cars, shipping barges and terminals; to train its own chemists and technicians; and to erect its own retailing network. "Standard Alone . . . From the Well Head to the House Wife's Door" was an early slogan of Rockefeller's kerosene business. It signified that every step in the process of delivering the company's principal product to the consumer was controlled by Standard Oil.

But not quite. Every step but one was under Standard's direct control by 1885. The missing link was the long-distance transport of oil, for although Rockefeller had built a fleet of railroad cars, he was still financially dependent on the railroad companies for their movement. It was in his solution to this final problem that Rockefeller effectively completed his monopolization of the oil industry. The solution was the cross-country pipeline. Curiously, the solution would provoke another fateful change of course in the direction industrial America was traveling.

CHAPTER **19**

THE GROWING PARADOX

By 1883, largely as a result of the achievements of Bell, Edison, Roebling, Rockefeller, and the creative moneymen of Wall Street, a symbiotic combination of organization, invention, finance, science and engineering had been hatched that would, over the next fifty years, complete the building of the framework of the United States as we know it today. During that mere eye-blink in the history of time, just about every vital device, machine, system, structure, technique and public service that has contributed to making contemporary America the most modern and materially comfortable nation on earth, and has bestowed similar beneficence on much of the rest of the world, was introduced and perfected. At the onset of the Great Depression in the early 1930s, almost everything we use today to convenience our lives was available, albeit not available to everyone.

But in 1883, for all the ebullient optimism triggered by the successful completion of the Brooklyn Bridge and by the life-enhancing discoveries of Edison, Bell, Drake and others, it was also clear that not everyone looked kindly on the prospects for the future. While some commentators hailed the bridge, oil, the light bulb and the telephone as favorable auguries of the material utopia to come, others complained of what they perceived as their negative symbolism.

Wrote Henrick Rhinelander, a member of an old New York family, in 1884:

I drove from that bridge yesterday into the snarl of beg-

245

gars, drunkards, and ne'er-do-wells that habitually pop-
ulate the streets surrounding its portal, and all I could
think of were the confounding contradictions that beset
the country. The bridge is a great advancement, no
doubt, but it only makes more vivid the ways in which
we have failed to advance.*

And Zebediah Cox, a visitor from Boston, observed in a letter
to his wife:

The East River Bridge is truly a wonder, my dear. But
more wondrous still are the blind encomiums which the
politicians and financiers here lavish upon it as a symbol
of the glory that is in store for the country. My fear is
that these overblown prophecies falsely elevate the expectations of the populace. The speakers treat of the
bridge as some miraculous emanation sprung full grown
from the brow of God. They forget that its construction
took many tortured years and consumed many
lives. . . . Their habit of likening the symmetry and
harmony and majesty of the bridge to what our society
will become is oratorically pleasing, but ignores the actualities. The actualities are that this giant structure,
along with its harmony and symmetry, were put together through great human sacrifice and are held together through a multitude of physical forces that are
constantly in equal opposition. Such an edifice may
function well when it is a collection of iron and stone. I
fear, however, that a society erected on like principles
would collapse in chaos, for human beings do not possess the inert qualities of iron and stone. If they did, the
society now foreseen by so many would grow as rigid
and immobile as the bridge.†

Both the optimists and the pessimists were right. America *was*
to become a material utopia, and much faster than most could
imagine. But in the process, many of the economic and political
problems already woven into the social fabric of the nation would,

*From a letter in the archives of the Brooklyn Museum, Brooklyn, N. Y.
†Ibid.

rather than be eliminated by material progress, expand and be exacerbated. In its size, diversity and complexity, the country would become figuratively what the Brooklyn Bridge was in real terms for its time—a man-made colossus. Like the bridge, though, its construction would entail great sacrifice and would suffer unexpected reversals, all due to what was clearly evincing itself as the paradoxical economic nature of free enterprise and competitive capitalism in a land devoted, at least in theory, to political democracy and social equality.

The building of the Standard Oil dynasty had four equally important impacts on the cultural and technological shaping of the United States after 1870. First, it accelerated the growth of a new and progressive industry that would otherwise have developed at a much slower pace. Second, a full decade before the birth of the electric power industry, it turned the nation's attention squarely to its need for organized scientific and technological education.* Third, it sowed the seeds of a great variety of new technologies— the internal combustion engine, for one—that in their turn produced scores of further new industries and subindustries, all of which contributed, quickly and momentously, to the country's material advancement.

Standard Oil's fourth major impact was, as it were, first among equals. It stemmed from the company's monopolistic character—indeed, from the very character of John D. Rockefeller himself. Along with the railroads, the monolithic expansion of Standard Oil during the 1870s came at a time when radical European social and economic ideas, first propounded by Karl Marx and Friedrich Engels in 1848, were beginning to invade the consciousness of the United States. The Marxist creed had been formulated in reaction to the social and economic evolution of industrial Europe, an evolution that Marx interpreted and condemned as having established a ruthless, antidemocratic enslavement of each country's huge working class by its small monopolistic capitalist class. Marx's solution to the baneful condi-

---

*There was a neat historical symmetry in the fact that Thomas Edison's invention of incandescent light was inspired, at least in part, by a kerosene lamp. No one ever thought to ask Edison if the fluid in the lamp from which he scraped the carbon for his successful filament was Rockefeller kerosene, but the odds are that it was. Edison's invention, of course, eventually did away with most of the market for kerosene. By that time, however, Rockefeller's petrochemists had discovered how to make gasoline from crude oil.

tions in Europe called for a revolution of the working classes that would enable them to seize control of the existing capitalist system and transform it into an economically equitable structure called socialism. The path to such a revolution was through the unification of the working classes. The vehicle of unification was to be the organized labor, or trade, union.

Little had occurred in the way of concerted labor unrest in the United States prior to the Civil War. This was due in part to the fact that the country had no single large organized industry; it was also because, with the constantly mounting rate of immigration, there were many more potential workers than there were jobs prior to the war. Those few work stoppages or strikes that did occur were minor, spontaneous, isolated, and generally unreported by the press.*

The country got its first taste of mass labor rebellion in the bloody draft riots of the Civil War. During the later stages of the war a few workingmen's unions were tentatively organized in the North in industries, such as railroads and ironworks, that were most vital to the war effort. In the first few years after the war, with the resumption of immigration from a Europe by then thoroughly infused with the anticapitalistic dogma of Marx and Engels, the nation's working classes began to acquire an organized labor consciousness. This consciousness spread and hardened during the early 1870s, particularly in those labor-intensive industries that, after the war, had set out on clearly monopolistic paths: railroads, steel, mining.

The chief goal of industrial monopolization was to minimize or, better yet, eliminate competition so that the monopolizing entity could unilaterally control the market for its products and thereby set the highest prices possible. Such a practice seemed to clash violently with the basic political and economic principles of American democracy. But at first, thanks to the philosophical confusion the conflicting impulses generated, there was little objection. Free enterprise meant absolutely free competition, it was thought, and if a single competitor managed to domi-

---

*A nascent American labor movement, spurred on by early religious social reformers, had gotten a start in the New England textile mills and shipyards in the 1830s. But with the exception of a few scattered short-term strikes, it had little effect except to raise the issue of whether such strikes were legal under state and federal law. This issue would preoccupy the nation's courts for the next hundred years.

nate a business or industry absolutely, restraining him would be a corruption of the cherished concept of free enterprise—it would be as though he were being punished for being too skilled a competitor.

Another goal of monopolization, however, was to reduce the cost of bringing a product to market and thereby, through the differential between its low fixed cost and high fixed price, to maximize the product's profit to the monopoly. One of the basic methods by which this goal could be achieved was by minimizing the cost of the labor required to manufacture the product—not just the direct labor in the factory, but all the way down the ladder to the labor that produced the raw materials from which the product was made, and all the way up to the labor that brought it to the retail market. It was as a result of this practice that a national labor movement began to coalesce in America's monopoly-prone major industries in the late 1860s. Although at first they did not subscribe to the Marx-Engels prescription of political revolution, workers' groups in the country's railroad, mining and steel industries formed loosely organized "brotherhoods," based on radical European trade-union models, and began to agitate for higher wages and better working conditions.*

The movement was disorganized and feeble in its beginning stages. And because it was an affront to the sensibilities of the owners and managers of the industrial enterprises, they ignored it. But then came the Panic of 1873 and the economic downturn that followed, along with the intensification of monopolism. With hundreds of thousands thrown out of work, labor unrest mounted and the infant brotherhoods and workingmen's societies grew in number and force. Early in 1874, police tried to disperse a mass rally of factory laborers at New York's Tompkins Square on the ground that such a public demonstration was illegal. The result was a riot. A year later a group of Irish-immigrant mine workers in eastern Pennsylvania were rounded up during a strike that had turned to violence. Several were convicted and executed for

---

*Generally, the workday in private industry of the late 1860s spanned an average of 10½ hours, and the work week remained at 6 full days. The average wage was less than today's equivalent of 10 cents an hour. These early industrial unions were encouraged in their goals by the fact that the federal government, in 1868, had enacted legislation mandating an 8-hour workday for laborers and mechanics who worked for the government. Several states also passed such laws, although they were not enforced.

murder, others sentenced to long prison terms.* In the summer of 1877 a wage protest on the Baltimore & Ohio Railroad spread quickly to other railroads east of the Mississippi and then to the lines beyond, producing the nation's first organized, industry-wide work stoppage. The strike triggered an escalation and ex-pansion of labor violence. Several major cities were wracked by rioting when federal and state militia, at the behest of the railroad companies, attempted to break up strike rallies and disperse picket lines. This first nationwide strike galvanized the labor movement. Thereafter it began to grow more organized, more widespread, and more radical in its political orientation.

The heightening mood of discontent was further fueled by revelations of financial corruption in the presidential administra-tion of Ulysses S. Grant. Although corruption had become en-demic in many city and state governments by the 1870s, the Grant administration was the first on the federal level to reveal patterns of blatant malfeasance. Several among Grant's Cabinet were implicated in a succession of scandals between 1869 and 1876, most of which had to do with the advancement of the na-tion's private-industry monopoly interests. What was perceived as the corrupt alliance between the federal government and big busi-ness was interpreted by many labor leaders as a fulfillment of warnings about the inherent evils of capitalism that had been broadcast by Karl Marx and his disciples during the previous thirty years, as well as a profound abuse of the country's demo-cratic ideology. As a result, the labor movement grew increasingly unified and more radically militant in the late 1870s and early 1880s. Its fervor culminated in the Haymarket Riot in Chicago in May of 1886, when a pitched battle between police and workers chanting communist slogans left seven policemen dead and sev-enty wounded.

The Haymarket carnage shocked the nation, as much because of its explicit revolutionary communist overtones as because of its violence. Suddenly the country was confronted by the specter of a segment of its society advocating the violent overthrow of the cen-

---

*Called "Molly Maguires," these coal miners were members of an offshoot of the An-cient Order of Hibernians, a secret farmers' and workingmen's brotherhood originally orga-nized in Ireland to break the tyrannical grip of the landlords there. Transposed to America, the Ancient Order had moved to the forefront of labor-organizing in those industries that employed large numbers of Irish. The Irish were still largely excluded from all but phys-ical labor.

tury-old American system and its replacement by either a communistic or anarchistic form of government, the latter of which meant practically no government at all. This was a prospect not favored by the majority among the labor movement; they simply wanted major reforms in the industrial system so that American workers could enjoy more fully and equitably the fruits of their labors.

Out of the ideological and legal turmoil that followed the Chicago bloodbath was born the American Federation of Labor, an alliance of twenty-five separate labor groups organized in December 1886 by Samuel Gompers, the president of the Cigarmakers' Union, for the purpose of bringing order, unification and moderation to the labor movement. Under Gompers's almost forty years of leadership, the A.F. of L. would become a potent force in the shaping of the modern American colossus.

The most significant immediate impact of Gompers's reorganization of the mainstream labor movement, though, lay in its transformation of both the people's and the federal government's perceptions about the private monopolization of industry and the national economy. Except during the Civil War years, the government had maintained the general *laissez-faire* attitude with respect to private enterprise that had been established by Andrew Jackson in the 1830s. If, periodically, the federal government had tilted at all, its tilt had been toward fostering unfettered competition and private industrial development through legislative grants and dispensations. Perversely, however, Jackson's prescriptions had had an opposite effect from the one he'd foreseen. Rather than deterring monopoly and the rise of the kind of economic ruling class the American Revolution had sought to make obsolete, the government's hands-off approach had in fact created a fertile field for private-sector monopolization and social exploitation. With the exception of agriculture, by 1880 every vital component of the nation's industrial infrastructure was monopolized, or well on its way to being monopolized, by a relatively few individuals.

The country was confronted by a deep philosophical dilemma. Carl Schurz, the social reformer and editor of the New York *Evening Post*, summed it up in an 1882 edition of that paper shortly after Edison began to light New York:

We have on the one side those advocates of monopolistic capitalism who contend that without the system such as it now exists our unique progress as a nation of invention and manufacture would be feeble, our position in the world without remarkability. To refute such contentions is not without logical difficulty. Yet we have on the other side those who hold vigorously to the view that the monopolistic system such as it now exists creates an ever-growing tyranny whereby the few gain a gross advantage over the many, and the many are subject to the whims and dictates of the few. To refute these contrary claims is, logically, equally arduous, and is made the more so by the plain evidence of the life that surrounds us. The next great test of our nation lies in its ability to make an accommodation between these conflicting currents, so that while the flow of progress is not retarded, the opportunities for all Americans' rightful and unrestrained share in that progress are increased.*

Moral and economic reform as against material and economic progress: By the 1890s the United States was confronted by two seemingly contradictory imperatives. The cutthroat system of *laissez-faire* capitalism and individual initiative had brought the country to its present state of material advancement, and it promised even greater and more rapid progress in the immediate future. But the very same system was also proving to be morally and politically regressive, threatening to plunge many of those who lived under it into a nineteenth-century version of the Middle Ages, of economic servitude and political paternalism. The initial attempts by citizen groups, and then by the government, to strike a balance between the two conflicting currents were feeble and generally ineffectual. The advocates of reform insisted that the political and social equality promised by the Revolution could

*New York *Evening Post*, November 13, 1882. Schurz, an emigrant from Germany in 1852, was a lawyer who had settled in Wisconsin before distinguishing himself as a Union general in the Civil War. Thereafter he combined a career in journalism with one in politics, serving as a senator and then four years as Secretary of the Interior under President Rutherford Hayes. He was editor of the New York *Evening Post* from 1881 until 1883, after which time he became actively involved in social and governmental reform. Although little-known today, he was a popular figure in late-nineteenth-century America.

not be sustained without governmental modification and control of the nation's fundamental private-sector economic processes. Their *laissez-faire* adversaries decried such notions, warning that any federal attempts to control the complex system of business, commerce, industry and finance would be a profound violation of the basic personal freedoms guaranteed by the Constitution.

It came down, then, to a conflict between equality and freedom. Each concept had been an ideological cornerstone of the political edifice built a century before. The question, thrown into sharp relief by the labor strife of the 1880s and 1890s, was: Could the two concepts coexist in an America suddenly and radically transformed by its own unique economic, technological and populational revolution? Although the question was vigorously and often violently debated throughout the last quarter of the nineteenth century, a definitive answer would not be formulated until the country was well into the first decade of the twentieth.

In the meantime the system continued to evolve and function generally as it had, with each tentative statutory attempt at governmental intervention and modification rendered ineffective by financiers, lawyers and accountants who proved as ingenious in the discovery and exploitation of legal loopholes as inventors had been in solving the riddles of mechanics and science. Federal interstate commerce and antitrust laws were easily skirted by the creation, in place of the overt trust, of the more covert industrial "holding company" and "interlocking directorate." Indeed, until 1890, the year of the enactment of the Sherman Antitrust Act, only 24 clear-cut industrial trusts had been formed. During the decade thereafter more than 150 additional such combinations arose, topped in size and centralized power by the formation in 1901 of the United States Steel Corporation, an amalgam of 228 smaller iron and steel companies that together controlled more than two thirds of the country's production. By the beginning of the century every major and vital industry in the nation was under the firm control of a few corporate titans. The nation's banking and financial resources were tightly concentrated, too, with the separate Morgan and Rockefeller interests wielding such immense power that hardly any new commercial enterprise of significance could be started without their participation or approval.

Although this concentration of wealth and power was viewed as an evil in a widening number of quarters, the country, perversely, along with the rest of the world, prospered and profited immensely from it. Selfish and atavistic the tycoons may have been, but never before, and never since, has the world seen such technological progress, improvement and diversification as occurred during their reign. Hardly a life-enhancing convenience we enjoy today—or the technological basis for it—was not developed during the forty years between 1870 and 1910.

To be sure, not every watershed mechanical invention and scientific discovery of the period occurred in the United States. But no country, no society, was better positioned to exploit every such invention and discovery. Even the most important medical breakthroughs of the time, although the great majority were European in origin, received their widest promotion and dissemination in America—this because the American rich were so eager to stay alive and well that they were willing to spend practically anything to obtain the benefits of the latest in foreign medical discoveries and treatments. And by the nature of the American economic system, what the rich at first appropriated for themselves eventually trickled down to the populace at large.

The cascade of invention and technological innovation reflected only a part of the country's genius for expediting material progress, though. Another vital part was its skill at exploiting those inventions and innovations—its ability to create financial, manufacturing, distribution, service and other such support systems and networks by which to spread the fruits of each advance among the populace. The time it took to get from Edison's invention of the light bulb to the establishment of a functioning electric power and light industry, mainly in the form of the trust-type General Electric and Westinghouse companies, was only a few years. The same was true for the myriad other convenience inventions of the period, from toilet paper to the telephone, as well as for the new industrial and scientific processes that were being discovered and developed. It was one thing to perfect a new invention or process, quite another to turn it into a useful and usable product, a valuable system or service. The latter required huge amounts of investment capital, most of which was generated by the financial titans of Wall Street, the increasingly despised architects of monopolies, combinations and trusts. Without the single-minded daring, avarice and arrogance of the country's financial and industrial "Robber Barons," as they came to be called, and without the pioneering if often ruthless legal, managerial and marketing skills of their surrogate business administrators, the material progress of the last quarter of the nineteenth century surely would not have occurred.

For every social sin American monopolism gave birth to, it could point to a compensatory virtue. Ironically, those who complained most bitterly about the business monopolists were able to make their complaints heard most widely and effectively through the very advanced devices and systems the monopolists had been so instrumental in creating. Those who advocated the destruction of American capitalism were best able to broadcast their radical programs and organize their dissident cadres through the very institutions American capitalism had perfected. The mechanized printing press, the telegraph and the railroad, each a product of monopolistic capitalism, were vital to the growth of the country's early political and economic reform movements. As were, later, electricity, the telephone, oil, the typewriter and the mimeograph.

John Hay, among the country's foremost statesmen-writers of the period, captured the paradox vividly in an article he published in a Chicago-based magazine called *The Dial* in 1889. An unabashed defender of American capitalism, Hay wrote:

> The radical pamphleteer sits at night at a desk made by machine laborers in a factory in Michigan. He writes with a pen made in another factory, this in New Jersey, using ink made and bottled in still another, this in Pennsylvania, on paper made in yet another, this in Massachusetts. He writes by the illumination of a kerosene lamp assembled in New York and fueled by a liquid distilled by Mr. Rockefeller in Ohio; or, if he is more fortunate, by the illumination of an incandescent bulb perfected by Mr. Edison. Once he has completed his preparation he brings it to a printer who produces for him, in no time, and at very little cost, five, ten, fifteen thousand printed copies by mechanized presses

devised by Mr. Tucker. Then he bales his pamphlets and puts them on trains for shipment to other cities; himself too, perhaps, so that he may distribute them personally. Or else he avails himself of the telegraph to broadcast the contents of his pamphlet. And what is his message? That the system that has provided him with all these conveniences is inherently foul and must be eliminated.

Nevertheless, if not eliminated, the system was about to be subjected to the "next great test" described by Carl Schurz: "to make an accommodation between these conflicting currents" of economic capitalism and political democracy, of freedom and equality.

CHAPTER **20**

THE GROWING PROMISE

Following the Civil War, many of the nation's political visionaries saw in the vigorous expansion of invention, scientific discovery and industrialism the solution to practically all of America's social and economic ills. But for every problem that was solved in the three decades that followed, a host of other, newer ones arose as a direct result. By the turn of the century this pattern became the central paradox from which all the other paradoxes of the free enterprise system flowed. More and more people benefited directly or indirectly from the country's fast-growing technological largesse. But at the same time, more and more failed to benefit, and even suffered. Nevertheless, the pace of material progress raced ahead with an energy and ambition that precluded thoughtful reflection about its negative consequences.

In addition to the telephone, the incandescent bulb, electrical power generation and the drilling and refining of oil, countless other uniquely American inventions and technological innovations were developed during the period. As early as 1866, Henry House, a Connecticut mechanic, built a self-propelled steam carriage that set off a race among inventors throughout the industrial world to perfect the first true automobile.

Mahlon Loomis, an electrical tinkerer from New York, demonstrated the first crude example of short-distance wireless communication in 1868, by fitting a telegraph machine with a special metal aerial. Loomis's idea of sending electrical impulses through the atmosphere predated the discovery of sound waves by almost twenty years, but it inspired the search that would result in radio and other forms of airborne communications.

In the same year a Pennsylvania printer, Christopher Sholes, put together the first practical typewriter. And in 1870, while Thomas Edison was perfecting his stock ticker, John Hyatt, a New York printer, invented a process for making celluloid that would revolutionize photography and lead to the launching of dozens of major new industries. Meanwhile, in Newark, New Jersey, scientist Edward DeSmedt paved the first American street with an asphalt he had developed from oil.

A year later a Connecticut farmer named Simon Ingersoll invented a pneumatic drill that used the power of steam-generated compressed air to cut through rock. Ingersoll's machine, along with the opening of Andrew Carnegie's first huge Bessemer-process steel plant in Pennsylvania in 1875, and the completion of the Brooklyn Bridge eight years later, endowed civil engineering and heavy construction with radically new parameters of possibility.

The year 1875 saw the advent of another kind of drill as well. This was the comparatively delicate, electric-powered dental drill, which was first perfected by Michigan inventor George Green. Together with the earlier American developments of ether, and then cocaine, as anesthetics, Green's instrument transformed dentistry into a healing art.

In the same year, Edwin Krebs, a German bacteriologist recently immigrated to the United States, discovered *pneumococcus*, the germ that caused the most common and lethal forms of pneumonia. Although, with the exception of surgery and anesthesia, just about all the major medical discoveries up to that time had been made in Europe, Krebs's indentification of the basic pneumonia bacterium, coupled with the expansion of pioneering operations by American surgeons during the 1880s, awakened the country to the potential of organized medical research in curing or eliminating at least a few of the diseases responsible for so many premature deaths and disabilities. Thereafter, centralized medical-care facilities in the form of hospitals, clinics and sanitariums rapidly proliferated, particularly in urban areas and, in the case of highly infectious diseases, in geographically remote sites as well.*

---

*A tuberculosis sanitarium was established by Edward Trudeau at Saranac Lake in the mountains of northern New York in 1884. Ten years later Trudeau added a research laboratory devoted to finding both a cure and a preventive for tuberculosis. In 1889 the Mayo brothers founded their soon-to-be-famous diagnostic and surgical clinic in the small town of Rochester, Minnesota.

The medical awakening also sharpened the nation's concern about public sanitation—again, particularly in urban areas—which in turn made the manufacture and improvement of private indoor plumbing appliances, and the construction of municipal underground sewer and water systems, major growth industries of the 1880s.

It was American surgical innovation and advancement that led most directly to the nation's medical awakening, however. As early as 1849, a few years after the development of anesthesia, Dr. James Marion Sims developed a safe surgical technique for the removal of vaginal tumors in women. In 1858, Ernest Krackowizer improved the laryngoscope, a European invention, and used it to good effect in the diagnosis and treatment of chest diseases. In 1861, Erastus Wolcott perfected a kidney-removal operation. In the mid-1880s several American surgeons introduced the spinal anesthetic. In 1885, Joseph O'Dwyer perfected a form of throat surgery which, although it didn't cure diphtheria, eased the painful consequences of that dread and widespread disease.

A year later appendicitis was identified by Dr. Reginald Fitz as the cause of a common and frequently fatal affliction, and a year after that Thomas Morton performed the first appendectomy, a life-saving operation that eventually became routine. An American surgeon, William Keen, in 1884 was the first to remove a brain tumor successfully. William Halsted, who introduced the use of sterile rubber gloves to surgery in 1889, was also a pioneer in arterial surgery and perfected operations for hernia and breast removal as well.

This is not to suggest that the intensification of medical research and surgical procedure had unalloyedly successful results. Just the opposite was the case—still more patients died than were cured by the medical advances of the period. Yet a favorable pattern had been established which would eventually lead to major breakthroughs in the immunological elimination of many dread diseases, in the surgical cure or management of others, and in the pharmacological treatment of still others.*

The crucial turning point in American medical accomplishment would come with the discovery of X rays by a German sci-

---

*It could be said that the emphasis by the early American medical establishment on surgery in the treatment of disease, rather than on chemistry and pharmacological potions, was due to the country's mechanical proclivities—its "Mr. Fix-It" mentality. For what is surgery but a higher form of mechanical repair work?

entist, Wilhelm Roentgen, in 1895. Although discovered by a foreigner, the technology and uses of X rays were developed and perfected most rapidly in the United States in the form of radiography (the X-ray machine) and radium treatment. Only a year after news of Roentgen's discovery was published, an American physician, Dr. Emil Grube, began to have some success with radium therapy in the nonsurgical treatment of breast cancer. Dr. Robert Abbe started to treat other cancers with X rays in 1903. And by 1913 an American researcher, William Coolidge, developed the first quality X-ray machine, a device that took much of the guesswork out of diagnostic medicine and advanced the art of surgery immeasurably.

The immediate beneficial effects of Coolidge's machine went still further. In league with the philanthropic sentiments of several industrial tycoons, John D. Rockefeller foremost among them, Coolidge's radiographical improvements launched the nation on an organized crusade to conquer the most bedeviling diseases of the time. Rockefeller spent millions to found the first organized medical research laboratory in the country: the Rockefeller Institute in New York. And Andrew Carnegie started a foundation devoted in part to improving and expanding formal medical education. Notwithstanding the fact that their motives may have been suspect, the financial contributions these men and others like them made to medical progress were enormous, albeit symbolic of yet another irony of the American system. On the one hand the monopolists earned their fortunes by exploiting and abusing the ordinary citizen. On the other, whether directly or indirectly, they produced improved products, services and amenities from which the ordinary citizen significantly benefited.

From the esoteric to the mundane, American risk-taking, ingenuity and organizational acumen in the last quarter of the nineteenth century brought an ever-widening range of material convenience and comfort to every aspect of personal and business life. Not a single advance failed to contribute to the profound alteration of the nation's cultural values and attitudes. Toilet paper, which did not begin to be mass-manufactured until the 1870s, was typical of the new American products that changed the country's— indeed the world's—habits.

Until the 1850s there had been no toilet paper as such. People used either old newspaper or coarse wrapping paper for their sanitary needs, substances that not only chronically irritated one of the more tender portions of the anatomy but also produced hemorrhoids and rectal infections in epidemic proportions. The first paper specifically developed for the toilet was manufactured in 1857, corresponding in time to the spread of indoor plumbing. Handmade, it was called Gayetty's Medicated Paper. It came in flat sheets enclosed in a plain wrapper that described it as "Unbleached pearl-coloured pure manilla hemp paper . . . a perfectly pure article for the toilet and for the prevention of piles."

But it was not until the 1870s, when machine technology was developed for mass-producing a softer, more tissuelike paper, that toilet paper became an everyday consumer product. The growth of the industry had ramifications far beyond mere toilet comfort however. During the generation in which it was first introduced, it remained a hard-to-find luxury, hand-fabricated in such limited quantities and priced so dearly—a typical early package of Joseph Gayetty's Medicated Paper cost 50 cents, half a day's wage for most workers—that only the wealthy could afford it. During the next generation, though, mass-produced, easy to find, and sold at much lower cost, it became a household staple.

Imagine today having to live without toilet paper. You would survive, of course, but it would be a messy inconvenience. The generations of the 1880s learned to feel the same way. After the essentials of food, shelter and clothing, toilet paper became the one material item no American family of the period contemplated being happily without, even before enjoying the benefits of indoor toilets. In a very measurable sense, the invention of toilet paper inaugurated yet another revolution—a revolution in mass-consumer needs and expectations.

And that was not all. Toilet paper manufacturers discovered that the key to profitable sales was not only their product's softness, but the package it came in. By the mid-1880s all toilet paper—there were close to a thousand different brands being made by then—possessed more or less the same quality of softness in equivalent price ranges. The ones that proved most popular were those marketed in the most appealing packages. Thus the toilet-paper industry gave birth to the concepts of commercial graphic design and mass packaging, which in turn led to the rise of the advertising industry, which in its turn further fueled the American consumer revolution. The doubly wry irony in this was that because social convention prohibited it, toilet paper, the world's first truly cheap mass-market product, could not be advertised directly or candidly as the product it was. Yet it was toilet paper, through its competitive mass-marketing techniques (packaging), that was the progenitor of modern-day advertising.*

Another American invention of the period that would make a profound impression on the nation's (and eventually the world's) social outlook was the typewriter. Here again, though, it was not just the invention itself but the entrepreneurial manner in which it was promoted that played a key role.

Mechanics and inventors throughout the industrialized world had been tinkering with the idea of a manually operated quick-printing machine since the mid-1700s; even Ben Franklin had sketched a few tentative examples of what such a device might look like. It was not until 1829, though, that a Michigan surveyor, William Burt, actually managed to build a crude machine based on the idea. Burt's creation was virtually useless, however, for it failed to solve the basic problem of manually operated machinery—that of translating a complex human motion of physical articulation into an equivalent but more efficient machine movement. A machine that required more work than the work it was designed to replace was of no value, even in an age when fascination with machines of all kinds was spreading like wildfire.

Yet Burt's "typograph," as he called his cumbersome mechanism, was a beginning. Fifteen years later Elias Howe devoted weeks of intensive study to the idea of a writing device while trying to solve the mechanical articulation problems associated with his invention of the sewing machine. During the same period Charles Thurber, a Connecticut mechanic, also tackled the problem and produced an improved version of Burt's typograph.

It was not until the late 1860s, though, that the idea of a writing machine began to approach the realm of feasibility. In 1867,

*Cooking pots, stoves, lanterns and other such "convenience" products became available en masse before toilet paper, of course. But because they remained considerably more expensive, they were items most people had to save carefully for in order to purchase. (A good kettle cost nearly $25 in 1875, a kerosene lantern $15.) As for such items as soaps and candles, these too preceded toilet tissue but were always considered necessaries which, if they could not be bought cheaply, were made in the home. Precisely because toilet tissue could not be made in the home, but grew to be viewed as a necessity of home life, it became the nation's first genuine mass-consumer product.

Christopher Sholes, a forty-eight-year-old Pennsylvania-born journalist and politician then active in Milwaukee, collaborated with two colleagues to build the first such practical machine based on ideas that had come to him while watching his daughter play the piano. Milwaukee was still a remote corner of the United States in the 1860s, however, and Sholes's machine went generally unnoticed and unappreciated until he sought out, in 1869, a financial promoter named James Densmore. By then, Sholes and his partners in invention, Carlos Glidden and Samuel Soulé, had built several more complex samples of their original prototype. Densmore, a florid, impulsive man, took one look at the most recent device and offered to put his entire fortune behind it. The mild-mannered Sholes agreed.*

Thereafter the development of the typewriter became as much the handiwork of James Densmore as Christopher Sholes. The dynamic Densmore hounded Sholes and his colleagues into producing a series of progressively improved versions of their machine. Some twenty-eight successive models were made, each of which Densmore sent away to be tested by various operators, most of them court stenographers in the East. Early in 1873, when the promoter was satisfied that Sholes had produced the best machine possible, he bought out the inventor's rights and began to search for an established machinery manufacturer with which to collaborate.

Densmore settled on E. Remington and Sons of Ilion, New York, a firearms maker that had prospered during the Civil War through its development of the repeating rifle. After the war the Remington firm had tried to expand into the manufacture of sewing machines, but with the national market dominated by the Howe and Singer companies, it had experienced only limited local success. Densmore guessed that Remington would welcome the chance to pioneer in the manufacture and marketing of an entirely new invention, one that promised to be every bit as significant and lucrative as the sewing machine, and to reward him handsomely in the bargain.

He was right. Along with a business colleague, George Yost,

---

*Sholes's first device had been a one-letter "imprinter" that looked much like a telegraph machine. It was only after watching his daughter practice on the piano that the idea of a multikeyed machine occurred to him. Sholes required the help of Glidden and Soulé to build such a mechanically complex prototype. Although much larger than today's typical typewriter, it operated on the same basic principles.

Densmore demonstrated the final prototype he had acquired from Sholes and Glidden to company president Philo Remington at the armsmaker's Ilion factory in mid-1873. After Densmore and Yost left Remington's office, Remington remarked to Henry Benedict, his financial adviser, "It isn't necessary to tell these people that we are crazy over the invention, but I'm afraid I am pretty nearly so."

After rewarding Densmore with a favorable royalty contract, the Remington company designed a few added improvements, mainly in the area of the machine's strength and stability, and in 1874 began to manufacture the Sholes-Glidden typewriter under its own name. Not surprisingly, it encountered considerable consumer resistance to its new offering at first. Although the typewriter's primary market was surely the business world, Remington salesmen found it almost impossible to persuade business managers of its virtues in expediting office labor.

In the first place, typewriter operators required special training for the machine's full speed and efficiency to be realized. Second, office administrators were more conservative than those who ran factories and warehouses. Offices were organized so as to present the most dignified front possible to a company's clientele, both actual and potential, an appearance of utmost deliberation and probity. A machine such as a typewriter, it was thought, would provoke the immediate suspicion of customers. To allow a machine to come between a customer and a representative of the business would be to erode the "personal touch." Further, limited experience had shown that many customers were insulted by typewritten letters and bills—did the senders assume they could not read handwriting? Others suspected that the typewritten letters they received were nothing more than personalized but impersonal circulars. Still another factor was expense. The handwriting of a hundred letters or bills cost only a few cents in pen, ink and paper, plus the cheap labor of a single clerk. The typewriter was a machine that required an outlay of at least $125 and the training of an operator, and it still did not supply the paper.

Not even the exhibition of the Remington typewriter at the 1876 Centennial Exposition in Philadelphia helped much. There, like Bell's telephone boxes, the device was treated more as a plaything than as a serious contribution to the age of progress. Oddly enough, it was a representative of that breed of American often thought to be among the most resistant to the mechanical imper-

sonalization and homogenization of society, the writer, who stimulated the first serious commercial interest in the typewriter—a
machine destined indeed to play a key role in the impersonaliza-
tion and homogenization of the nation's society.

The writer in question was Mark Twain. Twain boasted of
having composed his 1876 novel *The Adventures of Tom Sawyer* on a
Remington machine. He also provided a backhanded endorsement
of the typewriter when, in the same year, he sent a letter to the
Remington company declaring, "I have entirely stopped using the
Type Writer for the reason that I never could write a letter to
anybody without receiving a request by return mail that would I
not only describe the machine but state what progress I had made
in the use of it, etc., etc."

Twain's well-publicized success with the typewriter finally
generated an active market for it in the book, magazine and newspaper worlds in the late 1870s. Printers especially were grateful
for the chance to set type from mechanically produced rather than
handwritten manuscript. Courts also began to favor the acquisition of typewriters for the recording of their proceedings.* But
the most potentially lucrative market—the fast-expanding community of commercial business offices—continued to resist the
new machine well into the 1880s. It was not until the latter part of
that decade, when the discouraged Remington transferred its distribution interests to an aggressive independent sales company,
that the office market began grudgingly to yield.

This was because the sales company, one of whose principals
was Henry Benedict, Philo Remington's chief marketing and financial adviser, instituted a series of high-powered marketing,
promotion and training programs modeled on those of the major
sewing-machine companies and the McCormick Harvester organization. Special bonuses were offered to businesses that installed
typewriters in their offices, guaranteed service and repair contracts were included in the sales invoices, free typing schools were
established for office employees, and sophisticated advertising
campaigns, all emphasizing the "progressiveness" of the type-
writer-equipped office, were mounted. By the early 1890s, the

*Eventually the court system of the United States, through its various procedural and
statutory regulations, would mandate the use of the typewriter in the composition of all
court documents. The publishing industry would promulgate a similar if unofficial rule
with regard to "copy."

business-office market for typewriters began to flourish. Competing companies, offering their own versions of the machine, were launched. As the century turned, the typewriter gradually became a staple of American office procedure.

Two major consequences flowed from this change. The first had to do with the role of women in American society. Until the 1890s, most women who worked were limited by the country's social traditions, and by their economic or ethnic status, to unskilled or relatively unskilled occupations.* Nursing and teaching were the only pursuits capable of offering women "respectable" or "educated" work. But because organized schooling and medical-care systems were still in their infancy, such employment was open to only a comparative few.

The typewriter offered women a new kind of work. It was work that required sustained training and competitive skills. It was work that also provided competent women with the opportunity to remove themselves from the "blue-collar" environment of the workshop and ascend to the "white-collar" atmosphere of the business office, until then an all-male bastion, and to gain a modicum of respectability and economic independence. The long-term effect was to introduce women in increasing numbers to the dynamics of the American business system, with results that no one in the late nineteenth century could imagine. It is almost to belabor the obvious to suggest that the invention of the typewriter was the single most important event in the history of the emancipation of the American woman from her peculiar form of social, economic and political disenfranchisement.†

The other consequence of Christopher Sholes's invention was even more sweeping. It consisted first of the radical reform of business and management methods occasioned by the typewriter —for instance, the more efficient division of labor, mechanized bookkeeping, systematized filing and indexing, multigraphing and circularization (which were to become industries in themselves) —and, conversely, the phenomenon the world has come to know as "red tape." Second, and of yet greater consequence, were the numerous mechanical progeny inspired, if not directly sired, by the

---

*In 1890, of the total American work force of about 21 million gainfully employed, 3 percent were women. Of that percentage, about 95 percent worked at what today we would call menial jobs.

†Women would not even achieve the right to vote in all the United States until 1920, when the Nineteenth Amendment was ratified.

introduction of the typewriter: the checkwriter, the addressograph, the mimeograph, the calculator, the photographic duplicator, the intercom, the teletype, indeed even the modern-day electronic "state of the art" computer. All of these devices and more made it possible eventually for the mechanics of doing business to catch up with the speed of outside production, transport and commerce, which had already been increased by comparable mechanization.

The typewriter cleared the way for the intensive specialization that became so characteristic of the American business world. And it helped to generate the proliferation of countless new, specialized service industries and systems upon which the country came to depend for its economic, social and political organization. The typewriter, in short, was yet another vital paving stone on the road to colossus.

CHAPTER 21

THE CATALYST

The major American inventions and discoveries of the 1870s and 1880s were merely the tip of a vast iceberg of technological and scientific activity that was rapidly transforming the country into one of the world's most materially advanced nations. The metaphor is apt, for among other developments, a technique of making ice artificially, first devised by Thaddeus Lowe in 1865, had turned the mass manufacture of ice into a widespread and much-valued industry in the 1870s. Not only did Lowe's discovery revolutionize methods of preserving and transporting perishable foods, thereby creating a whole new branch of commercial agriculture, it also turned what had once been a luxury commodity into a common product, particularly in the nation's cities. What's more, it led to quick advances in many other areas of life, from the further expansion, specialization and diversification of retail food markets and leisure-time eating establishments to the facilitation of medical research (scientific laboratories required huge amounts of ice to freeze or refrigerate biochemical specimens) and the eventual development of electromechanical refrigeration.

The revolution in the distribution and retailing of food, brought about by abundant and cheap ice, led to a further revolution in the distribution and retailing of household and personal goods—at first mainly clothes, bedding, and other "soft" products, but later furniture, household implements and "hard" products, or hardware and appliances. Watching the urban marketing of food become centralized under single roofs and managements, dry-goods retailers began to expand on the earlier idea of department stores to include an ever-widening variety of commercial products. As a result, the modest dry-goods stores of the pre-

1870s quickly evolved into huge retail shopping emporiums, and not a city of any size was without at least one. The success of such mammoth centers then spurred the development, for the benefit of that sector of the population beyond easy access to cities, of the catalogue mail-order shopping industry, thus bringing millions of additional buyers into the consumer stream.*

The rapid growth of urban department stores, along with the intensification and diversification of other forms of commerce in the cities (banking, law, construction and real-estate development, for instance), also kindled a sharp transformation in the nature of public intracity transit. The horse trolley had remained the basic form of cheap transit in most cities of any size until the 1890s, although in San Francisco the cable car had been invented, its central machinery driven by steam, and New York had built a network of elevated steam railways. Edison's electrical discoveries changed all that, and in due course the electric-powered street trolley was introduced and was followed—at least in New York— by another Brooklyn Bridge-like miracle of engineering daring: the subterranean railroad, or subway.

The success of the department store and mail-order business had yet another transforming effect on the nation. That was the further stimulus it provided to "consumer-oriented" invention— the creation of new products of personal convenience and comfort—and to mass manufacture. As Schuyler Wheeler, the creator of the first electric fan in 1882, recalled in a personal memoir written in 1912, he received the inspiration for his invention by walking into the new Wanamaker department store in Philadelphia on an oppressively hot day in 1880. After inspecting the wide diversity of merchandise, he wondered what "was not available that could and should be." As he mopped his brow against the stifling heat made all the more intense by the store's arc-lighting system, the answer came to him.

It was upon mass manufacture, though, that the success of the stores and the later mail-order firms made their greatest immediate mark. The public appeal of the stores derived not only from their cheap bulk prices and centralized convenience, but also from the diversity and comprehensiveness of their inventories. This in fact

---

*In the 1870s, when the mail-order industry got its initial modest start with the founding of Montgomery Ward in Chicago, more than half the population lived beyond easy access to the nation's major cities.

became the central feature of their advertising. In an increasing number of cities, competing retailers vied for essentially the same customers, and such claims, along with announcements of the installation of the latest shopping "come-ons" (easy credit, elevators, ceiling fans in summer), were paramount. "Come to Stewart's Palace," implored a broadside for the eight-story New York department store of Alexander Stewart in the 1870s: "Guaranteed the Most Economical Prices in Town, Liberal Credit Terms on Consequential Purchases, The Richest Variety of Choices to Choose From." Stewart's main rival of the time, Haughwout's Department Store, would not be outdone. "Patronize the Haughwout Emporium," urged a circular for that store, which was smaller than Stewart's by three floors but was equipped with one of the first of Elisha Otis's new safety elevators. "Pick From the Most Generous Selection of Goods To Be Found in the City. No One Leaves Disappointed."

The competition among department stores to stock the greatest variety of merchandise—a strategy that quickly spread to all sorts of retail establishments specializing in consumer goods, including the catalogue companies—kept American workshops and factories humming in the 1880s and produced a remarkable expansion of new manufacturing enterprises based on improved or freshly invented consumer products.* And although the economic boom of the first half of the decade began to decay during the late 1880s, at least insofar as manufacturing was concerned, the attraction of falling prices kept consumer commerce at a relatively high level for several years more.

This was what so stunned the public when the country's overall economy again suddenly collapsed in 1893. Generally ignorant of the deterioration of the nation's overextended industrial and financial substructure, and having been able, through steadily declining prices, to maintain and even increase its rate of consumption, the public had grown firmly accustomed to material

---

*Schuyler Wheeler's portable electric fan was a graphic case in point. Invented in 1882, it was dependent on the installation of the electrical distribution systems pioneered by Edison. Once urban households and offices began to receive electricity later in the 1880s, Wheeler's fan—although more cumbersome, not unlike today's room fans—became a retailing sensation. Soon other inventors and manufacturers came up with their own "improved" versions, thereby circumventing Wheeler's patent. By 1890 dozens of different brand-name fans were being manufactured and marketed. People often bought one or more of them well before they had electricity, but in anticipation of receiving it.

acquisition. The 1893 crash was the first in the country's history to affect so large a segment of the population, if only because the two prior decades of invention, purchase credit, retail competition and industrial advancement had brought so many more Americans into the commercial marketplace. The public, much of it thrown out of work, all of it angry and disenchanted at the turn of events, was therefore all the more willing to join the small chorus of social and economic reformers who blamed the "greedy, socially irresponsible" business-industrial establishment for its woes.

Of course, in many respects the reformers were right. But also right were the apologists of big business who raised the defense that, had it not been for the daring and foresight of business and industry, the public would never have had the opportunity to enjoy the material progress and abundance it had. The competing claims were but another symbol of the basic paradox of the American system, the outlines of which had by then become deeply etched in the country's consciousness and were in the process of being further illuminated by the unpredictable economic dynamics of the nation's commercial and industrial revolution.

Seen in this new light, the paradox arranged itself as a conflict between the one and the many. The "one" stood for the rugged individualism and freedom from economic restraint that had formed the basis of American free-enterprise capitalism and brought the country so rapidly to its advanced material state. The "many" represented just what it implied—the tens of millions of Americans who, lacking the ingenuity and initiative of the "ones," were dependent for their well-being, if not their survival, on the benevolence of the system the ones had created.

On a more intellectual level, the paradox took the form of a bitter ideological conflict between the well-entrenched principles of survival-of-the-fittest capitalism, as espoused by Herbert Spencer earlier in the century, and the precepts of industrial socialism that had more recently washed ashore on the continuing flood tide of immigration from central Europe. If the paradox could not be fully resolved, at least it had to be tempered and balanced so as to accommodate the needs and impulses of the opposing factions. What was required was a catalyst.

And so a catalyst emerged. His name was Theodore Roosevelt.

*   *   *

Born in New York in 1858 to an old, patrician Dutch family, Roosevelt, after graduating from Harvard in 1880, decided to pursue a career in Republican politics and public service. He started by being elected to a term in the New York State Assembly in 1882. After losing a New York City mayoralty contest, he was successively a commissioner of the United States Civil Service and president of the Board of Police Commissioners of New York. In each of these positions he emerged as a dynamic public personality and an advocate of social and economic reform.* He resigned as New York's police commissioner in 1897 to become Assistant Secretary of the Navy at the beginning of William McKinley's Republican presidential administration, which had committed itself to including in its ranks a few token "progressive" Republicans in order to counter the growing mass-electoral appeal of the increasingly labor-dominated Democratic party of William Jennings Bryan. After preparing the navy for war with Spain, Roosevelt left to join the army when the Spanish-American War broke out. He became one of the war's foremost heroes when, as a colonel, he led a charge of unmounted cavalry during the battle for San Juan Hill in Cuba during the summer of 1898.

Capitalizing on his wartime celebrity, Roosevelt ran for the governorship of New York later that year and won. He distinguished himself during his brief term, and at the same time infuriated the state's old-line Republican bosses, by waging a vigorous fight for political reform within the state. As a result, he was nominated as vice-presidential running mate in McKinley's 1900 campaign to retain the White House—a nomination engineered by New York's Republican satraps eager to remove him from the state scene. Despite the cynical political motives behind his nomination, Roosevelt's progressive presence on the ticket was in McKinley's favor, for it did much to neutralize the magnetism of William Jennings Bryan, running again as the Democratic nominee.

It was less than a year after McKinley's reelection that the hand of fate again twisted the course of human-engineered events. On September 6, 1901, McKinley was shot by an anarchist assassin while attending an industrial exposition in Buffalo, New York. He died of his wound a week later and Theodore Roosevelt, by then known universally as Teddy, became President.

---

*The Civil Service had been the first institutional breeding ground of social reform in the United States in the early 1870s. Much of Roosevelt's later personal commitment to progressivism derived from his term as Civil Service commissioner between 1889 and 1895.

Shortly before these events, Wall Street had confounded the government's earlier legislative attempts to combat monopolization, and had flouted the public's sharpened sensitivities to monopolistic expansion, by forming the United States Steel Corporation and the Northern Securities Company—combinations designed to dominate the steel and railroad industries respectively. The principal concern of selective antimonopolists like Roosevelt had become that such huge combinations, by fixing the prices for their exclusively controlled goods and services, exerted excessive influence on the economy and inhibited the fair distribution of wealth. Democratic and socialist antimonopolists went beyond that to attack the monopolies' ability to perpetuate paltry wage scales and miserable working conditions, and to keep the majority of the population in economic thrall to a handful of financiers and industrialists.

By 1900 the nation's middle class had taken shape. Its attitudes embraced these fundamental concerns, and its values supported both the chance for industry to expand and flourish most efficiently, and the chance for every working citizen to share in and benefit from expansion. McKinley, despite his superficial political concessions to the antimonopolism of the 1890s, had remained basically a tool of the big-business monopolists. Teddy Roosevelt, in addition to his genuine progressivism, was motivated by political and historical ambition to distinguish his own presidency from that of McKinley.* To do so he had to part company with the nakedly pro-big-business Republican past. Yet politically he could not afford to identify himself too closely with the socialistic, anti-big-business Democratic present. His road was clearly a middle one between the two. Thus his constituency became America's expanding middle class, the strengthening instinctive thread of compromise and consensus in the country's political and economic fabric. It was around the two successive presidential administrations of Teddy Roosevelt in this century's first decade that America's middle-class social values, economic attitudes and political sentiments would crystallize and become institutionalized.

In his first major act as President, Roosevelt went before Congress to request powerful and comprehensive legislation that would, without weakening American industrial development, put a permanent end to the more sophisticated kind of monopolism symbolized by the formation of U.S. Steel and Northern Securities. To

---

*And also by the explosion of "muckraking" literature, which detailed the worst abuses of the big-business monopolism of the previous thirty years.

a Congress controlled by traditional McKinley Republicans who were financed largely by big-business interests, however, Roosevelt was viewed at best as an upstart and at worst as a traitor to the principles of McKinleyism. He failed to get congressional action.

As a result, in 1902 he set out to take matters into his own hands, first by using the Justice Department to seek the dissolution of Northern Securities under the provisions of the Sherman Antitrust Act, then by touring the country prior to that year's congressional elections to promote a new Republican political philosophy based on the slogan of "a square deal for all." Roosevelt's campaign produced a more sympathetic Republican Congress in 1903, and thereafter he began to get some of the stronger regulatory legislation he sought. First enacted was the Expedition Act, which facilitated the Justice Department's prosecution of antitrust suits by giving such actions precedence on the dockets of the federal courts and by relaxing certain traditional standards of evidence and proof.

Then, still in 1903, Congress created the government's first executive-branch department since the establishment of the Department of Agriculture in 1889. The formation of the new agency, called the Department of Commerce and Labor, clearly reflected the nation's growing preoccupation with its radically changed political and economic circumstances. The department's key component was the Bureau of Corporations, which was empowered to investigate and report on the internal operations of corporations engaged in interstate commerce.* This watchdog mechanism was included at the particular insistence of Roosevelt.

Finally in 1903, after seeing to the reorganization of the War Department, Roosevelt masterminded the passage of the Elkins Act, which put powerful enforcement teeth into the Interstate Commerce Act of 1887. Roosevelt's activist measures did much to blunt the negative impact on Republicanism of the muckrakers, whose disturbing books and magazine articles were reaching the height of their influence. As a result, in 1904, campaigning on an expanded Square Deal platform, Roosevelt was returned to the White House by a comfortable electoral margin. For the next four years he vigorously pressed his business and economic reforms, through both additional regulatory legislation and executive-branch legal actions. In 1904 the Supreme Court had upheld the govern-

---

*Several states had already established similar investigative bodies to monitor the activities of corporations doing business solely within their borders.

ment in its suit to dissolve the Northern Securities Company, thereby providing the Roosevelt administration with the impetus and rationale to spread its prosecutorial wings.

Indeed, the seven years of Roosevelt's presidency produced an enormous increase in the number of cases the Supreme Court considered with respect to the government's constitutional right to regulate or otherwise intervene in the private economic and business sector. For all practical purposes, the Supreme Court became the ultimate arbiter of America's future economic development. It began to function in lieu of a series of specific, restrictive economic amendments being added to the Constitution—measures that many social reformers had been proposing for the previous quarter-century. As time went on, the Supreme Court would play an increasingly determinative role in the *de jure* amendment and amplification of the Constitution, making it as much an economic charter for the nation as it had been a political one. Each such new amplification would pave the way, in the interests of greater domestic economic and social democracy, to equivalently more frequent government intervention in the affairs of the nation's populace.

If only for his trust-busting and other government-imposed reform and regulatory policies, Teddy Roosevelt's legacy to the country would have been enormous. But he was the author of another legacy as well, this one sharply contradictory in its nature and eventual impact on the nation.* It was a legacy of several vital parts—of heightened nationalism, patriotism and ethnocentrism, of vigorous domestic industrial expansionism, and of foreign economic and political adventurism. If the United States had been born as an international power in the wake of Matthew Perry's 1853 expedition to the Orient, and if it had come of age as such during the Spanish-American War, it became supremely conscious of its maturing global potency as a result of Teddy Roosevelt's presidency. The instrumentality of that awakening was Roosevelt's sponsorship of the building of the Panama Canal.

American interest in the construction of a canal across the narrow isthmus linking North and South America was as old as the

---

*Despite his antimonopolism, Roosevelt was in no way antibusiness. He always distinguished between "good trusts" and "bad trusts," and he had no tolerance for socialists or other apostles of radical reform. It might be said that he was the original American political middle-of-the-roader.

1848 Mexican War. What had stood in the way then was not a lack of engineering know-how but political barriers; the United States was quite confident of its canal-building capabilities but could not make appropriate arrangements with the British, who exercised the principal foreign control over the region. Proposals for such a canal, designed to connect the east and west coasts of the United States by a much-shortened sea route, were pursued until 1869, when the first transcontinental railroad was completed. For a few years the proposals were forgotten. Then President Ulysses S. Grant sent out naval exploring expeditions and established the U.S. Interoceanic Canal Commission in 1872. Interest further revived with the buildup of the American "steel navy" in the 1880s, and with the realization that the United States had a pressing strategic need for such a canal to expedite the movements of its modernized fleet between the Atlantic and the Pacific.

As Assistant Secretary of the Navy just prior to the Spanish-American War, Teddy Roosevelt was particularly adamant in voicing that need. The war itself, fought both in the Atlantic-Caribbean area and in the eastern Pacific, served to underscore it. By the time Roosevelt became President, the McKinley administration, under Roosevelt's prodding while Vice-President, had already established a policy designed to reach an agreement with the British whereby the United States could build a canal. Roosevelt made the achievement of such an agreement one of his first priorities upon reaching the White House, and in November 1901 an accord was formally signed.*

But that was just the end of one stage of the process and the beginning of another. The Anglo-American pact produced a complex two-year political and economic squabble with Colombia— which claimed sovereign rights to the Panamanian isthmus—that was not resolved until Roosevelt threatened forcibly to seize the isthmus with American troops and a naval armada. As it happened, the administration did help to engineer a sudden revolution in Colombia's Panamanian province. In 1903 the province declared its independence and was immediately accorded recognition as the independent Republic of Panama by the United States. Shortly thereafter, Panama granted the United States, in perpetuity, full

*The Hay-Pauncefote Treaty. The original plan of the United States was to build a canal across Nicaragua, but for financial and engineering reasons it later opted for the narrower Isthmus of Panama.

use and control of a canal zone ten miles wide across its territory, giving it in addition complete sovereignty over the zone. In exchange, the United States guaranteed Panama's independence and agreed to pay the new republic $10 million, plus an annual fee of $250,000 beginning in 1913, when, it was anticipated, the canal would be opened. Under the Hay-Pauncefote Treaty with Great Britain, the Panama Canal Zone was to be neutral and open to the shipping of all nations, and it could be armed and fortified by the United States only for defensive purposes.

The building of the canal and the events that led up to it had a galvanizing effect on the United States, both politically and industrially. Politically it solidified America's status as a major world power, particularly when the start of its construction in 1904 prompted Teddy Roosevelt to issue his so-called Roosevelt Corollary to the Monroe Doctrine. The Monroe Doctrine of almost a century before had endeavored to bar the intervention of European powers in affairs particular to the Western Hemisphere—North, Central and South America. The Roosevelt Corollary, an outgrowth of Roosevelt's "Big Stick" approach to foreign policy, transformed the Monroe Doctrine into one that practically assured American intervention in the affairs of the hemisphere.

But it was upon the further development of American invention, technological progress and industry, and upon all the domestic socioeconomic systems and processes that flowed from that development, that the Panama Canal left its most vital imprint. Although a politician, Teddy Roosevelt played as important a role in the building of the road to colossus as any inventor or business tycoon.

CHAPTER 22

THE TWENTIETH CENTURY

By the time the preliminary engineering surveys for the Panama Canal were started in 1902, the fruits of the wide range of American invention and technological innovation during the last quarter of the nineteenth century were well on their way to being disseminated, not only throughout the United States but across the world. These benefits had three essential applications. The first was to private-sector industry and consisted of all those new or improved processes, machines, and labor and financial systems designed to enhance and further diversify manufacture and production. The second was to the expansion of the nation's public-sector economic and physical latticework—mechanisms and processes that expedited the construction and improvement of the country's transportation, communications, electrical, water-supply, sanitation, health, commerce and other basic systems. The third application was to the consumer sector—all those industrially provided new goods and services which had the potential to make individual life more convenient, comfortable and diverting.

Of course, the three distinct categories were inevitably intermixed and interdependent. For example, a convenient new electrical appliance was of no use without the installation of an electrical generating and transmission system, without the mined and transported coal required to power the system, and without the human labor needed to operate and maintain it. But the three could be said to constitute the triangular base of America's own unique industrial revolution, the foundation upon which the co-lossal pyramid of the country's material, technological and scientific advancement was erecting itself.

The start of the construction of the Panama Canal marked the end of an era and the definitive beginning of the America we know today. The old era—the forty-year period since the end of the Civil War—had seen the transfer of the original Industrial Revolution from Europe to the United States. During that time America had vastly expanded the notion of invention and technological discovery, had perfected the basic techniques of mass production, heavy manufacture and their management, and had begun to spread the benefits of both beyond the narrow market of the economically privileged few to that of the masses. Indeed, among the nation's other watershed inventions was that of the mass market—the idea that the birthright of *every* citizen was ready access to the country's material largesse.

The only thing the country had not yet succeeded in doing was to appropriate Europe's nineteenth-century revolution in the pure sciences. The physical and material progress of recent history has been as much dependent on scientific discovery as on mechanical invention—if not more so. Up to the time of Teddy Roosevelt's presidency, almost every vital abstract scientific breakthrough had been achieved in Europe. The building of the Panama Canal was about to alter that fact. The transformation was sparked by the American conquest of yellow fever in Panama and the subsequent application of that victory to keep down the disease during the canal's construction. Thereafter, the United States would become one of the world's foremost bastions of organized scientific research, practical and abstract.

The most compelling effect of the canal, though, was its impact on the psychology of the country. The idea of constructing such a canal was not in itself revolutionary, to be sure; America had a long history of daring and proficiency in canal building. Besides, the completion of the Suez Canal thirty-five years earlier had made the prospect of a man-made interocean waterway no longer remarkable. Nevertheless, at the start of the twentieth century the idea of the Panama Canal loomed in the American mind as a monumental undertaking, the more so because it would be pursued far beyond the nation's borders and at a tropical site already infamous for its environmental inhospitability. Thus the prospect of the canal represented a pioneering new chapter in the history of American industrial and economic ambition, in breadth and scope far beyond the achievements in canal, railroad and bridge building so far made by the United States. Yet the construction of the canal, with all its environmental, topographical and engineering problems, was believed by Americans to be a project only the United States was qualified to undertake.*

What this popular mood of challenge and pride did was to reinforce the intense nationalism that had been produced in America by the Spanish-American War, and to inflate further the nation's industrial self-consciousness. The former effect, which was additionally stimulated in the decade after the war by Teddy Roosevelt's policy of plainspoken internationalism, drove American finance and industry more aggressively than ever into foreign trade and into the exploitation of foreign natural resources. It was during Roosevelt's presidency, for instance, that John D. Rockefeller began to think about competing with British, French and Dutch interests for oil discoveries in the Middle East, and it was in the same period that other American industries first developed their own bases abroad to extract vital natural resources that were scarce or nonexistent in America. These enterprises—the acquisition of foreign oil and other resources—would eventually play a crucial role in the expansion of American technology and industry.

The latter effect—the swelling of America's industrial self-consciousness—was of more immediate impact. Quite simply, the psychological gearing-up of the country toward the building of the Panama Canal spilled over into every area of domestic industry and finance. The canal was to be the most visible turn-of-the-century symbol of what the United States was capable of accomplishing economically and industrially. As such, it represented not just a portion, but all of the country's industrial ingenuity and potential. The metaphor of the canal had raised the stakes of the American gamble, and those who were the chief gamblers—the inventors, industrialists, financiers and investors—were ready to match the raise.

*Even the British had declined to consider constructing a canal across the Panamanian isthmus. The Suez Canal, coursing as it did through a flat desert landscape, had posed relatively simple engineering problems.

*   *   *

In today's retrospective terms, the discovery of oil and practical electricity were the two most important American technological developments of the nineteenth century. Perhaps because it was more recent, electricity and its commercial applications had remained almost exclusively within the American engineering, industrial and financial domains up to the start of the twentieth century; most foreign deployment of electrical systems and devices, including the telephone, was done under complex American patent licenses. The development of petroleum technology, however—not only because the discovery of oil had preceded that of electricity by twenty years, but also because oil itself was not a patentable substance—had already spread to Europe by the time Edison invented his light bulb.

European interest in petroleum stemmed particularly from the fact that oil, in addition to being a mineral substance, was a complex chemical as well. In the 1860s, research experience in practical chemistry in England, France, Germany and other northern European countries was still far ahead of that in the United States. So too was chemistry-based research in metallurgy and the development of new alloys. And so were ideas about devising a more efficient replacement for the steam engine as a source of small-scale mechanical power. The conjunction of these three research paths led to the creation of the world's first crude internal combustion engines, initially in France, then in Germany. Early experiments were conducted primarily with coal-based illuminating gases as fuel, as well as with other more recent, laboratory-discovered volatile chemicals. The experiments proved that internal combustion was feasible, but that available fuels were inadequate. Also, the experimental engines were still much too large and cumbersome to be of practical small-scale use.

News of the experiments reached the United States in the late 1860s. As a result, on the basis of sketchy descriptions, several inventors and mechanical engineers embarked on their own experiments. The one who would become best known was George Selden—neither an inventor nor an engineer, but a Yale-educated patent lawyer from Rochester, New York, whose legal practice had inspired him to try to join the ranks of his clients.* Selden,

---

*One of Selden's later clients would be George Eastman. Beginning in 1880, Eastman, a former bank clerk, would pioneer in inventions with celluloid—itself invented by John Hyatt, another American—that would transform still-photography into an everyday hobby and contribute mightily to Edison's and others' development of motion pictures.

also using illuminating gas, built and successfully ran his first engine in 1878 after visiting the 1876 Philadelphia Centennial Exposition and inspecting several of the huge European experimental samples. His engine was considerably smaller than its European counterparts and weighed much less—370 pounds as compared to the 1,200-pound average of the foreign machines. Thereafter, except for his legal work for George Eastman, Selden devoted all of his energies to improving his version of the internal combustion engine.

In the meantime, over the next few years the Europeans not only managed to reduce the size of their engines but also learned that petroleum, theretofore used only as a lubricant and source of kerosene, could be chemically refined in such a way as to produce a much more powerfully combustible and efficient fuel than illuminating fluid. This new petroleum derivative, first discovered by the German chemist Friedrich Kekule, was the precursor of what we know today as gasoline. Since the internal combustion engine depended for its power on the expansion and ignition of explosive gases within an enclosed piston chamber, the more explosive the fuel, the more efficient and powerful the engine would be.*

In 1876, while George Selden in America was still contemplating his ideas about internal combustion, Nikolaus Otto in Germany built the world's first four-stroke gasoline engine. During the next ten years Otto's engine was tried as a substitute for steam power in a succession of small factories in Germany, but without much success, since most of its power was spent in turning its internal machinery. During the same period, however, two other German engineers, Gottlieb Daimler and Karl Benz, were working on the idea of applying the Otto engine's basic principles to small-carriage locomotion. By 1885, Daimler had developed a smaller four-stroke engine and Benz had assembled the world's first gasoline-powered self-propelled vehicle, a three-wheel carriage with a Daimler engine attached to its axle.

In America, meanwhile, George Selden had been improving his own gasoline engine—a two-cycle device—primarily for the

---

*The mechanics of the internal combustion engine were similar to those of the steam engine—that is, the repeated compression of a gas, within an enclosed chamber, powered a reciprocating piston that was mechanically linked to a drive mechanism.

purpose of outdoing Nikolaus Otto's German factory engines. By 1883 Selden's engines were beginning to be used in a few small mills, shops and factories in America, in place of steam engines, to drive light machinery. American interest in internal combustion might have stopped there, however, had it not been for the advent of Karl Benz's first gas-powered carriage. The United States, with its expansive geography, was a natural locus for developing the concept of the self-propelled vehicle. Already American inventors had produced steam-powered personal road carriages, only to find them too bulky and mechanically complex to appeal to the general public. Steam seemed destined to be confined to mass long-distance transportation—boats and railroads—while the horse would apparently remain the principal means of personal short-distance conveyance.

Benz's German automobile, appearing in its first few manifestations as little more than an oversized toy, ignited the American engineering imagination when photos of it reached the United States in 1886. Shortly thereafter Charles Duryea, a machinist in Chicopee, Massachusetts, produced the first American prototype of a gasoline-powered vehicle. It too was toylike—a fragile, noisy, self-propelled open carriage operated through an array of levers, cranks and rods. But by 1892, Duryea and his brother Frank had put together a manufacturing and assembly shop and were able to sell a few samples of their road machine, which was powered by an engine modeled on George Selden's two-stroker. Although Selden had perfected the first such American engine, he had used his patent lawyer's wiles to delay obtaining an actual patent while still preserving his exclusive first rights to it. This bit of legalistic sleight-of-hand would play a significant role in the subsequent development of the automobile, and thus in the further transformation of American industry. The other vital ingredient in the crucible of transformation would take the form of a young Michigan mechanic named Henry Ford.

Henry Ford, born on a farm near the village of Dearborn in 1863, had left school at fifteen to become an apprentice in a Detroit machine shop, then a traveling repairman for a farm-machinery manufacturer. In 1887, after operating a sawmill for several years—one of the first mills in the Great Lakes region to use a Selden engine to power its cutting machinery—Ford was hired as chief engineer of the recently formed Edison Illuminating Company of Detroit, which was in the process of wiring that still-small city for electricity.

In the course of his employment with the local Edison company, the twenty-five-year-old Ford became an unabashed admirer of the "Wizard of Menlo Park" and resolved to pattern his life after Edison's—to organize and perfect a progressive mechanical and engineering system that was still in the experimental stage, and to make its end product available on a mass basis to the general public. That Ford chose the automobile to pursue his goal was because the automobile, still in its earliest experimental form, represented a future stage of progress that seemed potentially as important and profitable as Edison's development of commercial electricity.

Ford's initial venture in gasoline-powered vehicles came in 1892, when, after the Duryea Brothers had built their first models in Massachusetts, he constructed his own crude bicycle-wheeled version, using a Selden engine, in his backyard tool shed in Detroit. By 1896 he had improved his machine sufficiently to convince himself that the time was ripe to go into competition with the Duryea brothers, who had sold thirteen of their automobiles that year. Ford, dubbing his tiny, chain-driven, self-propelled carriage the "quadricycle," demonstrated it to potential investors in the company he set out to form.*

Although engineers and inventors were enthralled by the idea of the automobile (scores of other mechanically minded Americans were working on their own versions by 1896), the country at large was indifferent, even hostile, to the noisy new contraption. As a result, Ford was unable to raise enough money to charter a company until 1901, and even then the firm, due to financial squabbles between the autocratic Ford and his investors, failed to get off the ground. It was not until 1903, when public acceptance of the automobile had grown more certain, that he was able, with a group of new investors behind him, to establish the modest beginnings of the Ford Motor Company. By then there were nearly one hundred small establishments making automobiles. It was in that year, too, that the patent machinations of George Selden collided

---

*It was tiny in the sense that it was simply an open box on four bicycle-sized wheels; it was hardly longer or wider than a coffin and had room for only one person, the driver, who sat on top of the box and manipulated the steering tiller and power levers.

with the manufacturing aspirations of Henry Ford to produce the next installment in the transformation of American industry and society.

Selden had deliberately delayed seeking the grant of an absolute patent for his two-cycle engine in 1879 so that he would not have to submit the requisite final drawings and working model and thereby risk their being copied. Instead he had applied for a patent but had taken advantage of a provision in the law that enabled him progressively to amend his initial designs and drawings until he was ready to submit final specifications. Nevertheless, under the law, his right to legal protection began with the year of his provisional application, 1879. It was not until the early 1890s, after Selden saw that the internal combustion engine was about to become much more than just a limited-manufacture utility engine for mills and shops, that he submitted his final drawings and working model. And it was not until 1895, the year before Henry Ford produced his first quadricycle, that the U.S. Patent Office granted Selden the exclusive patent on the two-stroke "road engine." By virtue of his delaying tactics, Selden now controlled the rights to the automotive use of any such engine, no matter who made it, for another seventeen years, or until 1913.

As the infant automotive industry grew more active in 1899, Selden, while preserving for himself a royalty on each engine made, sold his patent to a group of financiers. In 1900 the group brought suit against dozens of individuals and shops that were making and selling two-cycle automobiles, the Duryea Brothers included. The suit was settled in 1903 by the formation, by ten of the leading automobile makers, of the Association of Licensed Automobile Manufacturers, which agreed to pay to the plaintiffs an engine royalty based on a fraction of the retail price of each auto sold by its members. Those automakers who did not join the association were effectively barred from continuing in the business of car manufacturing, even though they had been making their own engines.

Henry Ford had come of age during the time when political populism and economic antimonopolism were gathering force in America. Too, in the 1890s his personal business dream centered on bringing a popular new convenience to the masses, just as his idol Edison had done with electricity and other inventions. Toward this end, in developing his own automobile manufacturing plans, he had studied the history of interchangeable parts developed earlier in the century by Eli Whitney—that is, the assembly of the final product at a central location from a multitude of parts manufactured in other locations.* Ford knew that he could not invent the automobile per se, for that had already been done. What he now intended to invent was a system for mass-producing the automobile and making it available at a price low enough to create a large middle-class market. Until Ford conceived his plan, the relatively few automobiles that had been manufactured were laboriously hand-produced and expensive; the product was viewed as a personal luxury beyond the reach of all but the wealthiest class.

Ford was thus enraged when, upon forming his second company in 1903, he applied for membership in the Association of Licensed Automobile Manufacturers and was rejected on the ground that his plans for mass-constructing cars made him not a "manufacturer" in the true sense of the word but a mere "assembler." Claiming that the association was a monopolistic cartel designed to inhibit free enterprise and deprive the American public of the automobile, Ford began building cars at his recently erected small plant in Dearborn anyway. The association promptly brought suit, alleging that Ford was infringing the Selden patent. Ford answered by insisting that his automobile and the parts and processes that went into its assembly were the products of his own brain, that "no man on earth was entitled to any rake-off from that particular car," and by challenging the validity of the Selden engine patent on technical grounds.

As it happened, in the late 1890s, internal combustion engineers in America had begun to favor the principle of the four-cycle engine—invented by Germany's Nikolaus Otto and perfected for automotive use by Gottlieb Daimler—over the two-stroke engine. Although Henry Ford did not pioneer the development of the four-stroke engine in the United States, when the time came for him to begin mass-manufacturing his cars, the engineers he hired to assist him were committed to it. As a consequence, just as most autos

---

*Before Ford, Whitney's assembly system had remained confined largely to the manufacture of small-scale products. Large-item manufacture, such as that of railroad rolling stock and farm machinery, tended to be done in centralized factories or factory complexes where all the component parts were fabricated.

were being made with four-stroke engines in 1903, so Ford and his assistants designed and made a similar power plant for Ford's car. The lawsuit by the Association of Licensed Automobile Manufacturers was therefore eventually adjudicated in Ford's favor, for the Selden patent covered only automobiles based on the two-cycle engine.

The suit, the longest and most expensive infringement litigation in American history, was not resolved until 1911, eight years after it had been instituted. In the meantime the angry, obsessed Ford had revolutionized the primitive auto industry by developing the world's first large assembly-line plant and, in 1908, introducing the first cheap mass-produced car: the Model T. Thereafter, Ford's ideas about the automobile and its manufacture were to have a profound economic impact on the United States—on its industrial configuration in particular, and on its social and cultural outlook in general. Soon the automobile would become the centerpiece of the American experience.

The growth of the automobile industry, and of the scores of other old and new industries that became closely associated with it, were astounding in their speed and scope. When Henry Ford began turning out his first mass-produced cars in 1905, there were approximately 120 small car-manufacturing plants in the country, employing about 10,000 people. Ford's first vehicle was called the Model K and cost $2,800. In the year between the fall of 1907 and that of 1908, the Ford Motor Company produced and sold 6,398 versions. Five years later the company produced 163,304 units of the Model T, selling them at $600 apiece. Five years after that, in the year 1916–1917, Ford sold 730,041 Model T's at $360 each.

These figures were just one reflection of the automobile's sudden impact. By 1917 the Ford Motor Company was an industrial and business colossus unto itself. And rival automotive colossuses were also in the process of being created, all of them combinations of smaller manufacturers. With the competition came a rich diversification of markets, models and prices. Along with that came a succession of inventions, innovations and improvements in automotive comfort and operating convenience, such as the pneumatic tire, the electric starter, the hydraulic brake, the shock absorber, the automatic transmission and so on. By 1923 the number of automobile plants had risen to 2,471, and the number of people directly employed in manufacturing cars to nearly half a million, making the industry the largest in the country. Not only that, but the massive new industry started by Ford had become the single greatest customer, and therefore the most important stimulant of growth, of scores of other industries—from steel and rubber to chemicals and mining, from petroleum and plastics to carpeting and alloys.* Moreover, the automobile led straight to the truck and bus, triggering the start of yet another revolution in the transport of goods and people; and to the internal combustion-powered tractor and other farm machinery, thereby setting off, together with the American development of chemical fertilizers, an equivalent transformation of agriculture. It led also to a vast boom in road and highway building. Finally, the automobile engine, as perfected by Ford and others at the turn of the century, led directly to the aeronautical experiments of the Wright brothers, which culminated in 1903 in the first powered flight and the birth of the airplane.

Ford's realization of the idea of the automobile transformed the societies of the rest of the industrialized world too. But it was not just the automobile itself that accomplished this; to a greater extent it was the increasingly sophisticated techniques that Ford created to mass-produce it. Until Ford's time, mass manufacture had been accomplished by the process of the skilled individual factory worker putting together a given product in its entirety from a collection of machined parts supplied to the worker at a workbench. Ford's system called for low-skilled workers, each installing a single part as the evolving product moved slowly along a conveyor-like assembly line. Assembly-line manufacture proved not only faster and more economical with such a large, multiparted product as the automobile, for fewer workers were needed, but it ensured a uniformity and consistency never before attained in the mass

*In 1900, Charles Palmer, an American chemist, discovered a process for making a better grade of gasoline than that devised by Friedrich Kekule in Germany in the late 1870s. His process involved the use of high temperatures and pressures to decompose crude oil. In 1916 he sold the rights to his thermal process to John D. Rockefeller's Standard Oil Company, thus allowing Standard to set the pace in gasoline production. The success of competing oil companies, after the Standard trust was dissolved in 1911, would depend much on their development of improvements of the Palmer process. Indeed, the expansion of petroleum research and technology occasioned by the automobile would produce quantum advances in other basic chemical industries—chemical fertilizers, paints, plastics and so on.

manufacture of complex products. In essence, Ford and his engineers reinvented the machine, giving it a more human quality and giving humanity—at least in the industrialized world—a more machinelike quality.

Soon the desirability and techniques of assembly-line production spread to all forms of mass industry, from the production of parts for cars to the manufacture of countless other products and their components, large and small, consumer and industrial. Improvements in the technology of various types of assembly lines spawned entire new design and engineering industries, all devoted to power, machinery and production efficiency. By the second decade of this century thousands of products were being mass-manufactured by the assembly-line process, and not only the reality of factory work but that of mass consumption—first in America, then abroad as assembly-line production spread to industrial Europe—was undergoing yet another radical change. In Europe, but even more so in America, the change took the form of a further economic and material democratization of society. Added to all the prior equalizing influences were two new ones: uniformity and standardization.

Throughout the history of nationhood, national societies had always sought to unify themselves through various political formulas, usually totalitarian or monarchical ones that had the perverse effect of repressing the majority and provoking mass disunification. Although the American political formula had consciously eschewed monarchicalism and totalitarianism, the ethnic, religious and racial melting-pot character of American society, along with its ruthlessly competitive economic system, had made the nation's de facto social unification difficult nevertheless. Early in the twentieth century the United States was still struggling—often violently and painfully despite the equalizing influences of the previous three decades of industry and commerce—for moral, spiritual and political harmonization.

What it got as a result of the new assembly-line revolution was not unification, but an increasing trend toward uniformity. American society would never become morally, spiritually and politically unified. It would grow instead more "uniformized" and standardized as mass production and mass consumption became its principal socioeconomic *raisons d'être*. This process was an extension of the balancing mechanism American society had spon-

taneously invented to reconcile the fundamental paradoxes of life
it had earlier—also spontaneously—created. Thenceforth the balancing mechanism—this abstract, uniformizing social machine—
would become as dominant a force in the economic, political and
social evolution of the United States as invention and industrialism.

CHAPTER 23

THE NEW OUTLOOK

The spontaneous process by which the new American social mechanism acquired its preliminary design had evolved in the 1870s. The blueprint was completed during the presidency of Teddy Roosevelt. Thereafter its actual, if abstract, construction began. The construction was based on the reformist concept that government must function as the primary balancing organism of the American paradox—of the conflict between the individual and the group, between political liberty and economic equality, between personal striving and the "public interest." The various permanent regulatory agencies that were added to the federal system during Roosevelt's seven years as President, as well as his administration's more than forty antitrust suits, were popularly received. At first Roosevelt's personally handpicked Republican successor, William Howard Taft, carried on his predecessor's reform and regulatory programs, instituting an additional ninety government suits against business monopolies and backing further legislation intended to curb or regulate big-business practices.*

Temperamentally, however, Taft did not share Roosevelt's concept of the presidency as a stewardship of the public welfare. As he matured as President and grew less beholden to Roosevelt, Taft began to respond more positively to the counterpressures of the big-business interest groups that had become institutionalized in Washington during the 1890s. His first response came when he signed a new pro-business tariff act in the fall of 1909 which was

---

*Foremost among the new Taft-backed laws of the period was the 1910 Mann-Elkins Railroad Act, which placed telephone, telegraph, cable and wireless communications companies under government jurisdiction through the Interstate Commerce Commission and created a federal Commerce Court to rule upon rate disputes.

passed over the strenuous objections of the Roosevelt Republicans in Congress. This and subsequent actions taken by Taft produced a revolt in the Republican-dominated Senate, with a group of progressive Republican legislators, led by Robert La Follette of Wisconsin, eventually splitting off to form their own party, the National Progressive Republican League.

Equally angered was Teddy Roosevelt, who returned from his travels abroad in the summer of 1910 to attack what he condemned as Taft's reversion to old-fashioned and outdated Republican principles. Roosevelt reflected the rising political mood of the country—a mood he had been singularly instrumental in shaping during his seven years as President—in a speech he gave later that summer in Kansas. He coined the phrase "the New Nationalism" to symbolize the balance he insisted should be struck and maintained between the countervailing impulses of big business and the general populace. The New Nationalism, Roosevelt proclaimed, stood for the idea "that every man holds his property subject to the general right of the community to regulate its use to whatever degree the public welfare may require it."

Under William Jennings Bryan, the Democratic party, as well as its socialist and Populist offshoots, had been making such radical declarations since the early 1890s. Bryan had been the unsuccessful Democratic presidential candidate for a third time in the 1908 election, the one in which Taft succeeded Roosevelt. Nevertheless he had given Taft a fairly close run in the popular vote, a sign that much of the country now subscribed to the "public welfare comes first" imperative set forth in Teddy Roosevelt's 1910 Kansas speech. That one of the nation's most celebrated Republicans was now promoting such an idea was pure anathema to the traditional Republican big-business community, however. From its point of view, Roosevelt's New Nationalism verged on communism.

Roosevelt's statement declared in effect that the economic and social rights of the individual in America were now inferior to the economic and social rights of the group. And that the group in America had the obligation to regulate the rights of the individual in the interests of the group's general welfare. Of course, this was no different in form from what the big-business establishment had been insisting for decades—that is, that the rights of the corporation (the group) prevailed over the rights of the worker, the consumer and so on (the individual). It was different, however, in substance, and it was that qualitative difference that completed the blueprint for the country's new social mechanism.

Roosevelt's Kansas speech, made at the start of the 1910 congressional elections, kindled dozens of heated political campaigns throughout the country. With the widely admired ex-President's imprimatur on what had long been a fundamental tenet of Democratic party theory, the Democrats gained control of the House of Representatives for the first time since the party's first tilt toward populism in 1894. Along with the insurgent Progressive Republicans of Robert La Follette, they also dominated the Senate. What's more, in the various state elections of the same year, they elected twenty-six governors, including Woodrow Wilson in New Jersey. The nation, it was clear, had opted to begin formalizing what had, until then, been merely a trend toward increased governmental intervention in the fundamental processes of private economic and social life in America.

In the meantime, the pace of expansion in the country's already vast industrial and technological sphere had quickened in other ways. The feasibility of using radio waves (discovered by the German physicist Heinrich Hertz in 1887) as a communications medium was first demonstrated by an American, Nathan Stubblefield, when he transmitted his voice over the air, without wires, in 1892. Three years later Guglielmo Marconi invented a wireless telegraph that could transmit messages in Morse code. By 1899 he had succeeded in sending a signal across the English Channel, thus heralding the dawn of international wireless communications.

The most socially transforming breakthrough in radio came in 1906. That was when the Yale-educated American physicist, Lee De Forest, basing much of his research on knowledge gained in England from Edison's earlier experiments with the light bulb and the Edison Effect, created the vacuum amplifying tube. De Forest's invention, a three-electrode glass vacuum bulb, was the basis for the world's first commercial radio, which he called the Audion. In 1910 he was able to broadcast the voice of opera singer Enrico Caruso from the stage of New York's Metropolitan Opera House to the owners of the few Audion receivers in the New York area.

De Forest's development of the radio would become the basis for subsequent breakthroughs in other important areas of electronics. And it was a benchmark development in more ways than that. Oddly enough, though, the radio's refinement into its ultimate form as a broadcast medium was relatively slow when compared to the telephone and electric lighting. It had taken only a few years after Alexander Graham Bell's invention of the telephone for the service to begin to come into common use. Two years after Edison first threw the switch at his Pearl Street generating plant, electrical systems were being installed in cities throughout the nation. It was not until the early 1920s, however, nearly two decades after De Forest invented his Audion, that radio as we know it began to take hold. And it wouldn't have been introduced that quickly had it not been for a Russian-immigrant apprentice wireless telegrapher named David Sarnoff.

Sarnoff's rise to the pinnacle of commercial radio was typical of the serendipity of American invention and opportunity. In 1912 he was working as an operator of a wireless station that had been installed at Wanamaker's department store in New York. One day in April of that year, he intercepted a message from a ship in the North Atlantic: "S.S. *Titanic* ran into iceberg. Sinking fast." Sarnoff quickly established communications with another ship in the region which confirmed the *Titanic*'s message and reported picking up survivors from the "unsinkable" ocean liner. When news of the disaster reached Washington an hour later, President Taft ordered all other wireless stations in the Northeast to shut down, leaving Sarnoff as the only operator on the air. Sarnoff, remaining at his post for seventy hours while he reported the names of survivors, became an instant newspaper celebrity.

Just twenty-one at the time and with only an eighth-grade education, Sarnoff parlayed his fame into a job with the Marconi Company—which seven years later would become the Radio Corporation of America, with himself as its president by 1930. In 1916, Sarnoff proposed that the Marconi Company begin manufacturing "a simple Radio Music Box" that would "make radio a 'household utility' in the same sense as the piano or phonograph." Sarnoff's prediction that the company would sell a million electrically powered radio receiving sets during the first year proved to be a gross underestimate, and when RCA was organized in New York out of the Marconi and other small radio companies in

1919, Sarnoff was made its commercial manager for his perspicacity.

Like Edison's light bulb, though, a radio set was useless without a source from which it could receive the entertainment it was designed to provide. It was in this respect that Sarnoff once again profitably exercised his foresight. In 1926 he gathered a group of small experimental broadcasting facilities into a subsidiary of RCA, calling it the National Broadcasting Company. By then, improvements in De Forest's vacuum tube, in the microphone, and in other facets of radio technology—many of them made by Ernst Alexanderson, RCA's chief engineer—had made countrywide broadcasting feasible, and NBC became the first major national network. As much a result of businessman Sarnoff's efforts as those of Marconi, De Forest and other scientific pioneers of radio technology, the new medium was launched on a career that thoroughly transformed the entertainment world, as well as the worlds of advertising and news dissemination. By 1930 advertisers were spending $60 million a year on the radio, a figure that would multiply tenfold over the next ten years.* During the 1930s, radio became the most commonly shared economic, educational and informational experience in America, in effect opening up the country to instant aural access, interaction and response. The social, psychological and intellectual-bonding impact on the populace was enormous. Not the least of its effects was the still-higher level of material expectation radio stimulated during the dispiriting years of the Great Depression.

The story of the birth of RCA and the radio industry could, in its main outlines, be told about the rise of countless other major modern-day industries during the first three decades of the twentieth century. The story reflected the emergence of a new type of industrial entrepreneur on the American scene, one who was growing every bit as important to the nation's material progress as the old-fashioned inventor. The new entrepreneur was not a man of mechanical and scientific wizardry, but a person of organizational, financial and marketing ingenuity.

The democratizing trends of labor, education, expanded infor-

---

*In 1928 another business entrepreneur of Russian ancestry, William Paley, organized the Columbia Broadcasting System to compete with Sarnoff's NBC. Between them, NBC and CBS shared about 58 percent of the roughly $600 million spent on radio advertising in 1939.

mation and material consumerism in the late nineteenth century had reshaped popular thinking about the role of government in American economic life. That reshaped thinking, within the period of the first decade of the twentieth century, had produced the beginnings of a more activist, determinist and interventionist form of social and economic government. In the person of the charismatic Teddy Roosevelt, public welfare and public policy had become the dominant balance-weight concepts among all the conflicting impulses that had contributed to the creation of the American paradox.

Many modern observers insist that the actual social and economic changes wrought by Roosevelt were merely an upper-class individual's cosmetic way of mollifying a discontented lower-class majority infected by dangerous socialist-inspired revolutionary ideas, while at the same time conserving and preserving the privileges and advantages of the upper classes.* There is undoubtedly some truth to this, particularly in view of the fact that no matter how concerned with the public welfare Teddy Roosevelt's programs were, he still managed, with the help of Congress, to leave enough loopholes in the new regulatory legislation to enable big business and big industry to get on with their work. Roosevelt may have been a righteous reformer, but he was not out to destroy the country. Nor were those progressive Republicans who thought as he did. Nor were the even more socialist-minded Democrats who succeeded to power in 1910 and 1912.

Among Roosevelt's principal legacies, then, was a new class of industrial and financial entrepreneur that at least paused to consider the public interest as it reorganized and expanded existing industries, and organized and built new ones. Along with the publications of the muckrakers and the willingness of the Supreme Court to begin interpreting and amending the Constitution in economic terms, the Roosevelt-fueled drive to neutralize the power of the trusts had put an effective end to the era of the rapacious,

---

*It is a curious fact of twentieth-century American history that the elected Presidents who did the most to expand the social and economic roles of government were those who came from wealthy, or at least highly cultured, families. Theodore Roosevelt, Woodrow Wilson, Franklin D. Roosevelt, John F. Kennedy and, to a certain extent, William Howard Taft were such Presidents. Presidents born in poor or modest circumstances, on the other hand, tended to resist and often attempted to reverse government expansionism. Warren Harding, Calvin Coolidge, Herbert Hoover, Harry Truman, Dwight D. Eisenhower, Richard Nixon, Jimmy Carter and, most recently, Ronald Reagan have been such Presidents.

monopolistic Robber Barons who had built the foundation of the country's industrial and technological colossus. Thereafter, American capitalism, though still vigorously impelled by its traditional narrow-interest profit motive, would begin to consider the correlative interests of the masses on which it depended. Roosevelt had struck the balance through which America—all of America—could prosper and progress in more rapid fashion than ever. It would prove to be only a temporary balance, however.

The beginning stage of the modern American era spanned the period from 1900 to 1930. Again, never in the history of mankind did a people—so great a number of people—enjoy such material and economic enrichment in so brief a period of time. While the traditional capitalist drive for profit, property, possession and position deepened, the liberalizing and democratizing forces of social humanism deepened as well. Education, rather than remaining a narrow cultural conditioning device for the privileged or an equally narrow vocational training ground for the labor class, became the citadel of the new humanism as increasing numbers of citizens gained access to and exploited it. Education's principal adjunct became the university and the industrial research laboratory, in which abstract or practical scientific pursuits produced answers to pressing human medical problems with rapidly multiplying frequency. Paced by medical research and pharmaceutical manufacture, the experimental sciences themselves were in the process of becoming major industries, and group science began to supplant solo invention as the principal source of industrial and technological advance.

Thanks to the development of commercial radio, advertising, marketing and personal-credit finance grew more sophisticated and began to override the spontaneous dynamics of the free marketplace as the principal source of consumer demand. With this further spurt of mass materialism and economic democratization, though, another social paradox was born—the trivial became as important an object of consumer interest as that which was vital. Under the new pressures of mass marketing and advertising, the package became as compelling an attraction as the product it contained. It was not enough that almost anyone could now readily buy packaged soaps, beverages and other basic amenities. One now was pressured into making one's purchase primarily on the basis of a product's sensual allure. America was becoming a land in which increasing numbers among its society were easily persuaded that to go around smelling like a pine bough or the inside of a coconut was as desirable as living without illness or learning a production skill. Mass materialism was being transformed into crass materialism. The pursuit of physical comfort, the escape from physical discomfort were being transformed into the pursuit of psychic pleasure, the escape from psychic pain.

But "without the crass, there would have been no mass," as social critic Lewis Mumford dryly observed in 1954. He was right. Beginning in 1899 and lasting until 1929, save for a few brief downturns, the graph lines of American industrial production and economic expansion, as well as those of American employment, investment and consumption, soared to heights never before recorded, or even imagined, in any country of the world. Although the process of intensified industrialism had started well before 1900, within the thirty-year period thereafter the United States made itself into the Goliath it is currently. The period produced the essential completion of the organization and management of most of the basic industries and technologies that dominate America's cultural and economic life today. And those it did not complete, it gave birth to.

Aircraft manufacture and air transport came of age during the period, as did the automobile, automotive-equipment and home-appliance industries. Beverages—the giant beer and soft-drink companies—became an important component of the industrial base. Forestry, the building-products industry and construction boomed. Industrial chemical research and chemical manufacturing, pioneered by the E. I. du Pont de Nemours company, expanded and diversified with blinding speed, as did the manufacture of plastics and other artificial materials made from petroleum and man-made chemical compounds. Radio, though slower to develop, grew from an experimental pursuit into a major industry within a period of twenty years. Drugs, pharmaceuticals and medical care, along with perfumes and cosmetics, became a separate giant subindustry of chemicals. The mass manufacture of electrical and electronic products for both industrial and consumer markets, led by General Electric, American Telephone and Telegraph, and Westinghouse, grew by leaps and bounds. The production and distribution of what we today call energy and energy services by the major oil and gas companies raced ahead once the Standard Oil trust was dismantled in 1911. The food-supply industry took on its gigantic, complex modern-day configuration during the period. What are known today as the leisure-time industries—photography, motion pictures, tourism, lodging, restaurants and sporting activities among them—were organized. The manufacture of precision instruments and fine-tolerance machinery, each so vital to the rest of the industrial process, expanded apace. Package and container manufacturing grew infinitely more diverse in conjunction with the rest of the period's industrial explosion, as did other forms of miscellaneous mass manufacture, from key rings to toys. Mining and metals, steel and railroads, textiles and wearing apparel, merchandising and advertising, tires and rubber, tobacco, banking, telecommunications, publishing and office equipment—these and dozens of other major industries took their current form, developed their modern-day processes and systems, during the three decades between 1900 and 1930.

This massive expansion was inspired and made possible by many factors, not the least of which were the inherent inventiveness and industry of the American character, the economic and social democratizing trends those traits had earlier initiated, the drive for personal wealth, the pressures of a rapidly multiplying population, and the regimentation of society. But in addition to providing the country with a remarkable new material abundance, the thirty years of growth also imposed a host of new social and economic burdens on the country.

Since the time of the invention of the steam engine, the prime concern of mechanical engineers had been to create motors—steam, electrical, gasoline—that used less of their energy driving themselves than driving the machinery to which they were attached. Although improvements in engineering, metallurgical and fuel technology had greatly enhanced motor efficiency, thereby allowing engines to channel more of their energy into turning other machinery rather than their own moving parts, the ideal engine—the one that would apply all its energy to another machine and waste none on itself—remained beyond the realm of possibility.

As industrialism, consumer democratization, education and political reform transformed American society into a more systematized, interdependent, regimented and programmed organism during the first three decades of the twentieth century—into a more machinelike entity—a similar problem emerged. Despite the material abundance and prosperity the social mechanism bestowed on ever-larger portions of the populace, the social machine itself, because of the continuing disparities among its dynamic parts, was being forced to use more and more of its energy to run itself. This to a large extent was what produced the economic events of 1929 that brought so abrupt and traumatic an end to the nation's prosperity and plunged it into the Great Depression of the 1930s, hurtling the social mechanism into a state of near collapse in the process.

It was as a result of the Depression that American society began to recognize and accept its mechanistic nature. Out of that recognition came an acute awareness of the need to radically redesign and reorganize the social machine. The politicians and social leaders of the past who had made the first attempts to shape and control the functioning of the social machine—the men of Teddy Roosevelt's generation—had been nothing more, figuratively, than amateur mechanics attempting to keep it lubricated and in tune. But among the many effects of the latest phase of American industrialism had been the institutionalization in the nation's consciousness of the concept of professionalism. The first three decades of the century had created a huge new professional class: managers, technicians, doctors, lawyers, teachers and scientists whose badges of distinction were increasingly specialized educations and a consequent penchant to isolate, identify and solve complex problems in their narrow fields of expertise.

The Depression, under another Roosevelt, brought together in common cause a variety of such professional experts—political scientists and economists, sociologists and statisticians, managers and administrators, bankers and lawyers. In concert they conceived a new approach to the governance of American society. It was they who first identified society in mechanistic terms. Once having done that, they proposed to treat the malfunctioning social machine not as amateur mechanics tinkering with its parts, but as professional "social engineers" committed to the idea of completely redesigning and rebuilding it so that it would thereafter function smoothly, and without ever again failing.

CHAPTER 24

UNINTENDED CONSEQUENCES

In the 1930s the Austrian-born philosopher Karl Popper propounded the "law of unintended consequences" to describe a phenomenon that had occurred with increasing frequency during the
rise of industrialism in Europe. What Popper meant was that
every new technological development produced political, economic and social effects that were not only unintended but often
undesirable, requiring further technological developments, with
their own inevitably undesirable side effects, to cure. At the start
of the twentieth century in America, although no one had yet
identified or described it, the law of unintended consequences was
fully operative. Moreover, the process it connoted spilled over
into every area of life. The New Nationalism enunciated by Theodore Roosevelt during the Taft administration, for instance, had
the unintended consequence of enabling the Democratic party, in
1910, to regain control of Congress for the first time in sixteen
years. This was a markedly different Democratic party from the
one that had last ruled the national legislature; fourteen years of
immersion in populism, and in the quasi-socialism of the party's
William Jennings Bryan faction, had produced the difference.

Another unintended consequence of Teddy Roosevelt's New
Nationalism—itself a radical policy in the eyes of the nation's traditional Republican establishment—was his decision to challenge
the reelection of President Taft in 1912 on the ground that Taft
had betrayed the social gains of Roosevelt's term in office. With
Roosevelt running on a splinter Progressive party ticket against

both the regular Republican, Taft, and the Democratic candidate, New Jersey Governor Woodrow Wilson, the Democrats had no trouble winning the election. Not only did Wilson capture the White House, but he swept an even greater majority of Democrats into Congress with his victory. The stage was thus set for the implementation of additional pent-up social and economic reforms which the Bryan Democrats had been advocating for so long.

Wilson had campaigned on a platform whose principal slogan was "the New Freedom." The New Freedom differed from Roosevelt's New Nationalism in only one fundamental respect. Whereas Roosevelt favored the continuation of certain "good" monopolies under close governmental supervision, Wilson declared all monopolies to be evil and promised to work for their complete elimination. And so he did, in the process thrusting the government more deeply and widely than ever into a regulatory role over private-sector life. The steady stream of government-expanding legislation during the early Wilson administration, as well as during the prior Taft and Roosevelt reigns, had one consequence that, though unintended, was nevertheless inevitable: the adoption of a federal income tax.

Taxation had always been a nettlesome issue in America, particularly in the light of the country's colonial history. Income, consumer and inheritance taxes introduced during the Civil War had been justified by the Lincoln government as a temporary emergency measure needed to help finance the war, and they were repealed as quickly as possible at the war's end. Nevertheless the country, especially the North, had had a brief taste of such comprehensive taxation and had not exactly rebelled. At least the poor and low-income majority of the North had not rebelled, if only because taxation had not really affected them.

Most of the economic and social reform movements that grew out of the 1870s were launched by and among the low-income and poor majority of the Northeast. As reform sentiment spread and became more intensively laced with European socialist ideas in the 1880s, one of its major demands was that the federal government take responsibility for bringing minimal financial security to the economically disadvantaged majority. One of the means proposed for achieving this was a revival of the Civil War income tax and other levies on personal and corporate wealth and profit. To the monied classes, still well represented in Washington, this smelled of outright communist-style welfarism—the rich and middle classes paying for the poor—and they consistently and heatedly discredited the idea. In the 1890s, however, the notion began to enter the mainstream of American political thought, first through the platforms advanced by the reformist Populist party and other socialist labor groups during the elections of that decade, then through the reconstituted Democratic party of William Jennings Bryan.

Economic prosperity prior to 1893, coupled with Republican dominance of the government between 1895 and 1911, had managed to stave off any serious consideration of a revival of income and other forms of taxation. But by 1908 the legislative and executive expansion of the government had created steep yearly increases in the negative differential between federal revenues and the costs of running the federal establishment.* Thus, in the 1908 presidential and congressional elections, the need for an income tax—not only on individuals but on businesses as well—became a leading political issue. By then an increasing majority of the populace had begun to accept the inevitability of such a tax, and on July 12, 1910, the Sixteenth Amendment to the Constitution was proposed in Congress for the establishment of a permanent income tax.

The new amendment took almost four years to wend its way through the political process, and it was not formally ratified until February 25, 1913.† Although Woodrow Wilson had no direct hand in its creation, it could fairly be said that his near-landslide election in 1912, together with the strengthening of the Democrats' control of Congress, made its adoption certain. In that sense, then, it was the Wilson administration's amendment, and it would dovetail neatly with events soon to occur.

Woodrow Wilson presented himself to the people of the United States as both a forceful domestic leader and a contemplative international statesman whose only philosophical difference from

---

*Until then, the two principal sources of government income were excise taxes and customs duties, or tariffs.

†Later in 1913, on May 31, a Seventeenth Amendment was adopted as well. Also Democratic in origin, it provided for the popular election of United States senators and removed the Senate, at least somewhat, from the exclusive clutches of the business establishment.

the still popular Teddy Roosevelt was his intensely pacifistic nature. When war broke out in Europe in 1914, Wilson embroidered his lofty pacifism with a series of policy speeches pledging American neutrality. Old warrior Roosevelt, on the other hand, as the chief Republican opposition leader, traveled about the country urging the mobilization of a large American military force to stand ready to enter the war on the side of the Allies.

Their differences reflected a deep division of opinion within the country about the war. The Democratic party, by then comprised largely of the nation's immigrant and post-immigrant working classes, had little interest in the distant conflict; they were concerned mainly with improving their own lot in America and had scant sympathy for the continent they had recently left behind. Republicans, on the other hand, representatives of big business and of lucrative European trade interests, were eager to see the war end as quickly as possible. In their view, Wilson's neutrality policy was doing the American industrial and financial establishment no good, despite the sales of war matériel to the Allies.

Wilson assiduously maintained the country's official neutrality policy even when, on May 7, 1915, the British passenger steamer *Lusitania* was sunk by a German submarine off the coast of Ireland. More than 100 Americans were among the nearly 1,200 passengers who lost their lives. It was not the first time Americans had become fatalities of the war; just a week earlier two merchant seamen had died when an American tanker had been struck—mistakenly, it was explained—by a German torpedo off the English coast. But the *Lusitania*'s sinking galvanized even the most disinterested American public opinion against Germany and in favor of England and France. Later, speculation arose that the attack on the ocean liner had been orchestrated by elements within the United States and England eager to see just such a shift in American sentiment, but nothing on that score could be proved. Nevertheless the shift had occurred, and it was sharply intensified a year later when a huge explosion, attributed to German sabotage, destroyed an American munitions dump on an island in New York Bay. The Germans, while denying responsibility, praised the event on the ground that the munitions were being readied for secret shipment to England.

So sharply divided was the country by 1916 over the issue of

the war, and of Wilson's continued neutrality, that it nearly precluded him from being sent back to the White House in that
year's presidential election.* Wilson was matched against Charles
Evans Hughes, who had been drafted by the Republicans from
the Supreme Court to challenge him. Only a last-minute campaign boner by Hughes, coupled with the great number of women
who pressured their husbands to vote for Wilson because of his
promise to keep their sons out of the war, enabled the incumbent
President to eke out a victory. Once reinstalled in the Oval Office,
Wilson quickly abandoned his insistence on neutrality.

In the meantime, the reform-minded Democratic Congress remained busy enacting new domestic legislation. In June 1916 it
passed the National Defense Act, which provided for a quantum
increase in the size of the nation's military forces and equipment,
and for corresponding federal subsidies to military-related industries in the private sector. It followed this with the Farm Loan
Act, which furnished farmers with long-term credit facilities similar to those made available to private industry and commerce
through the Federal Reserve Act.† A number of other laws favoring small business and labor groups were passed in 1916 as well.

By early 1917, after Germany began a series of undisguisedly
deliberate attacks against American merchant ships on the high
seas, the United States' entry into the European war became assured. It was to be the country's first large-scale and concentrated
war in so distant and foreign a milieu. As a result, after the
United States formally entered the conflict on April 6, the administration and Congress promulgated a series of war-related statutes
and executive orders that, through the creation of dozens of large
new agencies, committees, boards and commissions, put control
of the country's industrial and economic base firmly in the hands
of the government. To finance this suddenly bloated government,
income and excise taxes were drastically raised and steep new
taxes were added in the form of levies on excess personal and corporate profits.

Few were the voices that objected to the spiraling tax burden.
This was because the intensification of patriotic nationalist feelings

---

*While publicly maintaining his hands-off attitude toward the war, Wilson had begun
privately to seek to mediate it in the hope of bringing about a negotiated peace.

†The Federal Reserve Act of 1913, and the government-controlled banking system it
established, were among Wilson's first economic reforms.

inspired by the country's first major foreign war diverted attention from it; and also because the mobilization of industry and finance in support of the war effort provided the home-front population with so much work and additional income that few were materially hurt by it. However, to use the modern-day business expression, there was a "downside" to the entire experience. The sharply increased taxation paid for only about 25 percent of the total expenditure by the government on the war; the rest of the roughly $35 billion total had to be raised by borrowing. At the end of the Civil War almost half a century before, the national debt had risen to just under $3 billion, a startling amount for the time. That debt had been steadily reduced over the next fifty years until it stood at just over $1 billion at the start of 1917. In August of 1919, a year after the armistice in Europe, the national debt had soared to an incredible $26 billion. American society found itself confronted by an entirely new era of economic values, and therefore social attitudes, as a result of the war.

The new era began with the continued expansion of the government in 1919 and 1920 as the Wilson administration struggled to return the country to normalcy. By then, the majority of the populace had become thoroughly accustomed to the reality of "big government" replacing big business as the central motive force behind technological progress and industrial largesse. Even the successive mainstream Republican administrations of Warren Harding and Calvin Coolidge, which followed Wilson's beginning in 1921, added to the expansion of the government without much popular protest.*

There was little reason for Americans to object, for the 1920s were proving to be a period of unrivaled industrial, technological and material bonanza. The Republicans had returned to stiff tariff protectionism. Consumerism boomed. Newer industries, offering a cornucopia of diverse new products and expanded work, multiplied ceaselessly. The country was building as it never had before: sky-scrapers, cities, highways, bridges, improved railroads, suburbs, cars, long-distance electrical and telephone systems, pipelines,

---

*Republicans made an overwhelming return to the White House and Congress in the 1920 elections when Warren Harding defeated the Democratic candidate, James Cox, in a landslide. The outcome was not an expression of the country's dissatisfaction with the domestic policies of the Wilson presidency, including internal government expansion; rather, it was a repudiation of Wilson's postwar foreign policy, particularly his sponsorship of the League of Nations.

power dams, reservoirs, urban and interurban transit networks and
so on. With repeated extensions of margin credit, the stock markets
were opening themselves up to ordinary citizens as never before,
and stock speculation became the new daily sport of the middle
class. Mortgage and automobile loans were just as easy to come by,
and home and car ownership grew increasingly common among
social classes that, just half a generation before, had been restricted
to cheap rental housing and public transport. Medicine, medical
research and medical education were at last beginning to make
genuine inroads into the treatment and cure of once fatal or debilitating diseases, with new American developments in organized
scientific research and education blazing the path. Leisure and rec-
reational time was well on its way to becoming an entrenched part
of the American experience, and income was suddenly available to
many among the middle and lower working classes to exploit it.
Indeed, Americans were proving they had a penchant for play and
recreation that was as powerful as their respect for work.

There soon appeared a familiar fly in the ointment, however.
So great was the speed and momentum of technological change
during the twenties that it began to accrue a dynamic and energy
of its own, a combination that tended to transcend the slower-
changing dynamics of American society itself. The founding of
the United States had been based in large part on the deep human
desire for social self-determination. At first, invention, technology
and industry had been viewed as having the potential to enhance
the quest for self-determination, to free each individual within society from the yoke of bare survivalism. But now the quest was
more perplexing and problematic than ever. Science and technology, along with the increasingly complex economic and social
problems that flowed from them, had acquired a force that tended
mechanistically to overpower individual and group self-determination. One development led so fast to countless others, often unintended, that society found itself, with rising frequency,
confounded and powerless to adjust. The American experience
seemed now to be shaped less and less by the conscious choices of
individuals and groups, and more and more by the impersonal
mechanical logic and impetus of industrial progress. Individual
self-determination was being dwarfed and overwhelmed by the
inexorable, compulsive, depersonalizing sweep of technology. The
very power that had made American society the most politically

and economically democratized in the world was now beginning to make many of its members feel socially inconsequential, somehow robbed of the right of self-determination. America had advanced enormously during the previous fifty years, at least in the material sense. But had it progressed in the spiritual, in the moral, in the human sense?

To be sure, these were not anxieties and questions that leaped en masse into the public mind in the 1920s. Only a few social and political Cassandras articulated them, and they were largely ignored for their against-the-grain pessimism or their political hereticism. But the heightening social, economic and materialistic frenzy of the 1920s hinted that the anxieties had at least penetrated the periphery of the public mind.*

The remainder of the American historical outline is more familiar. The frenetic twenties climaxed in the monumental financial crash of October 1929, soon after the start of the Republican administration of Herbert Hoover. The suddenness and massiveness of the collapse, and the bitter gloom of the economic Dark Age that followed, stunned and demoralized not only the American people but the government itself. Assigned the blame, Hoover was roundly rejected in the 1932 presidential election. Franklin Delano Roosevelt, a Democrat who promised a quick, government-engineered recovery from a Depression that by then had reached its most suffocating depths, was chosen in his place.

The Roosevelt presidency transformed the role, and the public expectation, of government once again—this time not in the modest, gradual fashion of his cousin Teddy's administration thirty years before, but in a sudden and radical one. While managing to combat some of the worst effects of the Depression, Roosevelt's mammoth New Deal regulatory and recovery programs thrust government directly into every American's personal life, often in a fashion that bordered on the totalitarian. Suffused with quasi-socialist principles, the new system of government—grown swollen with bureaucracy, legalistic process, regimentation, regulation and

*Some would have called that periphery the public "subconscious," a concept that was just coming into vogue in the America of the 1920s. Ironically, Sigmund Freud's system of psychology, upon which the notion of the subconscious was based and which was popularly interpreted to hold that the nature of every individual's life is mechanically preordained by his or her innate psychic character, later did much to reinforce American society's sense of alienation and powerlessness in the face of technological change.

standardization—was intended only as an emergency measure, or so the public was told. But when the original New Deal failed sufficiently "to put this nation back on its feet" by the mid-1930s, the vast majority of the populace opted for more. It reelected Roosevelt in 1936 and got a newer New Deal.

Clearly, American society had been forced to abandon its yearnings for individual self-determination and to rely more and more on the hopefully benevolent paternalism of the government's new regulatory and public-assistance bureaucracy for its material and moral welfare. Here was the "genuine American social democracy" Roosevelt had so boldly proposed in his New Deal sloganeering—an institutionalized system in which every group, and theoretically every citizen, would have access to government-guaranteed economic security and survival without the country's risking the further erosion of its industrial and material progress. Government was thereafter to be American society's paterfamilias—government the strict but charitable husband and father, society the obeisant, conforming wife; the obedient, conforming child.

Would the new system work? Only as society learned to accept it, which, it was believed, would take a generation or two of conditioning and adaptation. Fortunately, at least for the Rooseveltian blueprint, the Second World War intervened to put a definitive end to the Depression and speed up the conditioning process. The war dovetailed neatly in time and urgency with the monolithic system of government the Roosevelt administration had established and refined during the previous decade. The technology and conduct of modern warfare were as much the province of technicians, laborers, industrialists and bureaucrats as they were of warriors. A bureaucratic and mechanistically minded government was already in place. All that was required to wage the war was a shift in governmental emphasis from the domestic to the foreign sphere. Having become well-versed in the methodology of large-scale bureaucracy and technocracy, the nation's government machine had a head start on the war effort.

With the start of the war and the end of the Depression came, not surprisingly in view of the country's past, another unprecedented expansion of invention, technology and industry. Out of the military pressures of the war sprang the refinement, and in many cases the perfection, of the countless industrial and scientific processes that have endowed America with its present-day technological largess and sophistication. The technologies and systems of the computer, of television, of the commercial jet airplane and all-weather flight, of the comfortable and easy-to-drive high-speed car and bus, of automated mass-manufacture, of the communications satellite, of scores of cheap and efficient automatic household appliances—in short, of almost all of today's material abundance, comfort and convenience—emerged from America's participation in the war.

But out of the political and social pressures of the war there emerged as well the refinement and expansion of all those New Deal-inspired social and legal systems, private and public, that today arrange and order the conduct of American society. While such mechanistic systems often assure and expedite the imposition of mass equality, they do so just as frequently at the expense of society's traditional individual and even group ideals of personal freedom and self-determination. The real-life examples of this elemental contradiction of modern American life are so evident and numerous as to require no elucidation here. What is remarkable is the fact that American society, though perhaps grudgingly, has adjusted to the contradiction—just as it has always done. A key question remains, however. What are the future implications of the social changes that have been brought about by the evolution of the marriage of government, science, business and technology in America, and of society's willingness to adjust to and accept them?

Soon after World War II, the British writer George Orwell believed he foresaw the implications of the stranglehold that technology and social systematization even then seemed to be imposing on industrial society. He wrote a book and called it *1984*. In this fictional vision of the world thirty-six years hence, he drew a chilling portrait of a society seduced, spiritually lobotomized and physically tyrannized by the omnipotence of "the machine." Yet it wasn't so much the machine itself that brought about the future described by Orwell. Rather, it was society's apathetic addiction to the machine, and thus society's direct complicity in its own transformation into a machinelike organism.

Nineteen-eighty-four has come and gone. It is clear that Orwell's portrayal, though fancifully effective as an expression of the novelist's art, was wrong. Certainly those societies that have most intensively engaged themselves in advanced machine technology, at least in the West, have not assumed anything close to an Orwellian dimension. But exaggeration is the engine of all compelling fiction. Underlying Orwell's exaggerated rendering of the world of 1984 was a cogent message. The message was, and remains, that if society is not careful, it will one day be betrayed by its own technological ingenuity and by its addiction to the machine as the solution to all problems.

The accuracy of this insight has proved mildly true with respect to the technology of the ordinary machine, for modern mechanization and automation *do* frequently fail us, or strike back at us, in ways that cause havoc and otherwise tyrannize us. But it has proved morbidly true with respect to one device—the most awesome creation of America's technological genius—that even today transcends man's notion of the ordinary machine. For also out of World War II came the nuclear bomb, the result of the greatest mass scientific and technological research effort in history up to that time.

An invention, ultimately, of the new American scheme of regimentalized, compartmentalized, technocracized governance—it was government money, direction and organization that had made it possible, after all—the bomb, for all its terrible implications for the future, was the final scientific validation of the new system. In its perverse way the bomb represented the abstract *completion* of the democratization of America. Not only did it make everyone figuratively equal under its penumbra, it also destroyed the remaining institutional barriers between the pure scientist and the practical mechanic, between science and industry, and between the government and the people. Thenceforth—it was heralded in the euphoria following the war—science, industry, the government and the people would march forward together, in the tradition sired by Francis Bacon four centuries earlier, to enrich society, all of society, in unprecedented new ways.

All of which has come at least partially to pass in the forty years since the first nuclear bomb was detonated in the New Mexico desert. There can be no gainsaying the fact that the revised Rooseveltian blueprint for the nation, however uncertainly and haphazardly it was first patched together in the 1930s, along with its expansion and refinement by subsequent political administrations, has served American society well from the material and social point of view. Never has any society possessed so much in the way of material comfort, convenience, enrichment and diversity, or in the way of mass economic beneficence, than American society today.*

But the scientific and technological marriage that created the atomic bomb, and all the economic and material progress that has flowed from that marriage during the last forty years, have left American society more perplexed than ever. The vague sense of powerlessness that began to creep into the American consciousness in the dizzying rush and momentum of advancing technology during the 1920s was crystallized by the arrival of the atomic bomb. Since the time of the bomb, the sense of abstract mass foreboding and impotence has become even more sharply focused, and grown infinitely more pervasive. We have finally begun to realize that we are truly helpless and without the power of self-determination, and always will be, so long as we are at the mercy of the atom.

The ultimate American invention turned out to be the most malevolent betrayer of the original American political and social ideal, and the creator of the ultimate American paradox. It turned out, as well, to be the ultimate realization of the law of unintended consequences.

*Such an assertion does not ignore the fact that poverty still exists on a large scale. Yet even the material standard of living of America's poor has risen to a remarkable degree over the last century.

CHAPTER 25

COLOSSUS

Christmas was not celebrated in earnest in the United States until the decade following the Civil War, when the country took its first affirmative steps into the machine age. Thereafter, American society began to merge the rite's religious and spiritual symbolism with the symbols of the nation's intensifying technological and scientific materialism. By the early twentieth century, the holiday was well on its way to becoming synonymous with America's rapidly proliferating material wealth and variety. It has grown steadily more so ever since, and in recent decades the long "Christmas season" has been a countrywide metaphor of the vitality, virtuosity and productivity of American technological and scientific enterprise, a shiny emblem of the nation's material ingenuity, diversity and sophistication. Indeed, Christmas epitomizes the socioindustrial Goliath America has become.

But the once-gleaming badge of Christmas has lately been tarnished. It was during the Christmas season of 1981 that the United States Steel Corporation, one of the historic exemplars and traditional pillars of America's technological and organizational genius, announced that it was shutting down—probably permanently—its mammoth Edgar Thomson Works on the outskirts of Pittsburgh. That announcement turned Christmas into a disturbing new metaphor for much of the nation. It was a metaphor of yet another scare, one akin in dimension, gravity and future implication to that of the Great Depression. This time, though, it was not a decade of rising material expectation and consumer frenzy, climaxed by a stock-market crash, that produced the crisis. It was, rather, the increasingly sluggish dynamics of the nation's combined geographical, populational, technological, in-

313

dustrial, commercial, political and economic systems. All of these together constituted the modern American social body, the mechanism that had blazed, constructed and paved the road to colossus. Now the body, overloaded with the fat of half a century of unprecedented material glut and burdensome governmental appendage, appeared to be wearing out.

Although few were aware of it at the time, the 1981 U.S. Steel closure represented the end of an era for the United States. Since the early 1960s, the vigor and productivity of the postwar American industrial economy had been in an ever-steepening decline. Its principal components were being strained and distorted by competition from advanced foreign industrial technology, organization and management, most of which had been learned or copied from the United States; by the nation's daunting political and military commitments abroad; by the worldwide upheaval in the cost of energy; by a thickening forest of domestic regulation, systematization and social welfarism designed to keep the increasingly complex American socioeconomic paradox in equilibrium; by the advent of what has come to be known as high technology—computerized, automated production and services; and finally, by the spreading confusion and anomie of a culture grown sated by its own material abundance, yet profoundly perplexed by the many untoward by-products and unintended consequences of its rich technoscientific inheritance.

By 1981 the basic American industries were already suffering grievously at the hands of foreign competition. The shutdown of the Edgar Thomsom Works was just another traumatic symptom of the country's deepening economic, industrial and social distress. Subsequently, factory after huge factory in every important industry was forced to close or severely cut back production. Unemployment rose quickly to levels unmatched since the 1930s. And inflation, along with astoundingly high interest rates and soaring government deficits, left the nation powerless to explain or stem the tide of another demoralizing depression—or worse. The road to colossus appeared to have yet reached another destination. But once there, its builders—American society itself—found themselves confronted by the most nettlesome roadblock yet.

The obstacle was the rise of a revolutionary new form of international technology, production, communications, labor and commerce, a combination that in its earlier configuration the

United States had pioneered, refined and dominated for close to a century. The question now became: Did *destination* in fact mean "termination"? For some reason, America was losing its broad-scale preeminence in the world of technological, scientific and commercial achievement. Had the nation in effect reached the end of the road? Was the United States, by some perverse quirk of historical fate, destined to stagnate, its traditional problem-solving vigor too enervated by its own material satiation, too sapped by its century-long struggle to maintain the paradoxical balance, too emasculated by the psychic betrayal of its past technological brilliance, too fragmented and immobilized by its sheer size, diversity and complexity to enable it to surmount the new obstacle?

Most of the vital signs were pessimistic. Comprehensive studies in 1982 revealed that since the early 1960s, the United States had tumbled from its long-held world leadership in annual industrial productivity to the bottom of the list of all the free-world industrialized nations in this vital barometer of industrial vigor and growth. During the decade of the 1970s, productivity in all the American manufacturing industries had increased by only 28 percent, while in Japan such productivity had risen by more than 100 percent, in France and West Germany by 60 percent. Even the most favorable projections indicated that an additional half-dozen nations would surpass the United States in overall productivity during the mid-1980s. Moreover, in the span of the previous twelve years, America had slipped from first to tenth in the world in terms of gross national product per person; in 1983 it lagged behind every major noncommunist industrial nation except Britain and Italy.

The pace and variety of significant American invention and technological innovation, which for almost a hundred years dominated such surveys, have also slowed markedly as compared to such pursuits in many other countries. During the last fifteen years, patents issued to American inventors fell off by about 25 percent relative to the decade and a half before, whereas in most other industrialized nations the patent rates have spiraled. Furthermore, American patents granted to foreigners, once a negligible statistic in the records of the U.S. Patent Office, today constitute about one third of all patents issued during the past decade.

Similarly, American industry has seen its major share of the world trade markets erode considerably, along with its perennial, almost monopolistic grip on its own domestic markets. In the 1950s, the United States dominated the international trade in advanced-technology goods and services, in some years controlling as much as 60 percent of such commerce. That figure had plunged to 20 percent by the late 1970s, and it is still falling. Only in aeronautics and space technology does the country's global dominance remain, and even that is now being chipped away by Japan and Western Europe. Otherwise, America's onetime superiority has been overwhelmed by more innovative and aggressive foreign competition. In the 1970s, one out of every seven jobs in America depended on exports. The radical loss of export volume during that decade became a major and continuing cause of domestic unemployment and business failure into the 1980s.

What occurred in the home market during the same period has had an equivalent impact. In the late 1960s, Americans began to learn that many advanced-technology consumer and industrial products manufactured abroad—especially in Japan—were not only cheaper but of higher sophistication, quality, reliability and durability than their American counterparts. What had surfaced as a surprising revelation became an eruption of mass demand for such products in the 1970s. The results are readily evident throughout the country today: more pervasive, longer-lasting unemployment; the progressive atrophying of the nation's industrial backbone; economic schizophrenia.

Viewed from another perspective, the obstacle confronting the United States was nothing less than the advent of what has come to be called the capitalist world's "postindustrial revolution"—a prospective era not of huge, grimy manufacturing complexes, large-scale mechanical technology and vast labor forces, but of the small, pristine "production center," of esoteric, miniaturized electronic technology, and of lean, clean robotic manufacture and service. Could a United States shaped by—indeed, slavishly conditioned and tied to—more than a century of macrotechnology, profligate resource-wastage and social imprecision adjust to a future of microtechnology, ruthless resource-efficiency and the further social systematization such a future implied? Or was America, powerless to adjust, headed for a permanent decline and fall? Was the depression of the early 1980s simply that, a natural climax of another traditional "business cycle" to be followed by an energetic recovery, as has occurred so often in the past? Or was it more than that—a clear signal that American society had finally exhausted its vital lifeblood of technological resourcefulness?

A virtual army of experts in the political, economic and social sciences have soberly contemplated these questions and provided a plethora of well-thought-out answers during the past few years. In so doing they have advanced a rich array of explanations for the country's present-day ills, and an even richer panoply of solutions: everything from eliminating trade unions and the countless government-funded social welfare programs with which the nation is so heavily burdened, to the other extreme of creating a full-fledged socialist system of national life; from instituting an aggressive federal "industrial policy" along the lines of the successful Japanese model, to radically revamping a deeply encrusted national taxation system that encourages the "sheltering" of income and profit at the expense of capital reinvestment and research-and-development funding; from retraining the existing American work force in the arcane skills of the new technology, to doing away with the country's business schools, which have purportedly indoctrinated today's managerial class to value the corporate bottom line and quarterly statement more dearly than the old-fashioned tradition of entrepreneurial and technological daring, dream and innovation; from imposing stiff, punitive tariffs that would deter the importation of the cheaper, usually better-made and longer-lasting foreign products that have maimed the American industrial complex, to engaging in outright worldwide trade wars with America's chief foreign technological and industrial rivals.

Indeed, some specialists have even proposed that the United States incite another major military war—the seeming instant cure of previous industrial depressions. Not a global nuclear war, of course, but a "conventional" war of sufficient scale and complexity to remobilize and reinvigorate the American technological spirit. Although such a strategy has been seriously advanced, none of its sponsors has explained how the war they command could be conveniently contained so as to permit the United States to survive and benefit from the envisioned revitalization.

But overlooked in this contemporary orgy of diagnosis and prescription has been something crucial—the history of the road to colossus itself. If there is any value in the axiom that those who ignore the mistakes of history are bound to repeat them, America today must thoughtfully consider its own history if it hopes to recover its former preeminence as the world's main technological, scientific and industrial wellspring, and if it expects to restore in the future the pace of domestic material progress and life enhancement it has set in the past. In reviewing that history, however briefly here, we see that one significant element stands out.

The country's rise to the pinnacle of material sophistication and wealth would not have occurred had it not been for the fierce, individualistic spirit of invention, and the hunger for technological progress, that together became the hallmarks of the American character during the nation's first 150 years. Despite the fast-growing cultural and social diversity of the United States during that period, and despite the increasing and often conflictive complexity of its society, a singular unity evolved that was practically religious in its nature and impact. That unity was the deeply felt need, and a corresponding drive, to improve the quality of individual and collective life, whether for selfish or altruistic reasons. Its catalysts were, first, a class of people of technological and scientific vision working in what was virgin, and often lonely, conceptual territory; and then a class of people of financial daring and creativity who, motivated by their own peculiar lust for profit and comfort, took up where the inventors and technological innovators left off. Indeed, in the nineteenth century, inventors and business tycoons were the nation's chief celebrities, lionized, talked about and intruded upon much as leisure-time movie stars and sports figures are nowadays.

Today it would not occur to the American public to hold a technological or scientific pioneer, or an innovative business tycoon, in awe. A Jonas Salk or Albert Sabin, each of whom separately did so much to all but eliminate the scourge of polio in the 1950s, continues to function in relative, albeit well-to-do, obscurity. William Shockley, John Bardeen and Walter Brattain, each of whom had a vital hand in the birth of modern electronic-computer technology and communications with their joint development of the transistor during the same decade, are virtually unknown beyond the scientific community. A Thomas Watson or Robert Noyce or William Levitt attracts little interest outside the professional business press.*

*Watson, the principal creator of today's IBM; Noyce, the guiding spirit behind the growth of the modern semiconductor industry; Levitt, the father of a housing-construction idea that changed the cultural landscape of America.

Which is not to suggest that such figures should be lionized in the mindless fashion in which movie and sports celebrities are. It is to urge that they be recalled to mind when the country's "expert" economic, political and sociological analysts propound their diagnoses of, and cures for, America's present-day ills. The argument is a familiar one, to be sure, not unlike that which decries the fact that schoolteachers in America get paid vastly less than second basemen and fashion models. It is a tiresome and futile argument, many insist, for it is blind to the nation's cultural reality—which is that American society pays best for what it values most.

But is it so futile when viewed through the lens of the country's more compelling reality? There is no denying the fact that what American society values most is its essential material well-being. Ask any citizen what he or she would be most willing to live permanently without if forced to: the existence of the automobile or the existence of professional sports; that of the telephone or that of the fashion magazine; that of the electric light bulb or that of the electric guitar? For each category, the answer will invariably be the latter. When they reflect on it seriously, Americans discover that they value the essential comforts and conveniences of their everyday lives over the luxuries and nonessential gadgets. And when they reflect further, they see that the luxuries and gadgets are only possible because of the technological and scientific ingenuity that created the essentials.

It is in this realization, however gradually it may form, that the main hope for America's future lies. It is the realization that without a long, intense history of producing essential technological wheat, the country would not possess the peripheral material chaff by which it is so richly and facilely able to divert and entertain itself. America's economic, political and social scientists may be right in warning the nation that it is in deep and possibly irreversible trouble because its managers have concentrated on immediate profits rather than on long-term growth; or because it has cripplingly overburdened itself with government regulation, social welfarism and taxation in the cause of socioeconomic harmony; or because it has foolishly betrayed its own vital interests by succumbing to the lure of cheaper, more efficient foreign products. But such admonitions do not get at the heart of the problem.

What the nation must comprehend, beyond what have by now become the conventional diagnoses, is that technology and science, along with the inventor and innovative experimenter, have been the vital cement of America's road to colossus. It was not the sociologist, the economist, the political scientist, the statistician, the technocrat or the bureaucrat who built the America of material plenitude. It was the country's unique breed of inventors, creative technicians, engineers and, yes, financiers. And it is that very breed the country has grown progressively short of.

The evidence of this is no more readily apparent than in recent studies with respect to the relation between education and vocational or occupational opportunity in America. Of every 10,000 of its college graduates in the decade between 1972 and 1982, the United States turned out only 70 engineers of all varieties. In the same time span, out of every 10,000 of *its* graduates, the Japanese produced 400 engineers; and the countries of northern Europe, including several behind the Iron Curtain, generated almost as many. With a current population of 117 million, Japan graduated 75,000 engineering students in 1983 alone. Fewer than 60,000 were graduated in the United States, whose population is almost twice that of Japan. The fraction of scientists and engineers in the American labor force has declined steadily since 1960, while in the same period that fraction has doubled in Japan and Germany.

The annual number of postgraduate degrees awarded across the entire range of engineering studies has in the past been an unerring indicator of a country's future technological and economic vitality and growth. As every country in recent history has grown more technologically oriented, that number has increased at a steady rate. In America it dropped by a third during the 1970s among the native student population. On the other hand, almost half the engineering doctorates awarded by American universities in 1983 were obtained by foreign students, and roughly a quarter of the engineering faculty in American colleges under the age of forty were foreigners who had received their advanced degrees in the United States. As recently as the early 1970s, the majority of foreign-born engineering Ph.D.'s from American universities remained in the United States and eventually became U.S. citizens. Today the majority are returning to their home nations to apply their talents and learning there.

Quite simply, the number of engineers graduating from American colleges and universities has not grown fast enough to keep up with the country's basic technological-growth needs and potential. This is among the principal reasons for the country's economic decline. Today's engineers are the potential inventors and creative technological innovators of yesterday, yet their numbers are declining precipitously—even in the fabled high-tech industries, which accounts for the fact that most foreign high technology continues to outdo American versions of it. High technology could still grow at a rate of nearly 50 percent a year in the America of the 1980s if there were enough qualified engineers to fill the positions required to support that growth rate. There aren't—not even half enough. What's more, in 1984 there were more than two thousand unfilled engineering teaching positions in American universities, most of them in critical segments of the profession. Which is to say that even with the declining market in engineering students, the market in qualified teachers has dropped even more sharply. Should there be a sudden rise in interest in engineering studies on the part of the student population, the nation's instructional capability would not be sufficient to meet it.

The American government, along with the private sector, has devoted much of its domestic energies during the last decade to trying to explain and cope with the economic aspects of America's decline. In all their deliberations, however, they have ignored one prime lesson of American history. The lesson is that the country, and its vast, rich, once-vibrant economy, were created in the first place by the inventive engineers of yesteryear—many of them untrained, to be sure, some of them nothing more than backyard tinkerers, but all of them infused with what is basically a timeless engineering spirit and compulsion. A revival of those qualities in the American character will not alone return the nation to the vanguard of technological and material progress, and therefore economic vitality. But without such a revival, no amount of social, political and economic manipulation of our system as it exists today will salvage the future. If the country has any single most important practical imperative before it, it is to restore its scientific and engineering aptitude.

Can this be done? Will it be done? These are questions only the future will answer.

What seems certain, though, is that *unless* it is done, the United States will continue to grope in vain for an effective path through its latest roadblock. For, again, historically it was America's successive generations of technological and scientific visionaries who, more than any other group, had the major hand in building the road to our present colossus. If the road is to continue—despite the morbid shadow of nuclear holocaust under which we all must hereafter live, and despite the persistently unresolveable paradoxes of modern capitalism—it is upon future such visionaries that American society must rely.

It has been said that the past is but a prologue to the future. If so, then the words of Francis Bacon to his biographer, some 360 years ago, remain apt today:

> . . . it was plain that the good effects wrought by the founders of our cities, lawgivers, fathers of the people, extirpers of tyrants, and heroes of that class, extend but over narrow surfaces and last but for short times; whereas the work of the inventor, though a thing of less pomp and show, is felt everywhere and lasts forever.

INDEX